HOW TO RESTORE YOUR FARM TRACTOR

By Tharran E. Gaines

Voyageur Press

Contents

Chapter 1
Shopping for a Tractor

So you want to try your hand at restoring a vintage farm tractor? If you're like some antique tractor enthusiasts, you already have a tractor picked out, or at the very least, a particular model in mind. For many people, tractor restoration is a matter of nostalgia. The first model they want to tackle is the one they most fondly remember from their childhood. If they didn't grow up on a farm, perhaps it's a model their grandfather had owned, and they remember taking rides on it during the summer.

On the other hand, you may want to get into tractor restoration in order to take part in the growing number of clubs and activities that revolve around antique tractors. Whether your interest is in antique or vintage tractor pulling, tractor shows, or just driving your restored treasure in the county fair parade, there's nothing that generates pride like participating in such an event with a tractor that you restored with your own hands. The camaraderie that comes with being part of such a group is invaluable, as well.

There are some people, however, who just want a quality work tractor without the cost of buying a new or late-model machine. They don't have any interest in taking it to a show or putting it on display. They just want something to pull a rotary mower or a three-bottom plow. By restoring one of the rugged workhorses from yesteryear, they're able to get all the tractor they need at a reasonable cost.

Which category you fall into will make a big difference on which model is best suited to your needs. Some of the most collectible tractors make poor working machines whereas some less collectible tractors are fine workhorses. It makes little sense to put the time and money into restoring a rare model, only to put it in the field.

By the same token, extensive restoration of an extremely common tractor model may not be worth the cost and the many hours of labor it takes to restore it to running condition. Trying to break loose a frozen piston on a Farmall M is an effort in futility as you can spend a lot less time and money finding one in running condition at a farm sale.

With literally hundreds of tractors to choose from, the selection of a vintage tractor for restoration comes down to your personal preference and plans for the finished product. This beautifully restored Allis-Chalmers Model B is owned by Carmin Adams of San Jose, California. *Hans Halberstadt*

True rarities, however, are an entirely different matter. In those cases, the restorer is basing the tractor evaluation simply on what is left of the prospective tractor and what he or she can afford to invest. Mechanical and cosmetic condition are secondary.

There is one common rule of thumb for most restoration prospects: A complete tractor that doesn't run, especially if it has good sheet metal, is worth more than an incomplete tractor that does run, particularly if it has poor sheet metal. In most cases, it's a lot easier to get the engine running or replace the transmission than to repair or replace sheet metal that has been destroyed by rust. Ironically, it may cost more to replace the sidesheets or engine cover panels used on an Oliver Fleetline tractor than to have the engine itself overhauled.

WORKING TRACTORS

If you're buying and restoring a tractor for working an acreage, or to use as a backup tractor, the first thing you need to consider—even before selecting a particular model—is how the tractor and implements are to be used. If you plan to cultivate row crops, for example, you probably won't be happy with a Ford N Series tractor or an Oliver Super 55 since both are low-profile tractors with minimal ground clearance. On the other hand, if you plan to mow sidehills and road ditches with a three-point-hitch-mounted mower, you may want to steer clear of a narrow-front John Deere B or a high-crop Farmall; the maneuverability might be satisfactory, but the rollover potential is not worth any savings you might garner.

Once you've considered the jobs you have in mind, you need to look at the implements you plan to use. From this, you can calculate your horsepower needs and make sure the tractor model you select has the weight and power to do the job. Again, someone who is planning to pull a 10-foot disc harrow is going to be unhappy with a Farmall Cub or an Allis-Chalmers G. You'll need to consider, too, the need for hydraulic power or a three-point hitch.

The best insurance against buying the wrong model is to do your research and talk to a few farmers or tractor owners who have similar operations.

COLLECTOR TRACTORS

If you're buying a tractor strictly as a collector model, you need to realize that a whole different set of rules applies. You must also consider whether you're collecting the model for its value on the market or its sentimental value to you alone. As an example, some tractor restorers simply have a desire to restore and collect all the models

The quality of the restoration work that went into this International Harvester Farmall Super M shows over every inch of the machine. *Hans Halberstadt*

Antique tractor collectors often look for unusual models or variations within their favorite brand, such as this rare Wheatland version of an Allis-Chalmers D-17.

Any high-crop model is highly collectible. In fact, some restorers spend years scouring the country to find a model like this Farmall MV high-crop.

Tractors like this Ford 8N have always been sought after as solid work tractors for farms, hobby farms, vegetable gardens, nurseries, and the like. This 8N was restored by Palmer Fossum of Northfield, Minnesota. *Chester Peterson Jr.*

A WORD ABOUT HORSEPOWER

If you're planning to use your restored tractor as a working tractor, one of the things you'll want to be aware of is the horsepower rating. But what exactly is horsepower?

Technically speaking, horsepower is defined as the amount of energy or work required to raise a weight of 33,000 pounds to a height of one foot in one minute, or to overcome or create a force equivalent to doing that amount of work. Unfortunately, not all of the horsepower generated by the engine is available to pull a load or drive a PTO-powered implement. Part of it is lost to friction in the engine, inefficiency in the transmission, the power required just to turn the axles and tires, and so on.

Consequently, an engine's highest horsepower rating is going to be its indicated horsepower. This is the power developed in the engine cylinders as obtained from the pressure in the cylinder. A second horsepower rating is brake horsepower. This is the actual horsepower delivered by the engine to the shaft. Hence, it is equal to the indicated horsepower less the friction of the engine. Since the power-takeoff on many tractors is powered directly from the engine, rather than directed through the transmission, the figure is also frequently referred to as PTO horsepower.

Finally, you'll often hear a figure referred to as effective horsepower or drawbar horsepower. This is the final horsepower delivered to the drawbar to pull an implement. Considering that the tractor may also be powering pumps or auxiliary equipment for its own power production needs, the difference between indicated horsepower and drawbar horsepower may be as much as 25 percent.

Unfortunately, this fact alone often leads to confusion today. While the advertised horsepower on modern tractors is actually PTO horsepower or crankshaft horsepower, the horsepower of early antique tractors was generally measured at the drawbar. Consider, too, that drawbar horsepower may be as little as half of what the engine actually produced. The rest was lost to heat, inefficient gear drives, and the counterforces that had to be overcome just to move a heavy tractor, particularly if it had lugged, steel wheels.

Fortunately, horsepower was seldom a mystery to early tractor customers. In many cases, the horsepower rating was readily evident in the tractor model number. For instance, a farmer looking at a Twin City 27/44 tractor or an Allis-Chalmers 20/35 knew that the smaller number represented the drawbar horsepower whereas the larger number was the belt pulley horsepower. Even an International Harvester customer knew that an F-12 featured 12 horsepower at the drawbar.

Consider, too, that antique tractors were designed for high-torque output at low speeds. In contrast, modern tractor engines are rated at their maximum developed horsepower at speeds in the range of 2,200 to 2,500 rpm. That alone explains why an antique tractor rated at 20 horsepower can pull more than a modern compact tractor rated at the same horsepower.

within a certain series, such as the John Deere 60 Series models or the D Series in the Allis-Chalmers line.

Or maybe you just want to own a model like the one you drove while growing up on a farm. If that is the case, it's better to use the evaluation criteria outlined for a working tractor. Since many of these models are not rare, it's best to look for the best combination of sound mechanics, good cosmetics, and a decent price.

On the other hand, if you intend to buy a vintage tractor as an investment, you'll want to research its history. Study factory literature or tractor books to find out the number built of that particular model. This will give you an idea how rare that model is and what it might be worth when you are finished.

Chris Pratt, with *Yesterday's Tractors* online magazine, explains that working with rarities almost always rules out looking for the basics of perfect mechanical and cosmetic condition. "I have seen extremely rare tractors purchased that consisted of just the engine block, rear end, rims, and frame assembly," he says. "It often will take several purchases of components to build up a single machine. Indeed, many purchases of rare tractors and components take place without a preview, simply to ensure the piece isn't sold by the time the buyer can get there."

When shopping for a collector tractor, you will also want to take a look at the tractor's serial number. As a general rule, the lower the number, the greater its collector value. In the same manner, a high serial number might indicate that the tractor was one of the last models of its type to come off the assembly line. Again, it helps to know some history of the serial numbers assigned to the model you're inspecting.

A tractor recently restored by Allis-Chalmers enthusiasts Edwin and Larry Karg, from Hutchinson, Minnesota, is a good example. Built in 1970, their restored Allis-Chalmers Model Two-Twenty is far from being an old tractor. However, it's one of only 100 models that were ever produced with mechanical front-wheel assist. It seems American farmers weren't yet ready for front-wheel-drive tractors, so front-wheel assist was quietly dropped.

The Allis-Chalmers D17 Wheatland tractor is another example. Unlike the standard model, the Wheatland version featured full-crown fenders, larger tires on fixed rims and a heavy-duty swinging drawbar. But few were sold, since most grain farmers wanted more horsepower than the D17 offered. By 1960, the Wheatland no longer appeared in the price book. Today, it represents one of the rarities sought by A-C enthusiasts.

Of course the ultimate dream of every Minneapolis-Moline enthusiast is to own a UDLX Comfortractor.

While it would be an ideal work tractor, this wide-front John Deere 620, lovingly restored by Dennis Funk of Hillsboro, Kansas, is meant only for show.

Built in 1938, it was the most widely publicized tractor of its time, thanks in part to its sleek lines, automotive-style grillework and enclosed cab. Since only 150 units were ever built, it's considered a true collector's tractor.

Pratt warns, however, about buying a tractor on which the cosmetic components are the only things that make that specific machine rare.

"A common example of this is some orchard model tractors," he explains. "Frequently, there are no remnants of the orchard add-ons or anything but a model designation to distinguish the machine from its common utility version brother. Finding orchard models may be relatively easy, while finding the orchard components that make your project collectible are next to impossible. If an incomplete model is priced as a rarity, it may be wise to pass," he concludes.

SHOPPING FOR A TRACTOR

If there is one word of advice about locating and buying a tractor to restore, it's to take your time. Shopping for a tractor can be part of the experience and enjoyment of restoration. It's important to note, too, that the time you spend looking for the right model and inspecting each tractor will pay off later in the form of greater efficiency, less time and money spent on restoration, and increased satisfaction with the finished product. If it's a work tractor you're looking for, the benefits may also include increased safety; buying a tractor that is not ideal for your needs may not only be inefficient but dangerous.

One aspect to consider when looking for a prospective project is the geographic location from which the tractor originated. Eugene Mohr, a Minneapolis-Moline collector from Vail, Iowa, notes that, as a general rule, tractors from the eastern part of the United States are more apt to have rust problems and stuck engines, while those from the western part of the country tend to suffer more tire damage due to exposure to the sun and dry rot.

Estel Theis, a John Deere enthusiast from Savannah, Missouri, agrees that the dryer climate prevalent in the continent's High Plains helps preserve the classics. Nearly half of the vintage models he has restored to date have come from farms in Montana. In addition to having less rust, he insists western tractors also exhibit less wear on the steering mechanism and front axle, simply because the fields are bigger and flatter and the tractor has made fewer turns.

That's another reason Theis says it's helpful to know the history of the tractor you're buying. If, for example, the tractor was used to haul or load manure in a livestock operation, you can expect to spend some money on front wheel bearings and seals. And the steering mechanism on a row-crop tractor is likely to require more work than that of a Wheatland version.

There are other things, of course, that can tip you off to potential problems. One is the hose between the carburetor and the air cleaner tube: If it is cracked or missing, the engine may have sucked in a lot of dirt and will need work. Likewise, a missing or cracked shift lever boot can let water into the transmission, and everyone knows how many problems water that repeatedly freezes and thaws can cause.

In contrast, antifreeze in the cooling system and oil in the oil-bath air cleaner tells you right away that the tractor was treated well and is likely in good shape.

NEGOTIATING A PRICE
Before you even start dealing on any tractor, you should know your needs, your budget, and what is on the market. Become as knowledgeable about the prospective tractor as you can through research, conversation with

Rare tractors, like this 1938 Graham-Bradley, which was produced by the famous Graham-Paige automobile maker and sold through Sears, Roebuck & Company, naturally hold more value when restored. Locating parts, however, can be like a treasure hunt.

If a tractor is not in running condition, as is the case with this ancient Farmall F-12, you almost have to start your bidding price based on its junk value.

You'll find everything from junk-status tractors to fully restored models for sale in the flea market or swap meet section of antique tractor shows. Some shows have also begun featuring vintage tractor auctions, which is another source of a restoration project.

It almost goes without saying that a tractor in running condition, such as this Deere Model 60 LPG, is easier to assess for value and potential than one that won't even turn over. *Ralph W. Sanders*

If the tractor is equipped with hydraulics, as with this Farmall M, test the hydraulic system. Extend the rams on any hydraulic cylinder to test the range. If possible, use the system to lift a load, then let the load sit in the hold position for a few minutes to see if there is any leakdown. *Ralph W. Sanders*

The serial number plate alone can add value to a tractor, especially if it proves that the model was one of the first or last in the series to be produced.

other collectors, and physically checking out each tractor you are considering.

The *Yesterday's Tractors* website, found at www.ytmag. com, can be of value. The site includes a listing of recent tractor sales and lists a variety of models, their condition, and how much they sold for. Another source is www. tractorhouse.com, which provides a listing of tractors for sale throughout North America. With a few clicks of the mouse, you can find a number of Ford tractors, divided by model, for sale by individuals and dealers. If you can find a tractor in the listings that has a similar number of hours that is in a similar state of repair, you have a pretty good idea what the tractor should really be worth or at least where to start your offer.

This will allow you to go into the negotiations with a price in mind. If your preview of the tractor turned up any problems, you may find that the seller is willing

A nicely restored Case Crossmotor tractor. *Hans Halberstadt*

A beautifully restored Ford-Ferguson 2N. *Chester Peterson Jr.*

to come down on the price. However, you will need to decide if you have the time and the expertise to correct what you have found.

You may find, too, that the tractor is not running or won't start on the day you go to look at it. The seller may, in all honesty, tell you that everything worked fine when he or she last drove it; but when a tractor sits for very long, it can develop problems that even an owner is unaware of. In this case, you must start your bidding from nearly scrap level prices, since you have no idea what you're getting into, and go as far as your conscience and experience will allow.

Antifreeze in the cooling system and oil in the oil-bath air cleaner tells you right away that the tractor was treated well and is likely in good shape.

"Look at the left side of the block where the coolant draincock is located," he says. "Check all around the area in front of the draincock and above it for cracks or signs that a crack has been repaired. If someone has let the engine freeze up in the winter, this is where it usually cracks. Be wary of cracked blocks, especially if repairs have been poorly done. A cracked block makes the tractor worth substantially less, and trying to find a good used block for a reasonable price can be a very frustrating task. On the other hand, a crack that has been properly repaired won't affect the performance of a work tractor one bit."

Smith suggests that you do a lot of shaking and wiggling when checking out the tractor. You can start up front by wiggling the fan blade to check the bearings in the water pump.

"Shake the left and right tie rods," he adds. "All four ball and socket ends should be tight. Grab the front tire and push/pull inside and out on it. The wheel bearings and spindles should be tight with no play. Turn the steering wheel left and right to check for excessive backlash in the steering," he continues, using the Ford tractor as an example. "Does one front wheel start to turn before the other starts moving? This indicates a misadjustment or worn sector shafts in the steering box.

"Move to the rear tires," Smith adds. "Grab the top of the tire and push/pull toward and away from the center of the tractor. Does the wheel have side play? Do you hear a clunk when you push/pull?"

If the tractor is in running condition, there are several things you should check before and after you start the engine. It would be a good idea to turn to Chapter 5 and run through some of those procedures before you make your final decision.

If the tractor is not in running condition, you'll want to make sure the pistons are not rusted to the cylinder sleeve.

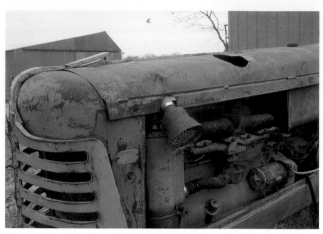

The condition of the hose between the air cleaner and carburetor on this Oliver should be a tip off to possible engine damage. In addition to not being the correct type of hose, it has holes that could have sucked in dirt before the tractor was permanently parked.

When shopping for a tractor, it helps to know what was original equipment. Obviously, the decals and seat have been changed during the long working life of this steel-wheeled John Deere Model A.

THE REALITY OF BUYING AN OLD TRACTOR

Tom Armstrong includes a humorous tractor buying guide on his N-Complete website that is sometimes all too true. A few sample entries are as follows:

Ad Says:	Really Means:
Rough condition	Too bad to lie about
Engine runs quiet	Using 90W oil
Many new parts	Still not running right
Slight surface rust	No trace of paint anywhere

Finding a vintage tractor with all the sheet metal still in place is often difficult—especially when side panels were used to enclose all or part of the engine. This Massey-Ferguson MF 25 is an ideal restoration candidate as it has retained all of its sheet metal in good condition. *Chester Peterson Jr.*

INFORMATION RESOURCES

Books on tractor history can be a great sources of information to help you become knowledgeable about a prospective tractor. Here are some recommended titles:

General Tractor Histories

The Farm Tractor: 100 Years of North American Tractors
by Ralph W. Sanders

Farm Tractors: The History of the Tractor
by Robert N. Pripps and Andrew Morland

The Field Guide to Vintage Farm Tractors
by Robert N. Pripps and Andrew Morland

Legendary Farm Tractors
by Andrew Morland

Specific Make Histories

The Bigger Book of John Deere Tractors
by Don Macmillan

Ultimate John Deere
by Ralph W. Sanders

Legendary John Deere Tractors
By Andrew Morland

The Big Book of Farmall Tractors
by Robert N. Pripps and Andrew Morland

Legendary Farmall Tractors
by Lee Klancher

The Big Book of Ford Tractors
by Robert N. Pripps and Andrew Morland

For some restorers, the challenge is restoring the oldest model they can find, which often takes them back to the steel-wheel era of this Farmall F-12.

One way to do that is to pull one or both of the spark plugs and shine a light inside the cylinder walls to check their condition. If the walls are shiny, the pistons are probably not stuck too badly, if at all. On the other hand, if you can't even remove the spark plugs due to rust, you might have cause for concern.

Many collectors also go into a negotiation with the idea that a stuck engine is basically "junk." If it can be freed, that's a bonus. Hence, your offering price should reflect that possibility.

Finally, know how much you are willing to spend on the whole project before you buy the tractor or start negotiations. Many people don't realize how much expense is involved in a restoration. Even if you get the tractor at a decent price, you have to anticipate the cost of engine repairs, bodywork, new wiring, replacement components, and so on.

Many restorers suggest that you assume the worst of any potential restoration. That way you won't be surprised if you can't find parts or if it takes more time and money to get it finished than you expected.

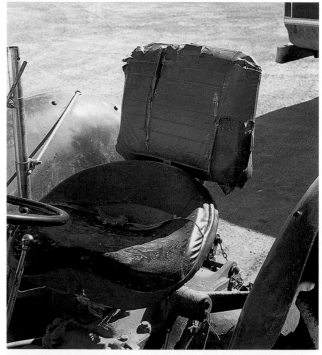

When shopping for a tractor, you'll find plenty of models that have been modified from their original states. Many times, the changes were made to improve comfort.

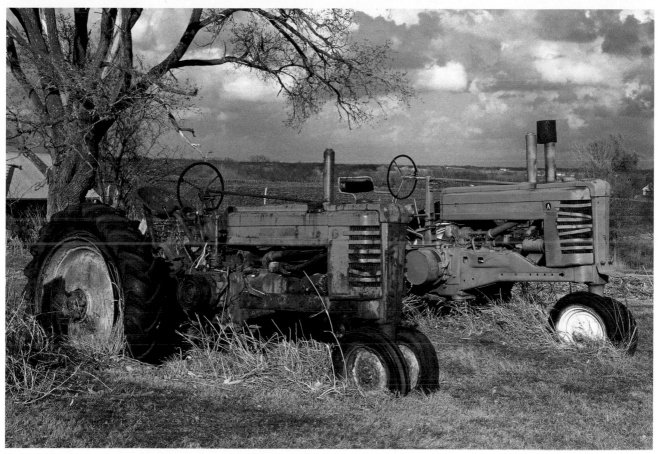

If a tractor is not in running condition, as with these styled John Deere Models A and B, you almost have to start your bidding price based on its junk value.

Considering there were only about 100 units built, this restored Allis-Chalmers Two-Twenty with Front-Wheel Assist is a real source of pride for Edwin and Larry Karg of Hutchinson, Minnesota.

Chapter 2
Setting Up Shop

TOOLS

It almost goes without saying that you're going to need a good set of tools if you're really serious about restoring a tractor. And make sure you put the emphasis on good. A cheap set of tools is only going to lead to frustration as they break, strip, or worse, damage a tractor part. Look for a set of automotive-quality tools that comes with a warranty, such as those offered by Sears (Craftsman), NAPA, Snap-On, and so on.

You'll want to start with a drive-socket set that contains sockets ranging from 1/16 inch to over 1 inch. In addition to a ratchet handle, you'll need a breaker bar to loosen stubborn bolts without risking damage to the ratchet.

You'll find that a set of combination wrenches will come in handy, too. There are some places you simply can't get a socket and ratchet into. You can decide which will work best for you and your budget, but choices include open-end, box-end, and wrenches that provide a box- and open-end configuration on each end.

To round out your tool collection, you'll want to add a couple of adjustable wrenches (often referred to as Crescent wrenches, even though Crescent is a brand name), a full set of regular and Phillips screwdrivers, a pair of adjustable pliers, needle-nose pliers, and a pair of locking pliers (again, often referred to by the popular brand name Vise-Grip). Other occasionally used tools that you'll probably need at some time or another include a good hacksaw, a punch set, and a cold chisel. And don't forget to pick up a couple of putty knives. You'll need those for scraping away grease and grime.

Don't assume you have to go out and buy all new tools, either. Due to the economy and changes in agriculture, farm auctions are far too common these days. So keep your eyes open for an estate sale or a shop liquidation where you can pick up what you need at a reduced price.

SPECIALIZED TOOLS

Depending upon how much engine or electrical work you get into, there are other tools that you may need. These include feeler gauges, a point dwell meter/tachometer, voltmeter, and compression and vacuum gauges. For tools and gauges that are only used on occasion, you may want to consider renting or borrowing them from a fellow restorer.

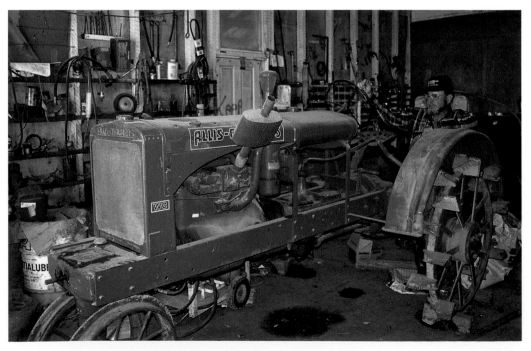

While your work area doesn't have to be anything fancy, it does help to have a place where you can keep the tractor indoors while it is being restored.

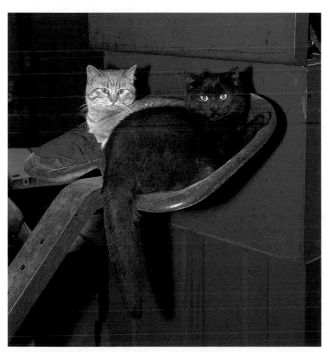

Four-legged companions don't always find restoration projects as fulfilling as their human counterparts, but they do find them equally relaxing at times.

Other tools that can make your life a lot easier while working on an older tractor include a gasket scraper, bearing and hub pullers, and a seal puller. A pickle fork can be a handy item, too, if you plan to separate the tie rods on the front axle.

If you anticipate doing much engine work, you'll also need a few tools for making precise measurements. At a minimum, these should include a micrometer for measuring items up to approximately an inch in width, a dial caliper to determine the acceptability of parts like the crankshaft and camshaft, a set of feeler gauges, and a dial gauge for measuring certain types of end play.

You'll also need a torque wrench. While most parts of the tractor don't require a specified torque rating, you'll find that many engine components, including the head bolts, must be tightened to a particular setting. This is important to reduce the chance of head warping and oil and water leaks. While there are several different types of torque wrenches, perhaps the easiest to use is the "click" type that makes an audible click when the correct torque rating has been reached. Since you preset the desired torque with a dial on the wrench, you don't have to worry about providing enough light to read a scale or being able to see the scale when working in a tight area.

Of course, you can get by with the older style of torque wrench that uses a stationary pointer and a gauge attached to the handle. As the bolt or nut is tightened, the handle bends in response to the applied torque. As a result, the needle, which is fixed to the socket head, moves up or down on the scale to indicate the amount of torque being applied; you just have to be able to watch the scale as you're tightening the fastener.

Depending upon how far you get into engine repair, you may also need specialized tools like a ridge reamer, valve-lapping tool, piston ring compressor, and cylinder hone. The use of each of these items is discussed in more detail in Chapter 5, "Engine Repair and Rebuilding."

Air Compressor

While an air-powered impact wrench can be a valuable asset when removing stubborn bolts, air-powered tools aren't quite as necessary as the air compressor itself. You'll want a portable air compressor with a tank for a couple of reasons. First of all, an air hose and nozzle are invaluable for blowing dust and dirt out of crevices and away from parts. You'll want to use it to blow out fuel lines, water passages, and the like, as well.

A good set of tools is a prerequisite for vintage tractor restoration. And having tools organized and close at hand can make a restoration project go much smoother.

Secondly, assuming you're going to be painting the tractor yourself, you'll need an air compressor to operate the paint sprayer. Here, tank capacity is even more important. If the tank doesn't have enough capacity and the pump can't keep up, you're going to be painting a few minutes, stopping to let the pressure build in the tank, painting a few more minutes, and then waiting again. Hence, you might want to put things in reverse order and shop for a paint sprayer before you look for a compressor.

Most restorers who do their own painting suggest using a compressor with at least 1/2 horsepower that is capable of delivering at least 4 cubic feet of air per minute at 30 psi pressure.

Vise

You don't have to own a vise to do tractor restoration, but considering the availability, reasonable cost, and the versatility that a vise provides, you'll likely find it worthwhile. Just being able to clamp a part in the vise while you work on it can be helpful at times. And you'll be especially glad you have one when you've got a part in which a bolt absolutely won't budge.

For versatility, many shop owners recommend at least a 6-inch vise that is bolted securely to a solid bench. You may even want to get a piece of plate steel to attach to the bottom side of the bench for extra strength and support.

Anvil

Another tool that you'll at times find invaluable is an anvil, especially if you have to straighten sheet metal. You don't have to invest in a commercial shop anvil, though. For what you'll need most of the time, a 2- or 2 1/2 -foot piece of railroad track rail will do. In fact, the rounded edge of the rail will work better for some metal fabrication than will a real anvil.

If you occasionally need a flat surface or a square end for bending, you can even weld a piece of bar stock across one or both ends of the rail so it will stand upright when turned rail side down.

Hoists and Jacks

Last, but certainly not least, you're going to need equipment to lift and support the tractor, engine, and other components. Naturally, your needs will depend to some extent on the type of tractor you're restoring. Some tractors, such as the Ford 9N, use the engine as a load-bearing member; in other words, there is no full-length frame. The front of the tractor attaches to the front of the engine and the rear of the engine attaches to

An angle grinder or stationary cutoff tool can be a valuable asset for sheetmetal work.

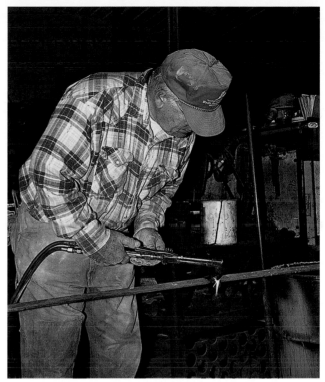

An oxyacetylene torch can be equally valuable for cutting metal and heating stubborn parts that refuse to budge.

A torque wrench is just one of those specialty tools you'll need to purchase or borrow when overhauling an engine.

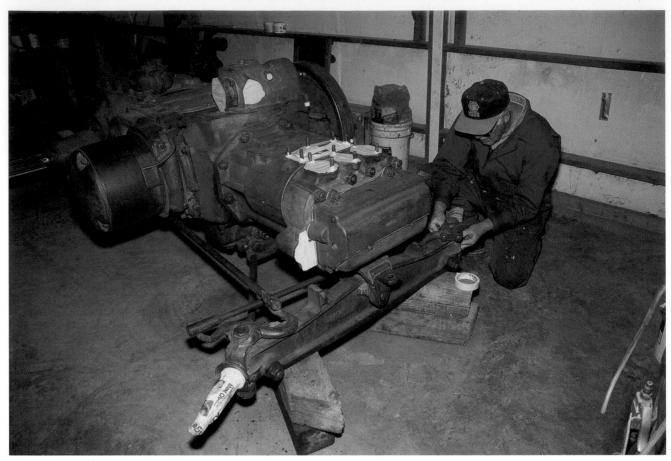

Even if it is just done on a temporary basis, placing the tractor on cribbing, or wooden blocks, will make it easier to work on the axle and steering components.

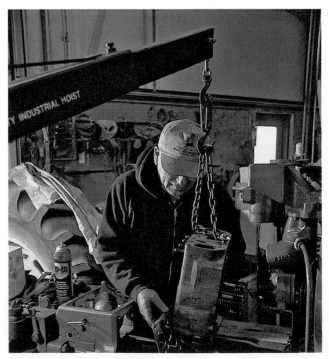

A hoist of some kind is a necessity when removing the engine or splitting the tractor for engine overhaul or transmission work.

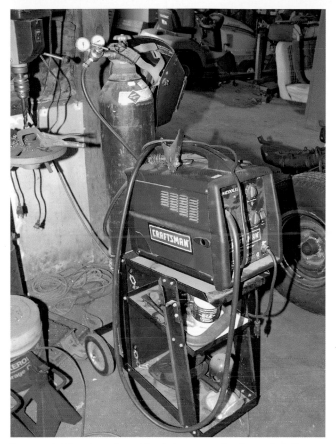

You may or may not need a welder during your restoration project. If you do, you can probably find a friend to help you out, rent a unit, or take the piece to a commercial welder.

the transmission. To remove the engine for an overhaul, you have to split the tractor in half. That means you need a floor jack or bottle jack to support each half of the tractor in order to remove the engine. If necessary, you can always reinstall the oil pan between the front axle and bell housing after it has been removed from the engine. This will give you a full chassis that can be moved around the shop for other restoration steps.

Other tractors employ a "bath tub" frame or frame rails that attach to the transmission. The engine then sets within this frame, which means that the entire engine can be lifted out while the tractor remains on its wheels. This type of arrangement, however, generally requires an overhead hoist or an engine hoist to lift the engine out of the frame.

There will come a time, too, when you need to remove the rear wheels and front axle and front wheels for cleaning, restoration, and painting. Again, you'll need some heavy-duty lifting equipment capable of raising the tractor to the level where you can block it up on stands or

wooden blocks. Don't try to get by with concrete blocks. They can crumble or crack too easily, posing a physical danger. Don't try to pile blocks up too high, either. The best bet is to build cribbing under the frame, which means you place strong wooden blocks log-cabin style under the tractor or axles as structural support until the wheels can be safely reinstalled.

Some restorers like to block up the entire tractor from the start, pull the wheels, strip the tractor down to the frame, and work on restoration from the ground up. Others like to leave the tractor on its wheels as long as possible, work on components as they go, and roll the tractor out of the way when necessary.

The bottom line is your lifting and cribbing needs will depend largely on the size and type of tractor you're restoring and how you prefer to work. Just be sure you keep safety in mind and that you have enough equipment to do the job. Don't try to lift the rear end of the tractor, for example, with a single bottle jack, even if it is an 8-ton jack. That's not what you would call adequate stability.

THE VALUE OF SHOP MANUALS
Considering all the different brands of tractors built since the early 1900s and the number of models made by each brand, this book obviously cannot go into detail on specific restoration procedures for each make and model—especially with powertrain restoration. There is simply no way to cover all the specifics and idiosyncrasies. Therefore, one of the first steps you need to take is to purchase a repair manual for your specific model, which should supply a source of specifications that includes tolerance limits, torque settings, wear limits, etc.

There are a number of good sources for service and repair manuals listed in the appendix. Intertec Publishing, for example, offers a complete line of their I & T (Implement & Tractor) Shop Service manuals, which are available for most of the popular tractor brands and models. Jensales Inc. in Manchester, Minnesota, also has service and parts manuals for virtually every popular tractor that was ever built.

You might check with your local farm equipment dealer, too. John Deere, for instance, carries repair manuals for a number of Deere tractors, including those built in the 1930s and 1940s. Likewise, AGCO still has a limited number of service and repair manuals available for certain Allis-Chalmers, Massey-Harris, and Massey-Ferguson tractors.

Finally, if you want to pay the price, you can still find original service manuals for sale by vendors at flea markets, tractor shows, and swap meets.

Chapter 3
Getting Started

TAKE YOUR TIME

The first step in restoring a vintage tractor, once you have it home, is to convince yourself that it's going to take some time. A lot of the people who restore antique tractors are retired farmers or mechanics who do it for the enjoyment of seeing an old tractor brought back to life. Some of the other restorers featured in this book are full-time farmers who spend much of their winter working on a tractor. Once spring arrives, however, their pet project tends to sit until ground preparation and planting are complete.

The point is, unless you're retired or have three or four cold winter months to devote to the project, you need to realize that a quality restoration is going to take up to a year or more. Trying to finish the project too quickly is going to lead to either discouragement or dissatisfaction later on with the shortcuts you have taken.

ESTABLISH YOUR GOALS

If you talk to many tractor restorers, you'll soon find that *tractor restoration* can mean lots of different things. And, indeed, one of the things you'll need to do right up front is decide how far you want to take the restoration project. To some enthusiasts, a vintage tractor restoration is nothing short of restoring the tractor to mint condition. That means they go through the engine, transmission, rear end, and every other component that might need attention. They also insist on accuracy in every detail and top it off with a quality coat of paint.

On the other hand, not everyone has the budget to do a first-class restoration. If you're in that category, you need to decide along the way what you can live with and what you can't. As an example, if you only plan to drive your finished product in a few parades a year and take

Some restorers get more enjoyment out of restoring tractors than owning them. Or, they simply restore them with the idea of reselling them when they are finished.

Before you get started, you'll need to establish your goals. Do you want to restore your tractor as a work tractor or as a show tractor, like this Oliver Model 88 Row Crop? Also, you'll need to decide whether you want to restore the engine and transmission to like-new condition, or if you can live with something like a missing gear tooth.

it to a few antique tractor gatherings, you may not need to replace that gear in the transmission that is missing a couple of teeth. But if you plan on using the tractor to mow the roadsides, plow the garden, and push snow in the winter, you'll want to restore the transmission to like-new condition, or risk further, more costly damage.

Don't try to cut costs where it doesn't make sense, though. If there is one common lament among tractor restorers who make their living restoring tractors for paying customers, it's that some clients don't want to spend the money to do it right the first time.

DOCUMENT THE PROCESS

As stated earlier, it may be a year or more before you get to the point where you're ready to reassemble the tractor. Consequently, it's important that you maintain good records as you disassemble the tractor. Keep a pad and pencil handy for recording measurements and taking notes. You should also consider taking pictures or shooting video as you go. Used in combination with a service manual, these images can be valuable several months down the road.

You'll want some good photos anyway, even if you don't need them for reference later on. One of the first questions people are going to ask you is "What did it look like when you started?" Showing them photos of the iron pile you dragged into the shop is half the enjoyment.

FINDING REPLACEMENT PARTS

Before you get too deep into the restoration project, you'll need to consider the challenge of locating and acquiring replacement parts. As you're disassembling the tractor for cleaning, begin making a list of all the parts you'll need to restore the machine to show or working condition. This will give you an idea of how much you may need to spend on parts like bearings, gaskets, sheet metal components, and so on. It will also give you a head start on locating some of those parts. By knowing what you need ahead of time, you can be searching the swap meets, salvage yards, and classified ads for the necessary components while you're working on other areas.

Record as much detail as possible, including part dimensions and their shapes and any serial numbers listed on separate parts. The good news is, parts for antique tractors are much easier to find today than they were just five or ten years ago, thanks in part to the growing interest in tractor restoration. AGCO, for example, recently initiated its Heritage parts program, which means that nearly 2,400 parts for Oliver, Minneapolis-Moline, Massey-Harris, Massey Ferguson, Allis-Chalmers, and Cockshutt tractors can be purchased or ordered through any AGCO dealer. Similarly, Case IH and John Deere dealers continue to stock parts for a number of tractor models that date back to the 1930s.

Keep in mind, too, that the part you need might just be available from an unusual source. Some tractor dealerships, including most John Deere dealers, for example, can reference the number on any bearing, regardless of what tractor brand or model it came off of, and tell you in a matter of seconds, via the parts computer, whether they have a bearing available to match it. Similarly, Jeff Gravert, a tractor restorer from Central City, Nebraska, says one of the little-known secrets in the tractor restoration world is that the bushings from certain Briggs & Stratton carburetor kits are the perfect alternative for those tractor carburetors that no one stocks kits for anymore. It's just one more reason to get involved in a club and ask questions of other antique tractor enthusiasts.

In addition to original parts, there has been a proliferation of small companies that specialize in restoration parts. Through the sources listed in the back of this book and in many of the restoration and tractor club magazines, you can find everything from reproduction grille medallions and rubber torsion springs to radiator caps and temperature gauges. There are numerous individuals and companies, too, that can repair your old magneto, carburetor, or distributor.

Before you spend a lot of money on new parts, though, spend some time searching the salvage yards and used parts dealers for original parts that can be refurbished. The swap meets held in conjunction with a number of tractor shows are a good source of used parts, too. Not only will used parts make your tractor more original, but they may save you money. Just don't rely on used parts in critical areas where a failure could jeopardize safety or cost you more money later on.

CLEAN IT UP

Just the word *restoration* implies that the tractor you intend to bring back to life needs a lot of attention. More than likely, it is covered with fifty or more years worth of grease, dirt, and grime. And that's assuming it runs or has been protected from the elements for a good portion of its life. If you're restoring a tractor that has been sitting in the fencerow for the last twenty years, you're probably looking at a lot of rust, too.

Hence, the first step in any tractor restoration is trying to find the potential that is hidden beneath years of neglect. If you haven't picked up the tractor already, you can start by running it through a car wash on the way home, unless you have a hot pressure washer of your own. Naturally, hot water or steam cleaning is going to do the best job of removing oil and grime.

Pride of work shows over every inch of this gloriously restored 1961 Massey-Ferguson 95 Super owned by Dan and Ken Peterman of Webster City, Iowa. *Chester Peterson Jr.*

Swap meets and flea markets at tractor shows are one source of parts for your vintage tractor. You'll be able to find everything from original parts that need work to reproduction parts and decals in the vendor section.

The first step in tractor restoration consists of stripping the tractor down and cleaning it up.

Bill Anderson, a full-time tractor restorer from Superior, Nebraska, likes to spray oven cleaner on some of the really greasy areas and let it soak before power washing the whole tractor. Others use a hand-pump sprayer to soak the tractor and engine with diesel fuel for several hours. Spray-on engine degreaser can be an asset, as well.

Chances are, though, it's going to take more than hot water and engine cleaner. Grease that has mixed with dirt and debris and has become baked on by engine or transmission heat can get as hard as rock. So you'll want to keep a putty knife and wire brush handy while you're cleaning.

If you're doing a true restoration, you should start disassembling the tractor at this point anyway. Start by removing the major components, like the hood, fenders, fuel tank, and so on. Not only will it make the job of mechanical restoration easier, but you will be able to do a more thorough job of cleaning and painting the part if it is already off the tractor.

While cleaning the tractor and stripping paint, keep in mind that any traces of grease, oil, rust, and old paint can create problems with paint adhesion. The goal is to make sure every surface will hold the paint you will be applying later.

Naturally, there are several methods that you can use for removing grease, paint, and rust, and each has its own place, along with advantages and disadvantages.

It is not recommended that you use gasoline or kerosene as a cleaner. There are cleaners and degreasers available at any automotive store that are both safer and more effective.

DISASSEMBLY

Either before, during, or after cleaning, you'll need to start tearing the tractor apart, beginning with things like the fenders, fuel tank, grille, hood, and so on. Again, take your time. Label parts, if necessary, so you can remember how they fit back together.

Obviously, you're going to have a number of bolts, nuts, and washers to keep track of, too. One way to organize them is to collect a bunch of egg cartons and put the nuts and bolts from different areas into individual egg compartments. You can even use and label separate egg cartons for different parts of the tractor (i.e., one for the grille and hood, one for the transmission cover, etc.). For bigger bolts or parts, you can use coffee cans, plastic butter tubs, etc.

Whatever you do, don't throw anything away while you're tearing a tractor apart. Even if a piece is rusted

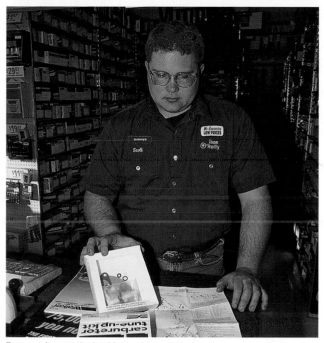

Farm equipment dealerships and automotive parts stores are also good sources of tractor parts, like this carburetor kit for an Allis-Chalmers Model WD. Notice that it also includes full instructions for carburetor overhaul.

beyond any possible use, it may be needed as a pattern for creating a new piece later on.

You'll also need to think ahead at times. As an example, some restorers have been known to leave the exhaust manifold attached to the head until they know for sure they can locate a replacement gasket.

Finally, be careful about using too much force when trying to remove rusted or frozen parts. In your haste to break things loose, it's easy to damage irreplaceable parts. Quite often, the best bet is to use a combination of penetrating oil, patience, and a proper tool. In other words, don't try to put a pipe or extension on a 3/8-inch socket handle and expect to break a bolt loose. It may take a 3/4-inch set or an impact wrench.

If the part can withstand the heat, a propane or oxyacetylene torch and occasional taps with a hammer can be as effective as anything. Alternately using heat and penetrating oil can also be helpful. Just don't apply oil to hot metal or direct an open flame toward a pool of penetrating oil. Be careful, too, about using a torch on a part where the heat can be transferred to a bearing. Using a torch to loosen the flywheel on a John Deere two-cylinder tractor is a good example. Unless you know you're going to be replacing the driveshaft bearing, the time you save may not be worth the cost.

REMOVING BROKEN OR DAMAGED BOLTS

One of the greatest frustrations of tractor restoration is dealing with a rusted bolt that simply will not budge. Fortunately, there are a few steps you can take to get that stubborn object removed.

First, determine if the bolt is actually rusted in place. It's not likely that this is the case with an antique tractor or implement, but some more modern equipment uses a thread-locking material on certain bolts. If that is the case, you will need to use heat to soften it.

If it is in fact a bolt that is rusted in place, use a wire brush to clean the area and to remove as much rust as possible from the bolt or nut and threads.

If possible, determine the type of material used in both the bolt and the surrounding material. Dissimilar metals have differing capacities for heat transference and dissipation.

Start by using a good-quality penetrating oil to loosen the threads. If you search the restoration forums, you can find a wide range of home formulas, including diet cola; a mixture of half acetone and half automatic transmission fluid; vinegar and baking soda; and even hydrogen peroxide. However, most restorers prefer one of two commercial products. The first is PB Blaster Penetrating Catalyst. PB Blaster is readily available at many locations.

The second option is Kroil penetrating oil, which many restorers swear by. Kroil is often a little more difficult to find. If all else fails, you can order it direct from the manufacturer, Kano Laboratories, at www.kanolabs.com. It's worth noting here, too, that Kano Labs has two additional formulations of Kroil available that provide some of the same benefits. One is Sili Kroil, which combines penetrating oil with dimethyl silicones. The other is Penephite, a combination of penetrating oil and graphite.

Several tractor enthusiasts have also mentioned a little-known product called Mouse Milk. Primarily used by the aircraft industry, it contains both a penetrant and lubricant, which also makes it ideal for freeing up cables, slides, and linkages. You can find it at several locations online, or it can be ordered directly from the company's website at www.mousemilk.com.

Be prepared to wait long enough for the penetrating oil to work—at the very least, several hours. Some tractor restorers have talked about waiting days, if not weeks, for the material to work its way down into the threads and break loose the rust, applying more fluid every day or so.

Use the right tool to remove the bolt. Pliers and Vice-Grips will only round off the flat sides of the nut or bolts. Open-end wrenches are also more likely to slip off and round the corners. A six-point box-end wrench is generally your best option. If the nut has become smaller due to corrosion, you might be able to get a better fit with the next smaller metric or SAE size.

Use a ratchet with a long handle or a breaker bar for more leverage on the wrench. Use smooth, continuous pressure and stop if the tension starts to suddenly feel soft, rubbery, or spongy. That's often an indication the bolt is about to break off, which will usually make your problem worse. The metal can only stretch so far before shearing off, so a change in the way it moves may be an indication it has stretched too far.

If all else has failed to this point, it's often time to break out what some restorers call the "blue wrench"—a propane or oxy-acetylene torch adjusted to a hot, blue flame. Just don't apply oil to hot metal or direct an open flame toward a pool of penetrating oil. And use caution when using a torch anywhere near the fuel tank or brake fluid. Be careful, too, about using a torch on a part where the heat can be transferred to a bearing. Unless you know you're going to be replacing the bearing anyway, the time you save may not be worth the cost.

Using a combination of heat and penetrating oil or heat and an impact wrench will usually take care of even the most stubborn bolt. However, an impact wrench should be a tool of last resort, since it just makes it easier to break the bolt.

Finally, be careful about using a torch on a part where the heat can be transferred to a bearing. Using a torch to loosen the flywheel on a John Deere two-cylinder tractor is a good example. Unless you know you're going to be replacing the driveshaft bearing, the time you save may not be worth the cost.

As another option, you can try a technique used by Paul Cummings, a tractor restorer from Amsterdam, Missouri. When faced with a bolt that is rusted in place, Cummings heats the bolt with a torch until it starts to glow red. Then, holding a small candle, like those you'd put on a birthday cake, by the wick with a pair of pliers, he presses it against the bolt. As it melts, the liquid wax flows down around the bolt and threads, finding its way into any open crevices. Others who have used this trick say they simply touch the end of a candlestick candle to the hot nut or bolt and let it melt. In most cases, the combination of heat and the wax coating on the threads allows Cummings to remove the bolt without much additional force.

As an alternative to heat, a couple of manufacturers have recently come up with a product that freezes the bolt, causing the material to contract. If you've ever heard of someone putting engine cylinder sleeves in the freezer so they're easier to slip into the cylinder bores, it's the same principle. One product is Loctite Freeze and Release. Another is CRC Freeze Off Super Penetrant. Both use a freeze shock action to freeze and loosen rusted and corroded mechanisms.

Jim Deardorff, owner of Superior Coatings, a sandblasting and painting business in Chillicothe, Missouri, says one of the advantages of the freezing technique is that it doesn't ruin the bolt, which can occur when a torch is used. With heat, he explains, the molecular structure of the metal can be altered, causing the temper to be lost. So the freeze shock method can be particularly valuable on antique tractor bolts that can't be replaced.

To use the freeze-and-release products, simply remove any dirt and loose rust, shake the can well, and spray the area for 5 to 10 seconds from a distance of 4 to 6 inches. That's sufficient to chill the part to around 20 to 45 degrees Fahrenheit below zero. Parts can generally be dismantled after allowing 1 to 2 minutes for the penetrating oil in the solution to act. Repeat the application, if necessary.

Deardorff says it has occasionally taken two or three applications to break a bolt or nut loose, but it normally works with a little time.

If you have a bolt or fastener that can't be removed by ordinary means, the only option left is to drill it out. One option is to drill a hole in the bolt, or what remains of it, and use an "easy-out" to back it out of the hole. Unfortunately, many restorers say easy-outs are more trouble than they are worth or cause more damage than if you just drilled the bolt out in the first place. "Easy-outs *aren't*," simply states one tractor restorer. "If you break one off, you have just created a bigger problem than you started with. The easy-out is made of some pretty hard steel, so once you've broken one off in place, you can no longer drill it out."

If part of the old bolt is still sticking above the surface, one alternative is to find a nut that is approximately the size of the broken bolt head. Place the nut over the broken bolt and then use an arc welder to fill the nut with weld, thereby fastening the nut to the bolt from the inside. In effect, you've created a new bolt head.

If you decide to drill out the old bolt, start by making a punch mark in the center of the bolt or bolt head. This will allow you to drill a starter hole through the center axis of the bolt. Now, begin drilling out the bolt using successively larger bits until the hole through the center is nearly as wide as the bolt. Be careful not to damage the threads in the parent material by using too large a bit or drilling through a hole that is off center. In some respects, this process isn't unlike that used by a dentist doing a root canal. Nice thought, huh?

One restorer says he has had good luck using a set of left-handed drill bits to drill out a bolt, once a pilot hole has been established. Since the bit is turning in the direction you want the bolt to move, it will often come out as the heat increases and the center is hollowed out by the bit.

A second opinion can be a valuable asset when restoring a vintage machine of any kind. That's why joining a collectors club can be beneficial for more than camaraderie.

Although this John Deere two-cylinder tractor has extensive fire damage, the sheet metal appears to be in good condition. However, since you can still see where the decals were located, it would be a good idea to take measurements before stripping and cleaning the panels. It'll make the job a lot easier when it comes time to position new decals.

While it's not as easy as using a sandblaster, Estel Theis finds that a wire brush on an electric grinder can take off years of accumulated rust.

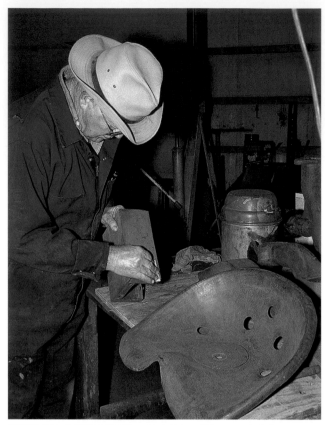

Almost every tractor restoration requires a certain amount of elbow grease—especially when cleaning smaller parts.

Sometimes, the only way to get a rusted bolt loose is to carefully apply heat and use a big wrench.

There are a number of materials on the market that can be used to repair metal parts that aren't subjected to a lot of pressure, including brands like Liquid Steel and J-B Weld.

Instead of heat, you can use Loctite Freeze and Release or CRC Freeze Off Super Penetrant to freeze a problem bolt, causing the material to contract.

One of the things you'll deal with most often in a tractor restoration is the replacement of seals, bushings, and bearings. Unfortunately, you may also run across the occasional shaft that has been damaged by a defective seal. This is generally evidenced by a groove in the shaft that is deep enough that you can feel it when you run your fingernail across it. In effect, replacing the seal at this point is not going to solve the problem. As long as the shaft is grooved, it's still going to leak.

The good news is you have a couple of options short of buying a new shaft. One is to sleeve the shaft with a sleeve such as a Speedi-Sleeve that fits over the original shaft to create a bridge over the groove. The Speedi-Sleeve is marketed by Chicago Rawhide, or CR for short.

To sleeve a shaft, you'll need to accurately measure the diameter of the shaft at a point where it hasn't been worn. Then, it's simply a matter of taking the measurement and the application information to your bearing or parts supplier. In most cases, the sleeve is thin enough that a different-sized bearing or seal is not required. The trick is just getting the sleeve installed on the shaft, using a special tool, since the fit is designed to be tight.

Another technique for repairing a groove or nick in a shaft is to fill it with a metal-type epoxy, such as Liquid Steel or J-B Weld. Generally, it's better to apply two or three thinner coats and build it up, rather than one thick coat. After the compound has cured, the shaft can be sanded down until the repaired area is flush with the rest of the shaft. Just be sure to use fine-grain sandpaper or emory cloth to start, so you don't scratch the shaft. Finish off the sanding with even finer-grit paper, in the neighborhood of 600-grit, for a smooth surface on the seal or bushing.

Chapter 4
Troubleshooting

In many respects, troubleshooting should be a supplement to your tractor-buying procedure. There are several steps that could be considered troubleshooting that you should have already done in the process of evaluating the tractor when you bought it. For the sake of finding out how serious the problems are, let's take a look at a few more things.

Whether you are an experienced tractor mechanic or a novice working on your first tractor, your senses can tell you a lot about what is wrong, if you know what you are looking for. Your sense of smell can tip you off to a problem with the radiator, clutch, or engine. Your sense of hearing can tell a distinct difference between a tick, a knock, and a grinding noise. There can be dramatic differences in the causes of such noises.

Start by looking on and under the tractor for traces of fluid. If what you find is a lighter hue, has the consistency of light maple syrup, and lacks the burned smell of combustion, it is probably from a leaking hydraulic fitting. A darker shade of brown that collects under the oil pan should be obvious. Engine oil is somewhat thicker and has the characteristic smell of having been in an engine; often it will leak out of the engine seals or leaky oil pan gaskets.

EVALUATING A TRACTOR THAT RUNS

Some restorers insist that unless the engine is totally locked up, it's best to start up the tractor and see how it runs in order to best figure out what it needs. If that means overhauling the carburetor or the magneto first,

Whether you are an experienced tractor mechanic or a novice working on your first tractor, your senses can tell you a lot about what is wrong with the tractor. *Hans Halberstadt*

or installing a temporary gas tank, that's what they will do. You can listen to the engine, run it through the gears to see how the transmission and final drive sound, and evaluate the various systems.

Chris Pratt, with *Yesterday's Tractors* online magazine, insists there are a few things you can check to avoid surprises later on. The following inspection points are just part of his troubleshooting and evaluation procedure.

Cooling System Inspection

Whether you're checking out a tractor before or after you've made a purchase, it's understandable that you want to fire it up without further delay. It will be to your advantage, however, to check out a few things while the engine is still cold. This includes the cooling system, oil pan, and transmission.

First, carefully remove the radiator cap and check for coolant. There should at least be some type of liquid in the radiator. The best thing you can find is an antifreeze solution. The next best thing is clear water. If you find only clear water, you have to wonder if it was added since last winter or if it has been in there awhile.

If you find rusty water, you can expect to find pitting inside the engine and possibly a radiator that is leaking or is about to leak. Rust in the cooling system is often an indicator that the coolant has become acidic, which means it could also start attacking metal components.

Last, but certainly not least, you'll want to make sure the coolant isn't oily. That can be an indication of seal failures; cracked parts that are allowing oil and coolant to mix; or pitted parts, which can do the same thing.

If you find that the system is leaking, look for bad hose connections in the cooling circuit, especially where the hose ends meet the radiator or connect to the thermo-siphon components. Also check the radiator core for cracked tubing or leaky ends. If leaks in this area are excessive, the core should be replaced, since the internal integrity of the core itself is probably not worth salvaging.

From the radiator, you'll want to move back to the water pump, if the engine is so equipped. Look for a steady but slow dripping or for antifreeze streaks down the front of the engine housing. Most water pumps have a hole at the base that will leak antifreeze and coolant if the seal on the pump needs to be replaced.

Oil, Transmission Fluid, and Hydraulic Fluid Inspection

Next, you should take a look at the oil, but don't just pull the dipstick to see if the level is where it should

When troubleshooting the engine and transmission, be sure to look for fluids that might have dripped onto the ground or shop floor.

be. Take a wrench and carefully loosen the drain plug to the point you could pull it out if you weren't holding it in place. Back off just enough pressure to drain out about a cup or less of oil and check it for water and antifreeze. If you get pure oil, you can rest a little more comfortably, knowing that water will settle to the bottom of a cold oil pan or gear case. A small amount of water can simply be condensation and may or may not be cause for concern. If you find antifreeze, it should raise a red flag concerning the mechanical condition of the engine. Repeat this process for the transmission/hydraulic reservoir.

Engine Starting Evaluation

Now you're ready to start the engine. Does the engine start easily when cold? Knowing that a tractor starts after just a few revolutions easily eliminates many of your concerns in one check. You may not have a guarantee on the condition of each component, but you immediately know that the battery, compression, ignition wiring, distributor/magneto, fuel flow, and carburetor are in reasonable condition.

If the engine doesn't start easily, you may still be looking at a good tractor, but you know there is a little more work ahead. Unfortunately, if you're looking at the tractor for the first time before buying it, and the unit has already been removed from the shed and warmed up prior to your arrival, you've lost out on a piece of information—namely, the cold start.

Engine Running Evaluation

Does the engine run well when it is hot? Taking the time to see how the engine runs after it has been warmed up is particularly important if you are going to be using the

Even if they are not this noticeable, oil leaks are often evident by the burnt-oil smell that comes off a hot engine.

Hopefully, you'll be able to spot bare wires like these before they reveal themselves through sparks or the smell of electrical shorts.

tractor to pull a load. Plan to spend at least a half hour running the engine to check for problems that can cause it to run poorly after it warms up. In the meantime, you can look for leaks in both the engine and radiator. After completing your inspection, shut the engine off and see how easily it starts when it is warm.

Exhaust Evaluation

Check for smoke from the exhaust. Blue smoke often indicates internal problems, such as problems with rings, pistons, or valve guides, that are difficult and costly to repair. White or black smoke can frequently be corrected with carburetion or ignition changes; however, white smoke can also mean that water is getting into the cylinders, possibly through a bad head gasket or worse, a cracked block.

Engine Noise Evaluation

Listen for noises from the engine. A ticking from the top of the engine may indicate the need for a simple valve adjustment, while a clunking or thumping sound deeper in the engine could indicate serious or expensive repairs. If possible, check if the sound becomes more pronounced under load. If a clunk becomes louder when the engine is put under a load, it may be an indication of problems with the crankshaft, bearings, or piston rods.

Oil Leakage Inspection

After the engine has been running for a while, shut it off and check the oil for foaming or the presence of water. Either condition is cause for concern. Check for oil seepage from the head and look for structural

cracks in the block. These procedures may be difficult to perform if the engine is encrusted in dirt and grease, but they can be time well spent. Check over the cast and steel components and look for hairline cracks.

Electrical System Inspection

There should be some charge showing on the ammeter when the engine is running. You should also see some change in the charging level when the lights are turned on if the tractor is so equipped. This indicates that the regulator or resistor switch and cutout are operating properly.

Governor Inspection

At some point, you'll want to make sure the governor is working correctly. Its job is to adjust the throttle to maintain engine speed as the load changes. One of the easiest ways to check the governor, assuming the steering, brakes, or tires are in good condition, is to go down and up a small hill in second or third gear, depending on the number of gears available. As you start downhill from level ground, you should hear the engine quiet down as the throttle backs off. It should automatically throttle back up to maintain the speed as you start back up the hill.

Transmission Check

Assuming the tractor is drivable, you should also check the transmission and final drive by driving the tractor around and listening to the gears. If the transmission is worn, you'll probably hear a whine when the transmission is shifted to a questionable gear.

Hydraulic System Inspection

If the tractor is so equipped, test the hydraulic system. Extend the rams on any hydraulic cylinder to test the range. If possible, use the system to lift a load, then let the load sit in the hold position for a few minutes to see if there is any leakdown. Chattering noises from the pump while lifting the load may indicate that the pump is getting an insufficient flow of hydraulic fluid. The pump will have experienced excessive wear if it has been run this way for long periods of time, and it may be on the verge of failure.

SIMPLE FIXES

On occasion, a simple fix is all that is needed to correct what may seem to be a complex or expensive problem. Always check the simple things first to avoid spending time and money on restoration steps that may not be necessary. Through his experience with tractor restoration, Chris Pratt, with *Yesterday's Tractors* online magazine, has come up with the following list of simple fixes.

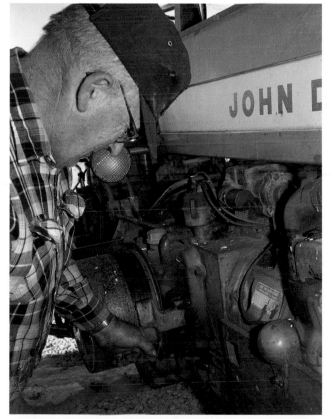

Checking the engine oil for traces of water, antifreeze, or foaming can tell you a lot about the condition of the engine and cooling system. Whitish oil often indicates water contamination in the engine.

Runs Poorly When Warmed Up

Before replacing the carburetor, check the fuel line, sediment bowl, and tank outlet. With old tractors, these often become clogged with rust sediment and cause the engine to run as if the float and float valve are damaged. Quite often the tractor will run fine when started but begin to starve out and miss after awhile.

Dies When Warmed Up

If the tractor warms up, then suddenly dies with no spark and you find that the spark does not come back until the tractor cools down, the problem is most commonly a bad condenser. Since testing condensers appears to be a lost art, it is simplest to replace them.

Good Battery Won't Actuate Starter

This problem may be most common on tractors with a 6-volt system. Before replacing the starter, check for warmth at the connections of the battery cables. It may be that the cables are of too high a gauge (the wire is too small), or the connections may be less than perfect. As a rule, 6-volt systems draw more amperage than 12-volt systems, and the connections and wiring need to be nearly perfect for the starter to function as it was intended.

Engine Is Getting Gas and Spark But Won't Start

If the engine is getting a spark at the right time and gas is getting to the plugs, yet the tractor won't start, it is likely that your gas has gone bad—particularly if the tractor has been sitting for some time. The solution may be as simple as draining and replacing the gas.

Won't Start, Water in Distributor Cap

If you have trouble with your tractor during high-moisture times, such as during a thaw or in damp conditions, check under the distributor cap for moisture. In most cases, all you have to do is dry it out and hit the starter. Since it displaces moisture on electrical connections, WD-40 sprayed on the inside of the distributor cap can also do the trick.

Overheating or Not Charging

Before you replace your water pump, thermostat, and radiator cap, be sure that you have the correct width and profile V-belt for your cooling fan. Also, ensure that it is tensioned properly. This can also cause the charging system to appear to be faulty.

Boiling Out Radiator Fluid

If the tractor is boiling out radiator fluid every time it warms up, the first thing you should do before replacing the thermostat is make sure the radiator cap is rated correctly for the system and that its spring and seal are still in good shape. The cap may be letting off steam under what was supposed to be normal pressure.

Burning Oil

A compression test indicated good compression on all cylinders, indicating that the valves, pistons, and rings are in good shape, but traces of oil smoke are coming out of the exhaust. This can be caused by the oil-bath air filter. Be sure that you are running the correct weight of oil. If the oil is too light, it will be drawn into the engine. Don't go overboard the other way, however; if the oil is too heavy, it won't clean the air. To learn more about oil-bath air filters, refer to Chapter 11 on the "Fuel System."

COMPRESSION TESTING

If you've had a chance to start or drive the tractor, you probably have an idea how well the engine runs. But for a real test, before you make the purchase or start tearing it down, you should run a compression test. This measures the pressure built up in each cylinder and helps assess the general cylinder and valve condition. It can also warn you of developing problems inside the engine.

Before you begin, you should start the engine and let it warm up to normal operating temperature. Now, shut off the engine and open the choke and throttle all the way to provide unrestricted air passage into the intake manifold. Remove all of the spark plugs and connect a compression gauge to the No. 1 cylinder following the gauge manufacturer's instructions.

At this point, you need to either have someone else crank the engine or use a remote starter switch that has been connected to the starter relay. Always follow all manufacturer's safety instructions, and make sure the transmission is in neutral and the wheels are blocked or locked prior to engaging the starter.

Crank the engine at least five compression strokes or until there is no further increase in compression shown on the gauge. Remove the tester and record the reading before moving on to the next cylinder. In addition to the psi rating, you should also note whether the needle goes up all at once, in jerks, or a little at a time.

You'll need to check the service manual for your tractor for the recommended pressure, but generally the

A compression check measures the pressure built up in each cylinder and helps assess the general cylinder and valve condition. It can also warn you of developing problems inside the engine. When performing a compression check, you'll want to record both the pressure reading and the rate at which the pressure increased. You should also compare the pressure readings between cylinders.

lowest pressure reading should be within 10 to 15 psi of the highest. Meanwhile, engine compression specs can vary anywhere from 80 to 150 psi. A greater difference indicates worn or broken rings, leaking or sticking valves, or a combination of problems.

If the initial compression test suggests a problem, you might want to confirm your suspicions with a "wet" compression test. This is done in the same way as your previous test, except that a small amount of heavyweight engine oil is poured into the cylinder through the spark plug hole before the test. Since this will help seal the rings from the top, it should help pinpoint the problem.

For example, if there is little difference between the wet and dry tests, the trouble is probably due to leaking or sticking valves or a broken piston ring. However, if the wet compression reading is significantly greater than your first reading, you can assume the problem is worn or broken piston rings.

If, on the other hand, two adjacent cylinders have similar low readings during wet and dry tests, the problem is more likely a defective head gasket between the two cylinders or a warped head-to-block surface.

TROUBLESHOOTING CHECKLIST

Sometimes the source of a problem is so simple, we overlook it. Hence, it helps to run through a checklist. Always make one adjustment at a time, and if the adjustment made does not improve the condition, return to the original setting before proceeding to the next adjustment.

GASOLINE ENGINES
Engine Fails to Start or Runs Unevenly
- Fuel valve is shut off
- Incorrect fuel in tank
- Float valve sticking
- Fuel tank empty
- Clogged fuel filter or fuel lines
- Dirty or clogged air cleaner
- Leaking or loose manifold
- Engine flooded
- Broken wires from distributor to engine
- Wires not in proper position
- Switch not turned on or defective
- Spark plugs wet, dirty or broken
- Distributor weak, or out of time
- Spark plug points pitted, dirty, or improperly spaced

Engine Overheated
- Low water level in cooling system
- Radiator clogged
- Fan belt slipping
- Collapsed radiator hose
- Thermostat stuck
- Tractor overloaded
- Improperly timed ignition
- Fuel mixture too lean
- Weak spark
- Diluted lubricating oil
- Pulling heavy load at reduced engine rpm
- Water pump impeller vanes broken

DIESEL ENGINES
Hard Starting
- Cold air temperatures
- Insufficient fuel
- Air traps
- Incorrect timing
- Loss of compression
- Dirty nozzles
- Battery charge low
- Valve clearance incorrect
- Fuel transfer pump faulty
- Fuel injection pump faulty
- Fuel injection pump out of time

Engine Overheating
- Low water level in cooling system
- Radiator clogged
- Fan belt slipping
- Collapsed radiator hose
- Thermostat stuck
- Engine overloaded
- Diluted lubricating oil
- Pulling heavy load at reduced rpm
- Water pump impeller vanes broken

Loss of Power
- Insufficient fuel
- Air in fuel line
- Restriction in fuel line
- Clogged fuel filters
- Transfer pump defective
- Late injection pump timing
- Loss of compression
- Sticking valves
- Valve clearance incorrect
- Faulty nozzles
- High idle rpm too slow

Irregular Operation
- Governor control linkage binding
- Compression pressure uneven
- Valves not seating properly
- Faulty fuel nozzles
- Low fuel pressure
- Low operating temperature
- Fuel injection pump out of time

Excessive Exhaust Smoke
- Engine overloaded
- Clogged air cleaner
- Too much fuel to engine
- Faulty fuel nozzles
- Oil consumption

Engine Knocking
- Engine overload
- Incorrect fuel
- Incorrect timing
- Air cell plugged or leaking

Your notes on how the needle moved up can tell you a lot, too. If the needle action came up only a small amount on the first stoke and a little more on succeeding strokes, ending up with a very low reading, burned, warped, or sticky valves are indicated. A low pressure buildup on the first stroke, with a gradual buildup on succeeding strokes, to a moderate reading can mean worn, stuck, or scored rings.

There can be good news, however. If the readings from all cylinders are within reasonably close proximity,

you can assume that the upper end of the engine is in good condition and may not warrant an overhaul. A simple tune-up may suffice.

If you're checking the compression on a diesel engine, the process is basically the same, except you will need to remove the injectors and seal washers. Plus, since the compression is higher on a diesel engine, you'll either need to use a different compression gauge or an adapter for diesel engines.

Chapter 5
Engine Repair and Rebuilding

The first real step in engine repair and restoration is to find out what you are dealing with and what repairs are necessary. If you're lucky, you are restoring a tractor on which the engine is already in running condition. If that is the case, all that may be needed is a good tune-up. Chapter 4 on "Troubleshooting" should have given you some ideas about how much repair is necessary.

On the other side of the coin is the engine that is completely frozen. Or the tractor may have been parked and left to rust after a piston rod broke or the engine block cracked. In either of those situations, you better figure on a complete engine rebuild.

The more common situation, though, is the engine that will run or start, but performs poorly. Perhaps it smokes, or has a distinct knock. If you're like some restorers, you may choose to overhaul the engine as part of a restoration. And if you're like others, you may be on a budget that demands just fixing what needs to be fixed. Either way, this chapter will hopefully guide you through some of the processes.

FREEING A STUCK ENGINE

Ask a dozen tractor restorers how to free a stuck engine and you're likely to get a dozen different answers. Each one seems to have his own favorite method. Unfortunately, few of them are quick fixes; they all take time and patience.

Most often, engines get stuck because the pistons and cylinder walls or sleeves have rusted together. This can occur as a result of water directly entering the engine or by condensation, or "block sweat," inside the engine, which leads to flash rust.

With a little time and work, flash rust can often be broken loose fairly easily. Unfortunately, pistons that are practically welded to the cylinder walls are a much bigger challenge.

The head on this Buda engine, which powered numerous Cockshutt and Co-op tractors, has already been removed in preparation for engine overhaul.

One advantage of Minneapolis-Moline and John Deere two-cylinder engines is that the block can be removed from the tractor and placed in a press when a piston is frozen in place.

One innovative method used to free a stuck piston is to fill the cylinder with diesel fuel and then pump grease and the accompanying pressure into the cylinder through a modified spark plug/grease zerk.

Before you attempt to break anything loose, though, there are a few things to keep in mind. First, be careful about towing the tractor in gear in an attempt to free the pistons. Even if you have soaked the pistons for some time, you run the risk of damaging the engine. One possibility is that you will bend the connecting rods or components in the valvetrain, should the pistons come loose but the valves do not.

You also need to be careful about putting too much pressure on any one piston—such as with a hydraulic press—if all the pistons are still connected to the crankshaft. If the piston on which you're pushing comes loose but three others are still stuck, you not only risk damaging the piston, but the connecting rod or the crankshaft as well.

One tractor restorer says he likes to soak the piston heads and cylinder walls while leaving the connecting rods attached and the tractor blocked up on one side and in gear. Then every few days, as he walks by the tractor, he gives the back wheel a push to see if anything has loosened up. Others have devised ways to put leverage on the flywheel or belt pulley. If you do attempt to tow

the tractor at this point, make sure you are using a slow speed and you're pulling it over soft ground or gravel so the wheels will skid. Letting the wheels get a firm grip is a sure way to bend something.

Soaking the cylinders and using a press or hydraulic ram to force them loose is another option. Some tractor manufacturers, such as Minneapolis-Moline, even made this process easier for you. In the case of M-M, a center section of the engine block, which houses the pistons, can actually be removed and taken to a shop where it can be placed on a press or a bench. The center section on most John Deere two-cylinder engines can also be removed with the pistons still in the cylinders.

Another method practiced by some is to put a chain around the engine while it is still in the tractor and pour oil into the cylinders. A round, wooden block is then cut to fit the cylinder. Finally, using the chain as a brace, a hydraulic jack is placed against the block and pressure is applied to the piston until it comes loose.

Rex Miller, a tractor restorer who lives near Avenue City, Missouri, has developed his own way of breaking

Usually, the best method for breaking a piston loose is letting it soak with penetrating oil for weeks or months and applying torque along with a few taps with a hammer and block of wood.

Most Minneapolis-Moline engines were unique in that they used a separate block for every two cylinders.

With its two-cylinder, overhead-valve engine, the 21-horsepower Models M and MT represented a departure from most early John Deere tractor designs.

the pistons loose on a John Deere two-cylinder tractor. He starts by pouring as much diesel fuel as possible into the cylinder through the spark plug hole. Then he installs a spark plug, which has a hole bored through the center of it into which he has soldered a grease zerk. Miller then pumps the remainder of the cylinder full of grease, adding it to the diesel fuel that already fills most of the cylinder. As he continues to pump grease into a full cylinder, the grease gun generates several hundred pounds of pressure against the cylinder head.

When it comes to the type of lubricant or penetrating oil to pour into the cylinders, everyone seems to have their favorite recipe. Some simply use diesel fuel, while others prefer something as exotic as olive oil. Still others prefer a mixture of ingredients that may include brake fluid, penetrating oil, automatic transmission fluid, kerosene, Hoppe's gun solvent, oil of wintergreen, Marvel Mystery Oil, and Rislone. One restorer claims to have freed the pistons on fifteen different engines with a mixture of one-third automatic transmission fluid, one-third kerosene, and one-third Marvel Mystery Oil. Another prefers to use Seafoam, a solvent available in most automotive stores that is used for everything from cleaning carburetors to lowering the gelling temperature of diesel fuel.

Of course, if those solutions don't work, you can always try Coca-Cola, as some would suggest. Although

Since the block rests within the frame, it's fairly easy to work on a John Deere two-cylinder engine. Most times, all you have to remove is the head.

For a complete overhaul, most engines will need to be removed from the frame—or the tractor will need to be split if the engine block serves as a load-bearing member.

DETERMINING PARTS SERVICEABILITY

One of the greatest challenges when overhauling an engine is determining which parts need to be replaced, which can be reused, and the sizes to order when you do replace them. This is particularly difficult for the main and rod bearings, piston and sleeves. Moreover, the help you get from the service manuals ranges from detailed to non-existent, depending on the manufacturer.

According to Chris Pratt, with *Yesterday's Tractors* online magazine, the factors that go into determining the serviceability are the manufacturer's specifications for what is considered serviceable and the condition of the various surfaces involved. For example, you may have a main bearing surface that is within the recommended tolerances, but it may be scored too badly to use in a restoration.

Another example is a sleeve and piston that are within tolerances at the bottom, yet the upper portion of the sleeve is wider and out of specification, so instead of cylinders you have upside-down cones. An extreme example may be a piston

that looks and measures perfectly but has a hairline crack. Consequently, you may need to measure the entire surface and not stop at a single reading, watching for damage that goes beyond simple wear as you proceed.

Obviously, you'll need different tools for different surfaces, but most measurements will be given in thousandths of inches. The primary tools are a set of calipers, Plastigage, an inside micrometer, and feeler gauges. Some manufacturers also require you to use a spring scale to measure pounds of pull since they show specifications such as piston wear in terms of the pull required to remove a certain-size feeler gauge from between a piston and sleeve wall.

The first step is to locate the specifications and determine the method by which the manufacturer expects you to arrive at them. The owners and service manuals of most tractors show the required specifications. In some cases, these can also be obtained from the dealer that carries the appropriate parts.

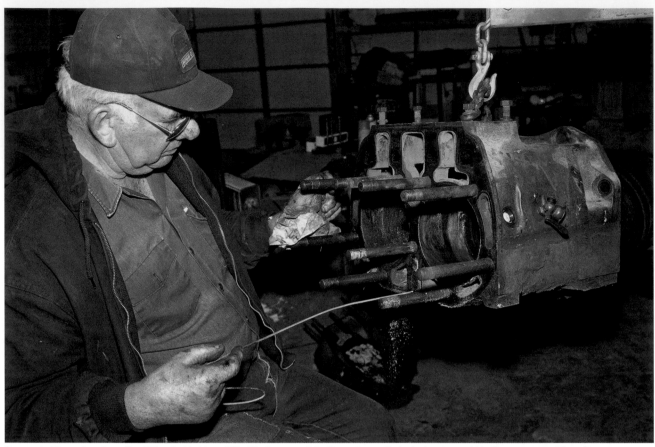

Savannah, Missouri, restorer Roy Ritter decided to pull the block on one John Deere two-cylinder just so he could better remove rust from the water passages.

they recommend the diet variety to keep sugar from gumming things up, they insist it is as effective at cutting rust as anything on the market.

The important thing to remember when trying to free a stuck engine is that it took time for the engine to set up and it will take time to free it.

RING JOB OR COMPLETE OVERHAUL?

If you have seen traces of blue smoke coming from the exhaust and the engine has been using quite a bit of oil, chances are pretty good that you are in the market for a set of piston rings. Before you can know for sure, though, you will need to check the piston-to-sleeve tolerances and surfaces, plus make sure the valve guides are not sloppy. The valve guides can exhibit the same symptoms as worn pistons and sleeves.

In most situations, it is not advisable to replace only the rings in an engine, because by the time you do the tear-down and measurement of the components, you'll find something else that justifies the need for a complete

rebuild. If you are planning to replace only the rings, however, you need to first verify all of the following:

- Bore of cylinder is not scored

- Piston is not scored, cracked, or its top surface is not eaten away

- Rings are not stuck to the cylinder wall(s)

- Bottom flanges of sleeve are not cracked

- Sleeves are not leaking oil into cooling system

- Bore is within tolerance throughout piston travel (up and down and across right angles around the bore)

- Piston ring grooves are within tolerance and not damaged

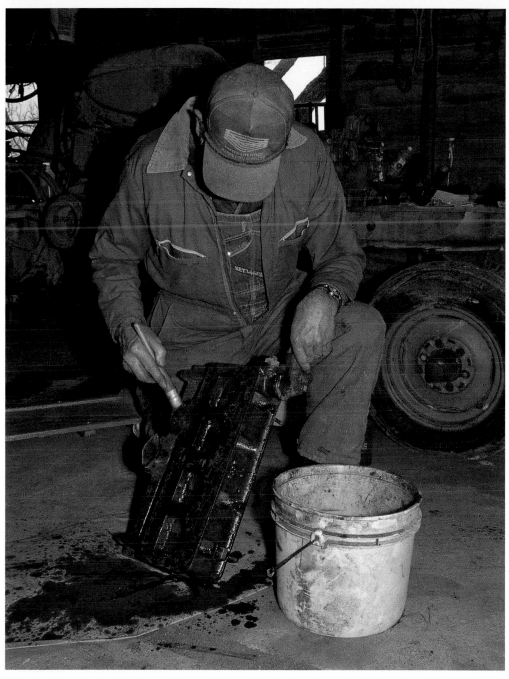

Once the head is off, you'll need to remove as much carbon and grease as possible before proceeding with a valve job.

ENGINE DISASSEMBLY

If you have a service manual for your tractor, it is best to follow the disassembly process outlined by the original manufacturer. In the absence of that material, though, the following procedure and tips should apply to most tractor models.

First, if you haven't done so already, you will need to drain all the fluids from the engine. This includes water and antifreeze, fuel, and oil. You'll also need to remove the engine hood, grille, radiator, and fuel tank to expose the engine.

Now, you may want to move to the bottom of the engine and remove the oil pan. This is fairly straightforward in most cases, but if the oil pan is made of cast material, you should loosen the bolts in an alternating pattern to prevent any warpage. As you remove the oil pan, look for any pieces of metal or shavings that might be a clue to engine problems.

A couple of the sleeves on this four-cylinder engine came out of the block easily. But the other two required a little persuasion after the engine was pulled.

Once the pistons have been removed, check the cylinders for signs of scoring or wear. Whether you're just replacing the rings or doing a complete overhaul, it's important that you carefully examine the pistons for damage.

To determine how much the ring grooves have worn, insert the new piston ring in the appropriate groove and measure the side clearance. Your repair manual should list the allowable tolerance.

At this point, you have a decision to make. If you're only replacing the piston rings, it is possible on some tractor engines to pull the pistons out from below by simply removing the rod bearing caps. Unfortunately, if you don't remove the head, you will not be able to remove the ridge at the top of the cylinder. This process can only be done from the top with a tool called a ridge reamer.

This ridge is formed naturally as the piston and ring travel up and down thousands of times in the cylinder. In essence, the area of piston travel wears, while the portion above it does not. If you don't remove this ridge, though, there is a possibility that the new, larger, sharp-edged rings will be broken by contacting the ridge. This means another tear-down, another set of piston rings, and the chance of sleeve replacement due to scoring. So for the sake of doing it right from the beginning, it's usually best to go ahead and take off the head. This will also let you remove the pistons from the top; plus, you can test the valves for proper sealing and measure the tolerances of the head and block surface.

First, remove any components or accessories attached to the engine, such as the coil, spark plug wire brackets, etc. Also remove the valve cover. If the engine utilizes a valve-in-head design, you should remove the intake and exhaust manifolds at this time, as well.

Now, begin loosening the head bolts a quarter turn at a time in an alternating pattern. If you have a service manual for the tractor and it shows a tightening pattern, simply loosen them in reverse order. This will slowly relieve the stress on the head and lessen the potential for warping or cracking.

If it becomes necessary to pry the head off to get it loose, make sure you are prying against the gasket, and not the block. You'll be replacing the gasket later anyway.

Once you have the head off the block, you can remove the ridge at the top of the cylinder using the

Before honing the cylinder, make sure the cylinder walls and hone are free of particles that could cause scoring.

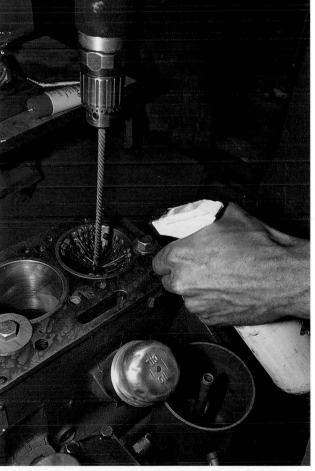

While honing the cylinder, keep the drill moving to create a nice cross-hatch surface. You should also keep the hone well lubricated.

The fact that this two-cylinder John Deere block had rusted through where it contacted the frame wasn't noticeable until the block was pulled.

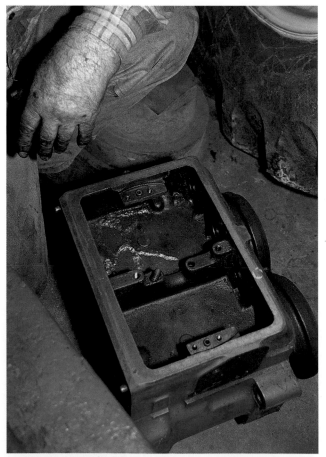

At some point, a previous owner had decided to have this John Deere two-cylinder block welded. Rather than reuse it, though, Estel Theis chose to replace it with a used block.

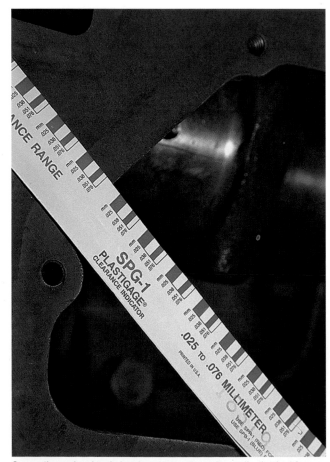

Connecting rod and main bearing clearance can be easily checked for tolerance using the appropriate size of Plastigage.

ridge reamer. Since this is one of those tools that is only used on occasions, perhaps you can borrow or rent one.

Now, you can remove the rod-bearing caps and pull the pistons out the top of the block. Then, examine both the pistons and the cylinder walls for scoring that would suggest the need for more than just ring replacement. In the process, try to keep carbon from getting into the cylinders, particularly the water and oil passages.

PISTON RING REPLACEMENT

Once you have removed the pistons and checked them for scoring, you'll need to remove the rings by carefully spreading them from the break or ring gap. This is most easily done with a special tool called a ring spreader. An inexpensive ring spreader looks like a pair of pliers that open when squeezed. More-expensive ring spreaders have the same design but also have a band to wrap completely around the circumference of the ring to ensure that you don't elongate or spread the ring gap too far. This is not that important on your old rings since you are throwing them away, but on the new ones it is critical.

Once the rings are removed from the pistons, examine the grooves that the rings fit into and make sure they are not damaged. You will also need to carefully clean the grooves to remove carbon and dirt that would hamper the correct seating of the new rings.

Next, you'll need to determine the size of the new rings by measuring the bore and determining what oversize will completely fill the gap when the piston is at the top of its stroke. The manufacturer's required ring gap should also be taken into account. The ring gap is the clearance left at the split in the ring when the ring is as compressed as it will be in the cylinder. This usually occurs at the top of the piston's stroke.

In most cases, going one oversize up from the existing rings is sufficient, since ring replacement is done only when there is little wear on the piston and cylinder. If it takes more than one size increase, you might want to consider a more thorough overhaul.

Once you've determined the ring size, you'll need to hone the cylinder to remove the smoothness—generally referred to as a *glaze*—from the cylinder bore. Otherwise, the new rings will not seat properly. A cylinder hone that fits into a 1/4-inch drill can be found at most any auto parts store.

The intent of cylinder honing is to get a nice cross-hatch surface on the cylinder. This requires moving the hone up and down as the drill operates. Never allow the drill to run in one spot, and keep the hone lubricated and

The stripped flywheel splines on this John Deere two-cylinder crankshaft have rendered it useless.

cooled with a fifty-fifty mixture of diesel fuel and kerosene, penetrating oil, or other thin lubricant. Be sure there are no large particles on the bore or hone surfaces that will cause scoring. Also, cover the crankshaft rod journals while honing to keep them protected from falling debris.

Now, it is time to check the ring gap. As stated earlier, the ring has to have the minimum specified compressed gap when it is in the cylinder bore to allow for expansion that occurs when the engine reaches operating temperature. Otherwise, the ring ends might butt together and cause scoring and ring breakage. Check your repair manual for the exact specification, but generally, it is considered to be 0.002–0.003 per inch of cylinder bore diameter.

To measure the gap, you'll need to compress the first ring and place it inside the bore. Don't put it on the piston. Now, push the ring into the cylinder using an inverted piston. This not only makes it easier to push the ring into the cylinder or sleeve, but it ensures that the ring is square with the cylinder wall. Take your feeler gauge and measure clearance between the ends of the ring. Compare this with the specifications in your manual and determine what changes, if any, are necessary. Insufficient clearance will require that the ring gap ends be filed down to tolerances.

One of the best ways to do this is to take a file and mount it vertically in a vise. Take the ring and, holding it firmly in both hands, draw it downward over the stationary file. After removing a small amount of metal, check the ring in the bore again, repeating this process as often as needed. Follow this procedure for each ring making sure you note each gap specification for each particular ring.

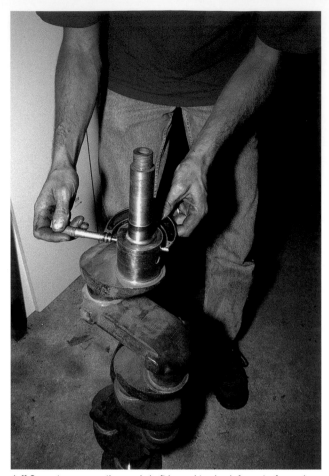

Jeff Gravert measures the crankshaft journal to check for out-of-round, taper, and wear.

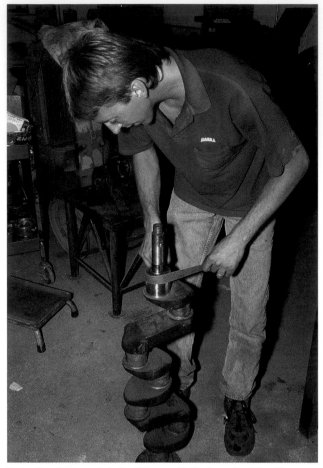

Having found the crankshaft within wear limits, Gravert polishes the journal surfaces with fine-grit emery cloth.

After the gap for each ring has been established, take each ring, insert the edge of it into the corresponding ring groove in the piston, and measure the side clearance to determine if the ring grooves are worn. There should be ample room for the proper feeler gauge between the ring and piston lands. This will be another case where you need to check the manual for the specifications. Too tight a fit will keep the rings from proper rotation and movement as the piston moves up and down. Excessive side clearance, on the other hand, will allow the rings to flutter in the piston grooves when the engine is running. This can result in poor sealing of the combustion chamber or, worse, eventual ring breakage. Make sure you place each ring in corresponding order with each piston groove and check the ring for a mark indicating the correct side up. If the ring side clearance exceeds specifications, you'll need to replace the piston.

Once everything has checked out and the ring gap has been established, it's time to install the new rings on the piston using the ring spreader to prevent overexpansion or distortion. If you're not using a ring spreader, carefully spread them by hand and slip them into the ring grooves starting with the lowest ring (the oil ring), ending with the top ring (the compression ring). Be sure to stagger the piston ring end gaps around the piston for maximum sealing.

Now, it's time to reinstall the pistons back into the cylinder. Remember, all components—especially the pistons—should be reinstalled in their original positions if they are being reused. Also, you'll need to note in your service manual whether the pistons need to be installed in a certain direction. Some have a notch on the crown that has to be oriented toward the front of the tractor. Finally, lubricate the pistons and cylinder walls with clean engine oil.

Using a suitable ring compressor to compress the piston rings, place the piston into the bore. Basically, a ring compressor is a sleeve that fits around the piston to

It doesn't take a measurement to determine that these cam shafts are unusable. Missouri restorer Roy Ritter relates that much of the damage was caused by mouse urine, which tends to be highly corrosive.

Although this two-cylinder head is salvageable, water damage has already ruined at least one valve.

Valves need to be carefully checked for warping, burning, pitting, and out-of-round wear, even if they don't have rust damage like some of these.

If you find that the cylinder bores or sleeves are scored or worn beyond specification, you have several choices. One is to bore out the sleeve or cylinder bore to the next larger size and install larger pistons. In mild cases, a larger set of piston rings will suffice to take up the gap. However, the limit with sleeves is generally in the range of 0.060 inch or less.

Still, you can usually bore dry sleeves a little thinner than wet sleeves, simply because they have the block behind them as a support. Dry sleeves, in fact, are pressed into bores in the cylinder block itself and never touch the coolant directly.

Wet sleeves, on the other hand, simply bridge the gap between the top and bottom of the block and are surrounded in-between by coolant. For this reason, they also must seal at the bottom with an O-ring.

Lastly, there are the engines that simply use a bored block without any sleeves at all. In this case, the bore size is limited only by the structural strength and thickness of the cylinder walls and the availability of replacement pistons.

Before you make any decision about boring the cylinders, though, you need to make sure the appropriate-sized pistons are available. You need to realize, also, that boring sleeves and cylinder bores is beyond the scope of even talented mechanics. You'll need to find a qualified machinist. In fact, it would be a good idea to locate both the machinist and the pistons first, and let the machinist bore the block to match the pistons.

If you're dealing with an engine with sleeves, you'll have to weigh the difference in cost between a new set of pistons and rings and a new set of sleeves. With dry-sleeved engines, you can also discard the sleeves and use pistons that fit directly in the bore.

Conversely, if you have a non-sleeved engine on which the bore is severely damaged or scored—beyond what can be repaired by overboring—you can have a machinist bore the cylinders to accept a set of custom dry sleeves. Again, you'll have to weigh the cost of custom machining and special components against that of a replacement block. But if you're dealing with a unique engine that is in short supply, you may not have a choice.

---

compress the rings enough to allow the entire piston to be slipped into the bore. Be sure the ring compressor is perfectly clean on the inside, and gently tap the piston down into the cylinder. Be careful to ensure the connecting rod studs don't scratch the cylinder walls or the crankshaft journal as you're installing the pistons. As extra insurance, you can always place pieces of plastic or rubber tubing over the connecting rod studs during piston installation.

At this point, all that is really left is to apply a light coat of engine oil to the connecting rod bearing inserts and install the bearing caps on the connecting rods.

Before you reassemble the engine, you should slip a feeler gauge in between the camshaft and its bushings to see if they have exceeded their useful life.

Since the rod bearing caps are already off, it's a good idea to also perform measurements to see if the journals need adjustment or replacement. On many machines, adjustment will simply involve removal of one or more shims, but if you don't do it while you're replacing the rings, you may have to go through the whole process again in the near future. For more specifics on determining serviceability of these components, refer to the following section.

ENGINE BLOCK PREPARATION

Before you do anything else with the block, you'll need to check it for hairline cracks. Depending upon the size of any cracks you find, you have a couple choices. One

Unless you have the equipment and experience to grind and reseat the valves, it's recommended that you take the head to a machine shop or an experienced rebuilder.

is to find a new block at the salvage yard. The other is to have the block welded by a competent welder.

Pratt notes, "Although there are probably weak points on several machines, a common example is the lower right corner on a Farmall Cub engine. This flange commonly cracks and will be a persistent oil leak once the engine is assembled."

A valve-spring compressor is used to compress the valve springs for access to the keeper. The keeper is a small pin, clip, or wedge that needs to be removed in order to remove the spring.

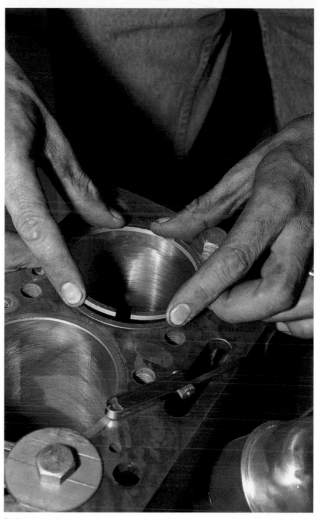

Before installing new rings on a piston, insert each one into the cylinder to check for proper end gap.

Another more common problem, he says, is the lack of flatness of the mating surface between the head and block. To check both surfaces, you'll need a straightedge, feeler gauges, and your tractor shop manual, which will provide the allowable tolerance. If the engine is sleeved, this tolerance takes on an extra importance because the sleeve stand-up (or how far the sleeves stick out of the block) must be taken into account. If there are radical differences between the cylinders following assembly, you'll need to locate the problems. These can include dirt under the sleeve flange, the sleeve setting down where the O-rings fit, or distortion of the lower mating surface. This can cause leaking at the head gasket, seepage of oil into the coolant at the base of the sleeve, and distortion of the sleeve that hampers free movement of the piston.

MAIN AND ROD BEARINGS

The main and rod bearings can generally be lumped together, since the methods used to measure them are identical. The measurement you are looking for here is the existing size of the crankshaft pin or journal. Using this figure, you can calculate which undersized replacements will bring the crank or rod journal tolerance back to factory specification.

The first step in measuring the crankshaft and bearings is to check the surfaces for scoring. If scoring is minimal, it can generally be remedied by having a machine shop turn the crank on a lathe. However, this will cause the journal to be undersized to its original specification. If the scoring or damage is too bad, you'll simply have to look for a replacement crankshaft.

Once the piston ring has been squarely positioned in its respective cylinder, measure the end gap as shown and compare it to the engine specs.

Assuming the crankshaft passes the initial inspection, use a caliper to determine if it has equal wear across the surface. If the journal has more wear on one side than the other, you will again have to look at having it turned or replaced. Finally, check to see if it has worn unevenly around the diameter of the journal, creating an oblong cross section. This can be done by taking a measurement, rotating the caliper around a quarter turn, and taking another measurement. Repeat this process a few times and you will quickly get an idea whether it is serviceable. The better manufacturers' manuals will even explain what are acceptable tolerances in this respect.

If the crankshaft does exceed the manufacturer's wear tolerances, you have two options. The first is to purchase a reground crankshaft. While this is expensive, it has the benefit of simplifying your measurements, since new bearings that have been pre-measured for the shaft are nearly always provided with the replacement. In this case, you are done with this job.

The less-expensive alternative is to have the crankshaft ground by a local machine shop. While the price is generally reasonable, there is often a wait, especially during certain times of the year, since many of these shops also work on specialty engines, such as those used for racing or tractor pulling.

Before you take a crankshaft in to be ground, though, be sure you can get the right-sized bearings to cover the amount of material the machinist will remove before you have the shaft ground. Otherwise, you may have wasted your money on the machining.

The other journal- and bearing-measurement process is accomplished by putting the whole assembly back together with Plastigage inserted between the bearing shell and the crank journal. Some manuals will talk about using shim stock to measure the clearance. However, since the advent of Plastigage, this technique is seldom, if ever, used anymore.

You should be able to find Plastigage at any good auto parts store. You'll find that it comes in different colors, like red, green, and blue. The color is a universal code for the range of clearance each particular plastic thread is capable of measuring. For example, red Plastigage is designed to measure a bearing clearance of 0.001 to 0.004 inches. If you take along your service manual, or tell the parts person how you want to use it and how much clearance you need, you shouldn't have to worry about colors. Any knowledgeable parts salesperson should be able to help you find the right size.

Basically, Plastigage is an impregnated string that squishes flat as it is squeezed between the journal and bearing shell. To use it correctly, cut a strip of Plastigage wide enough to go across the journal; then reassemble the shell and cap with the strip placed between the journal and shell; and torque the bolts to the proper specifications. Never turn the crank during this process.

Next, remove the bearing shell and compare the width of the Plastigage against a scale on the package to determine your exact clearance. Once you find this value, you can determine how much oversize will be required to bring the clearance back to that required by your manual.

"If you take the cap off and find that the Plastigage is almost round yet, you've got some problems," jokes tractor restorer Eugene Mohr.

As you've probably noticed, you have now measured the journals twice, once with a caliper and once with Plastigage. But with many old tractors, this is important. First, the caliper finds the irregularities and gross

With the rings compressed with a piston ring compressor, and the piston lined up with the bore, carefully drive the piston into the bore using a soft tool or the end of a wooden hammer handle.

When reinstalling the journal bearings, coat all the bearings with assembly grease and torque the caps to spec.

CAMSHAFTS

Although camshafts can bend, it's not likely, since the push rods tend to sacrifice themselves much sooner. The more common problem with the camshaft is worn or scored bushings. This can result when the surface went too long without oil or if a foreign object lodged in between the bushings and camshaft.

While it is possible to get the shaft turned, you'll need to first check to see if oversize bearings are available, since only standard-size bearings are normally sold for old tractors. If no oversize bearings are available, you can still have a machine shop make new bushings. Another alternative is to purchase a used or reconditioned camshaft.

ROCKER ARMS

Like the push rods, you'll need to check the rocker arms for straightness and smooth profile. Rocker arms can be distorted, which can not only make adjustment difficult, but cause the push rod to slip when combined with a slightly bent push rod.

VALVES AND VALVE SEATS

Faulty valve action is one of the main reasons for loss of power in an engine. Although carbon, corrosion, wear, and misalignment are inevitable products of normal engine operation, the problems can be minimized with high-quality fuel and valve tune-ups.

Carbon is a byproduct of combustion, so it's always going to cause some problems, like fouling spark plugs, which make the engine miss and waste fuel. But valve seats can also become pitted or be held open by carbon particles. Carbon deposits can also insulate parts and cause them to retain heat, compared to clean metal, which tends to dissipate engine heat. This increases combustion-chamber temperature and causes warping and burning.

Finally, unburned carbon residue can gum valve stems and cause them to stick in the guides. Deposits of hard carbon, with sharp points on them, can even become white hot and cause pre-ignition and pinging.

Consequently, valves need to be carefully checked for warping, burning, pitting, and out-of-round wear, especially on the exhaust valve, since it is exposed to the high temperatures of exhaust gases.

Burning and pitting are often caused by the valve failing to seat tightly due to carbon deposits on the valve seat. This in turn permits exhaust blowby, although it may also be due to weak valve springs, insufficient tappet clearance, warpage, and misalignment. Warpage occurs chiefly in the upper valve stem due to its exposure to intense heat.

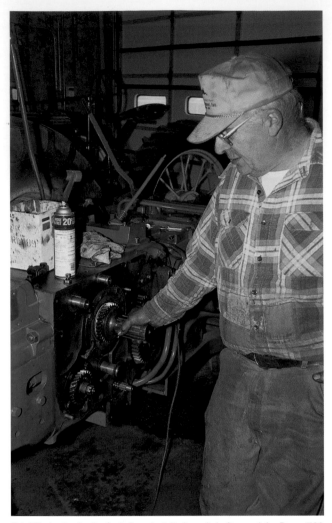

Estel Theis checks the feel of a reinstalled crankshaft on a John Deere 720.

undersizes that necessitate crank welding, grinding, or total replacement. The Plastigage process is needed to determine whether shimming is required during reassembly. If Plastigage is the only measurement you use, it may be hard to spot irregularities like conical or oblong journals. On the other hand, you virtually can't measure for the proper clearance without Plastigage.

PUSH RODS

Push rods can bend if the valve timing was off or even if a valve was adjusted to be open all the time. Visibly bent push rods should be replaced and all others should be checked. Checking them can be done with a perfectly flat surface and feeler gauges.

Although some people claim they can straighten push rods, it's usually best if you replace them, even if it means going to a salvage yard for better ones.

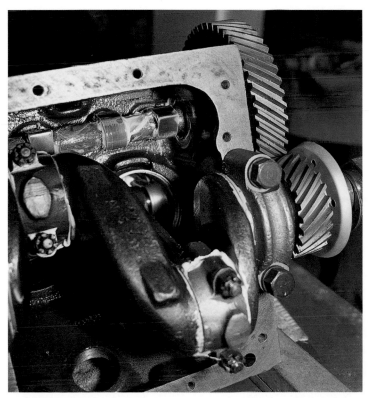

Once tightened, the cap bolts should be locked in place with cotter pins or mechanic's wire, depending upon the design.

Out-of-round wear follows when the seat is pounded by a valve whose head is not in line with the stem and guide. Oil and air are sucked past worn intake valve stems and guides into the combustion chamber, causing excessive oil consumption, forming carbon and diluting carburized fuel.

Misalignment is a product of wear, warpage, and distortion. Such wear, which is often hastened by insufficient or improper lubrication, will eventually create sloppy clearances and misalignment. Distortion, on the other hand, is generally caused by unequal tightening of cylinder head bolts.

VALVE GUIDES

Valve guides tend to warp because of the variation in temperatures over their length. Consider, for example, that the lower part of the guide is near combustion heat, while the upper is cooled by water jackets.

Any wear, warpage, or distortion affecting the valve guides destroys its function of keeping the valve head concentric with its seat, which obviously prevents sealing.

VALVE SPRINGS

Valve springs must be of a uniform length to be serviceable. To check the springs, place them on a flat, level surface and use a straight-edge ruler to determine whether there is any irregularity in height. Unequal or cocked valve springs should be replaced.

Spring tension that is too weak will also allow the valves to flutter. This aggravates wear on the valve and seat, and can result in valve breakage. If the springs are less than 1/16 inch shorter when compared with a new one, they should be replaced.

PISTONS AND SLEEVES

Just as you did with the crankshaft, you'll want to examine the piston and sleeves for any visual damage, such as scoring, out-of-roundness, and greater width on the sleeve at the highest point of piston travel (not including the ridge that forms above the high point of travel). Scoring will indicate the need for replacement regardless of the measurements. The other conditions can be determined through precise measurement.

Valve seats that are damaged or severely rusted can be renewed by machining a recess and pressing in a new seat, which is then ground to match the valves.

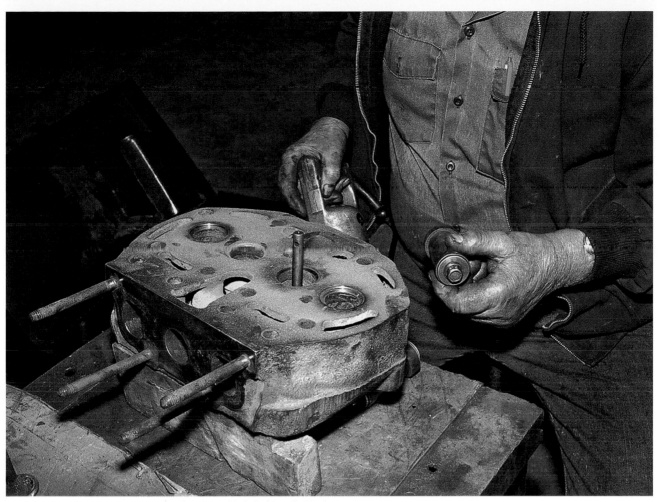
To ensure the valve seats are evenly resurfaced, a guide is first installed in the seat.

To check for out-of-roundness, use an inside micrometer to take a measurement at the top and bottom of the cylinder. Then repeat the process at right angles to the original measurements. With these numbers, you can see how conical the cylinder is and how oblong it has become. Repeat the process using your caliper on the piston. There will usually be a factory specification for what is acceptable.

Some pistons are cam ground, meaning they are supposed to be slightly out of round. Similarly, there is generally more wear at the top of the bore than at the bottom. However, the amount of deviation from the factory specifications on both the piston and the bore will determine whether the parts need to be replaced. If the engine is the type that doesn't use a sleeve, which is often the case in older tractors, the only option will be to have the block bored out and a sleeve installed in the cylinder bore.

If the differences at the top and bottom are acceptable, you may still need to determine if there is too much distance between the piston and the sleeve/bore. This will be most noticeable at the top of the stroke. Most shop manuals suggest using a long feeler gauge of a certain size placed between the piston and sleeve with the piston inserted in the sleeve. A scale is then used to pull the feeler gauge out of the bore. The amount of drag required to pull it free, as measured on the spring scale in pounds of pull, determines its serviceability. This process needs to be done without the rings in place, and the measurement is usually taken 90 degrees from the piston pin hole.

There is an additional series of sleeve measurements still to be made. You may be wondering why these measurements are needed beyond those you have already taken. Well, the real goal is to avoid any unpleasant experiences when purchasing new pistons and sleeves, like having to send them back and try again. The reason

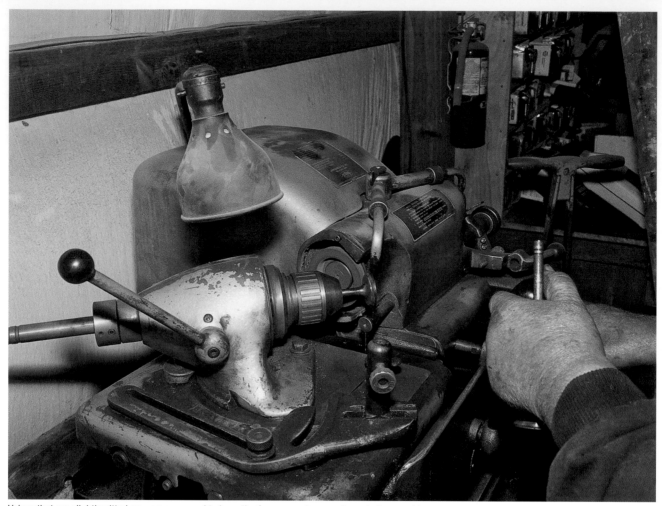

Valves that are slightly pitted or worn may need to have the face ground on a valve-grinding machine.

this happens is that many tractors had more than one sleeve size for a given model. A few tractors even had different sizes embedded in the middle of their serial number ranges.

To make matters worse, it can take some serious research to ensure that your engine was not replaced with one that is two years older and, thus, has a different block. The helpful measurements here are the bore and stroke. This is the distance across the piston and the distance the piston travels. You should also measure the thickness of the sleeve. Lastly, a few engines can be identified by measuring the outside diameter of the sleeve or the outside diameter of the base of the sleeve where it seals to the block.

According to Pratt, tractors that should always be checked for these types of differences are the Farmall A, B, and C, Super A, A-1, Super C, and the Ford N Series machines. "These are ones that I have commonly had the serious problems with, but there are probably many more," he says. "Simpler problems occur with the Allis-Chalmers D Series and the B, C, IB, and CA, where the sleeves will all fit, but you may end up with a smaller cubic-inch displacement and less power when your overhaul is complete."

PISTON PINS

The piston pin is difficult to measure without using calipers to measure the pin—and the results of this may be meaningless to the home mechanic anyway. If your tractor does not use bushed piston pins, then bearing replacement may be inexpensive and quick. If it does use bushings, then refer to the service manual for indications of wear and acceptable tolerance. The main objective is to ensure there is no detectable looseness. Some manuals, for example, state that the piston pin should be a "thumb push fit" in the piston pin bore.

Resurfacing the valve seats with a valve seat grinder can improve valve seating and combustion to like-new condition.

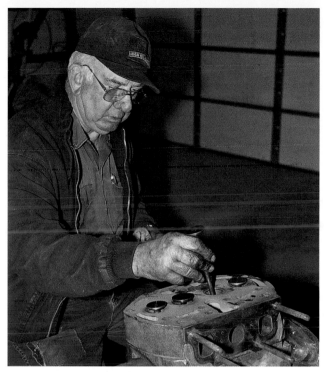

To lap the valves, coat the valve face with lapping compound, which contains fine abrasives, and place the valves in the appropriate valve guides (without any of the springs installed).

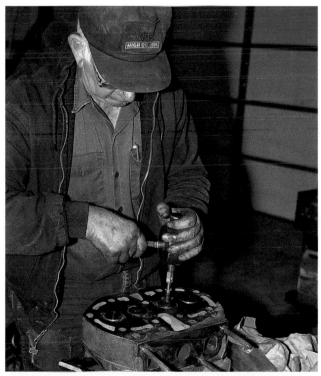

Using the valve-lapping tool, which usually has a suction cup on one end, rotate the valve until the face and seat have matching polished areas that are smooth and clean.

REBUILDING THE ENGINE

If you're planning to completely overhaul the engine, you may want to consider purchasing an engine rebuild kit—assuming there is one available for your tractor. Most have all the replacement parts you'll need for overhauling an engine without going to the store to purchase separately gaskets, special measuring tools, or miscellaneous parts. But don't let the matching sleeves, pistons, rings, and bearings lead you into a false sense of security. They, too, need to be measured and installed in a workshop environment.

If you are going for a total rebuild, your best bet at this point is to have the engine block, head, and any other major grease-carrying components professionally cleaned in a hot chemical bath. This process will not only strip those components of grease and paint, but it will also remove carbon, varnish, and oil sludge from both the inside and outside of each part.

While the engine components are out for cleaning, it's also a good idea to have a professional magnaflux the engine block and head for cracks that are not visible to the naked eye and, as a result, would have been overlooked in your original inspection. This investment alone could save you a lot of time and money.

Meanwhile, smaller parts can be cleaned in the shop using a solvent tank, then dried, inspected for integrity, and placed on a clean rag. When the engine comes back from the machine shop, it should ideally be mounted on a rotating engine stand and prepared for reassembly.

Use an air hose from your air compressor to blow out the engine block. Be sure to hit all the openings and bolt holes to remove any residue that may be left. A clean solvent rag can be used to wipe off the internal surfaces to remove any film left over from the tanking process. Hopefully, the machine shop has reinstalled the casting plugs (sometimes called *freeze plugs*) and oil galley plugs.

It is generally recommended that the head be reworked in its entirety by the machine shop, as well. Pressing in valve guides, getting the correct angles on the valve seats, setting the proper valve-to-head recession, and measuring and milling warped surfaces, among other things, are really beyond the scope of the average home shop level.

Crankshaft and camshaft measuring, grinding, and polishing are also out of the realm of the home shop. It is wise, though, to always double-check the machine shop's work with a feeler gauge, dial indicator, and Plastigage. It is important to check the crank end play with a feeler gauge and also to check each bearing journal with Plastigage before starting the reassembly procedure.

If your rebuild includes cylinder sleeves, you may also want to look at having the machine shop install these, as well. The need for cylinder sleeves, of course, will depend on your engine model and the amount of wear on the engine. Some engine manufacturers used replaceable sleeves, or liners, on all their engines, while others relied on the ruggedness of a cast-iron block to resist wear.

If you're going to be putting in a set of cylinder sleeves yourself, one restoration specialist recommends putting the sleeves in the freezer for a couple of hours. This will cause the metal to shrink just enough to slip into the cylinder bores a little easier. Place the block on a hydraulic press and line it and the ram up with the sleeve. Place some cylinder sealer around the upper end of the sleeve, install an adapter on the top of the sleeve

Having been cleaned and lapped, the valves are reinstalled in the head or block, depending upon the engine configuration.

The last step in valvetrain overhaul is reinstalling the valve springs and adjusting the tappet clearance to specifications.

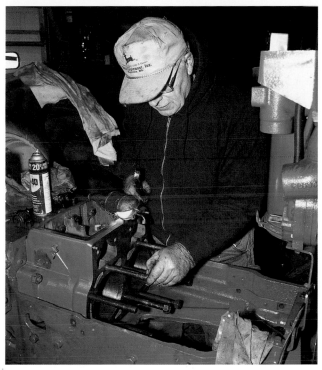

Before reinstalling the head, make sure the threads on the head bolts are clean and reusable.

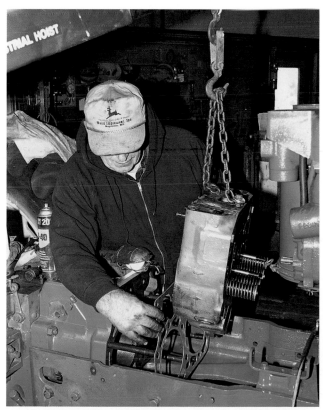

Install a new head gasket, making sure it is oriented correctly. Then, position the head back on the block.

that will mate to the ram, and quickly but gently press the sleeve into the bore.

Don't stop midway for any reason as the natural heat from the block will quickly cause the sleeve to expand, increasing the risk of breakage. Only stop when the sleeve is flush with the top of the block.

If you're simply honing the old sleeves or the cylinder walls, you can refer back to the piston ring replacement section for this process.

Now that the sleeves are in place or the cylinders have been honed, the next step is to match the pistons to each cylinder. Refer to your shop manual and locate the piston-to-cylinder wall measurement. Generally, it should be around a 0.004-to-0.007-inch sidewall clearance. To obtain this measurement, you'll need to locate a long feeler gauge, commonly called a ribbon gauge. Install the piston in the bore and see if the specified feeler gauge will slip in next to the piston. The proper fit is when the ribbon gauges can be pulled from between the piston and sleeve with a specified inch-pound pull as verified by an inch-pound scale. If you don't have the recommended scales, you should at least make sure the feeler can be pulled out freely with moderate pressure and without binding. You should also check the piston at the top and at the bottom of the cylinder for proper clearance in case the sleeve is tapered. Don't assume that if the piston freely falls through the bore that the clearance is adequate. If the clearance is inadequate, the cylinder bore (or sleeve) will have to be honed and then rechecked. Take the time to do it right.

Each piston will come with a certain number of piston rings. Unwrap the rings and lay them next to each piston in the order of installation. Basically, the instructions for measuring and installing the piston rings are the same as for piston ring replacement, so refer to the previous section in this chapter about piston ring replacement.

Once the piston rings have been installed, the next step in assembly is to check the piston pin-to-bushing tolerances. Once again, this is a close tolerance and is best done by a competent machine shop. An insertion pressure of pin to bushing will be slightly looser than that of the pin to piston. When dealing with clearances of 0.0002 inch or less, it is important to have the proper measuring tools. A pin too tight or too loose will cause a piston and rod to break apart under the stresses of engine operation.

VALVETRAIN OVERHAUL

Depending upon the condition of the engine when you started, you may or may not have to do major work on the valvetrain. If the engine was running when you acquired the tractor, a good visual inspection and adjustment of the tappets may be sufficient.

However, when water gets into an old engine, it seems that the valves are among the first components to suffer. As a restorer who likes to focus on orphan tractors, Bill Anderson of Superior, Nebraska, has seen his share of valvetrains that not only required one or more new valves, but valve seat restoration, as well. Generally, this can be accomplished by using a valve seat tool to regrind the seats. However, if damage to one or more valve seats is severe, it may be necessary to have a

Adding the valve cover should finish up this John Deere two-cylinder overhaul.

machinist cut recesses into the block or head that will accept special hardened valve seats.

To inspect, grind, or lap the valves and seats, you'll first need to remove them from the head or block, depending on whether it is an overhead-valve engine or a valve-in-block engine. To do this, you'll need a valve-spring compressor so you can compress each of the valve springs. Once the spring is compressed, you can remove the clip or keeper from the base of the valve spring. At this point, the valve can be lifted out. Be sure to keep the valves separate so each one can be replaced in the original seat.

Depending upon the condition of the valves, you'll have one or more options. If the valves have notches or burned sections, you'll need to replace them. However, if the valve faces and seats are simply a little rough and dirty, they can be cleaned and renewed with valve lapping. To do this, make sure the valves are returned to their original position after inspection, so you're lapping each valve into its original seat.

Before you install the valve, though, place a small bead of medium-grit valve-lapping compound around the face of the valve where it mates to the valve seat. Now, using a valve-lapping tool, rotate the valve back and forth in the seat, alternating between clockwise and counterclockwise rotation. In the simplest form, a valve-lapping tool is little more than a suction cup on a stick that you spin in your hands. Other, more sophisticated versions have a suction cup on a shaft driven by a device that looks a little like an egg beater. Some older-style lapping tools, however, engaged a slot or recesses in the valve head.

At any rate, you can move on when you have a smooth, clean surface all the way around the valve face with a matching surface on the valve seat. If necessary, add more compound during the process.

These, in turn, can be ground to the correct seating angle for your engine. Of course, some people like to install hardened seats as a routine, so the tractor can handle unleaded gas without fear of later damage.

Valve lapping should not be a substitute, though, for having the valves professionally reground. If they're in rough enough condition such that a few minutes of lapping doesn't polish up the mating surfaces, you're probably better off having a machinist grind the valves and seats. This basically consists of clamping the valve stem into what looks like a large drill chuck and turning them against a grinding wheel that renews the face to the correct angle.

When tightening the head bolts, be sure to alternate the tightening pattern and torque the bolts to spec.

All that is left now is to thoroughly clean all the parts, including the keepers. Then, check the valve springs to make sure they meet service manual specifications and reassemble the valvetrain, coating all parts with clean engine oil as you go.

Once the valves and springs have been assembled back into the head or block, you'll need to finish up by adjusting tappet clearance according to specifications. Correct clearance contributes to quiet engine operation and long valve-seat life. Insufficient clearance causes the valve to ride open, resulting in lost compression and burning. Too much clearance retards timing and shortens valve life.

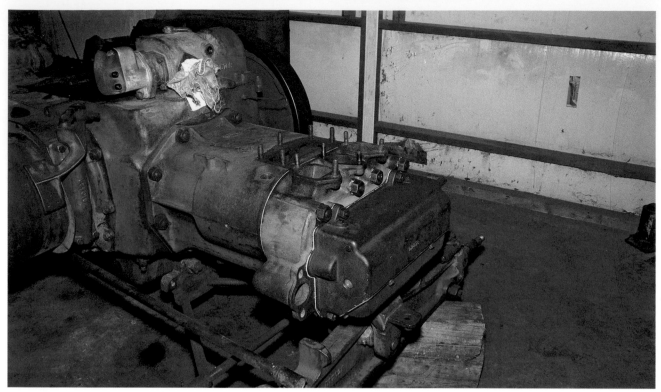

Having overhauled the engine, Ed Hoyt, who owns this John Deere Model D, is ready to move on to other parts of the tractor.

Engine overhaul sometimes involves more than one engine. Many early diesel tractors used a pony engine to start the main diesel engine.

It took a little help from another tractor linked to the belt pulley to get this old John Deere Model D started for the first time. There were plenty of observers to offer suggestions, though.

Massey-Harris smallest series, the one- and two-plow Models 81 through the 102 Junior, used a Continental four-cylinder L-head engine. This Model 81 had the 124-ci (2,031-cc) version of the engine. Owner: Ron Hoffmeister. *Ralph W. Sanders*

SPARK PLUG SUBSTITUTION

It should come as no surprise that many of the original spark plugs used in antique tractors are no longer available—at least not under the number listed on the old plug. Fortunately, a group of antique tractor enthusiasts has come up with a list of sutstitutes.

The following chart, which can be found on *Alan's Old Tractor and Steam Engine* home page on the Internet, was first published in the *K & O Steam and Gas Engine Association Newsletter*. In each case, the "new plug" is a Champion replacement number for the "old plug."

Old Plug	New Champion Plug	Old Plug	New Champion Plug	Old Plug	New Champion Plug
0 Com	W-10	8 COM	D-16	XJ-12Y	XJ-13Y
1 Com	W-14	D-8	K-97F	F-14Y	UF-14Y
2 Com	W-18	DL-8C	K-98F	C-15	D-21
J-2	J-57-R	JT-8	CJ-8	J-18Y	UJ-18Y
K-2	J-57R	L-8	L-14	20	W-20
3 Com	W-18	Y-8	UY-6	36	C-97B
J-3	J-62R	9	D-21	C-36	B-86N
K-3	J-62R	F-9Y	UF-9Y	44	W-89D
4 Com	D-6	H-9	H-8	45	W-95D
C-4	C-16Y	J-9Y	UJ10Y	49	D-89D
Y-4A	UY-6	10 Com	D-23	J-79	J-2J
Com	D-9	L-10S	L-7	S-79N	RS-79N
5MJ	D-9J	F-11Y	UF11Y	L-82Y	UL-82Y
6 Com	D-14	H-11J	H-11	J-91	CJ-8
6 MJ	K-15J	L-11S	L-7	73 0	L-87Y
Y-6	UY-6	H-12J	H-12	813	D-21
XY-6	UY-6	J-12	UJ-12	901	W-85N
7	D-16	J-12Y	UJ-12Y	H-9J	J-8J
XL-7	XL-85	L-12Y	UL-12Y		

This illustration shows how the oil pump on a Minneapolis-Moline Model U is positioned and held in place.

CAP SCREW

PUMP SCREEN

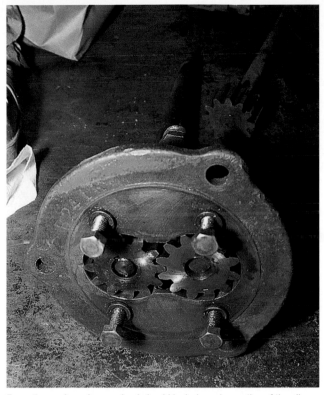

Every thorough engine overhaul should include an inspection of the oil pump, since it provides the life blood to engine parts.

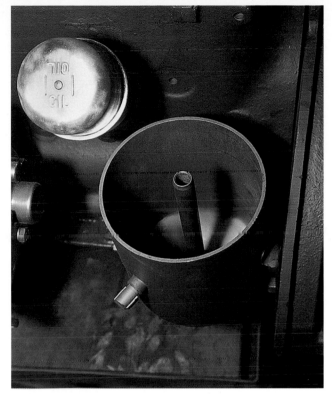

Finally, make sure the oil-filter housing has been cleaned and that all oil passages are open.

OIL PUMP RESTORATION

Any thorough engine overhaul should include an inspection of the oil pump. Although oil pumps can be of the vane type or gear type, almost all vintage tractors use the latter. Like the gear pumps used in some hydraulic systems, the pump uses two gears that mesh together to create an area of high pressure on one side of the gears and low pressure on the other side. As one gear drives the other and the teeth mesh, oil is carried around the outside between the gear teeth and housing.

Inspection involves cleaning or replacing the pickup screen and checking the gear surfaces and housing for wear and cracking. Be sure to also check for worn bushings

or bearings and ensure that all oil passages are clear. The oil pump on the Allis-Chalmers WD and WD-45, for example, includes a groove up the body and shaft that lubricates the cam-drive gear. Hence, excessive wear on the shaft or body can cause low pump pressure. Check your repair manual if you have any doubt about wear criteria.

Finally, make sure you use the correct thickness of gasket between the pickup screen and gear housing when you put everything back together. This not only affects the clearance, but it can affect oil pressure. Ideally, the pump should also be primed before replacing the oil pan. One way to do this is to pack it with a lithium-based grease, commonly called white lube, before replacing the oil pan.

Chapter 6
Clutch, Transmission, and PTO

When it comes to transmissions, it's usually a good news, bad news situation. The good news is that transmissions were probably the toughest-built items on antique tractors. In fact, about the only time a tractor restorer faces a big problem is when a transmission failure was the reason the tractor was permanently parked in the tree row in the first place—and that's the bad news. As an example, some tractor models, including the Farmall M and H, have little clearance between certain gears and the bottom of the transmission case. In the event of bearing failure, ball bearings were known to occasionally drop to the bottom of the case. Now, picture the gear teeth catching that ball bearing but having insufficient clearance to move it out of the way. The only place for the little steel ball to go was through the bottom of the transmission case.

If the tractor is in running condition, you should have had the opportunity to drive it and run it through the gears before you made the purchase. Hence, you should have an idea where the trouble lies. Often it will be with one of the gears that saw a lot of field work, particularly if there were only three or four gears in the transmission.

Other things to watch out for are the effects of dirt and water. Just as with a modern-day transmission, dirt is the gearbox's biggest enemy. If the shift boot has worn or rotted away, then there's probably water in the transmission, too.

Still, there's a good chance that you will get lucky and find that all it takes to get the transmission in working order is to drain it, clean it up, and refill it with fresh transmission fluid. In fact, most tractor enthusiasts say that's all that has been needed on the majority of the tractors they have restored.

If the transmission appears to work satisfactorily, but is just a little noisy, replacing the transmission fluid with a heavier-weight product—going from GL5 to GL4 lubricant, for example—may take care of the problem. That's assuming you're primarily going to use the tractor on occasion for parades and shows. If you plan to use the tractor as a work machine, this may just cover a larger malady.

That's probably not the case with the clutch, though. If during your test drive—assuming the tractor is in running condition—you found the clutch slipping or chattering, you'll need to take a closer look. Most likely the problem is a worn clutch plate. At any rate, the clutch is probably going to need more attention than the transmission.

When working on a John Deere two-cylinder tractor, you have the luxury of being able to overhaul the transmission and clutch without pulling the engine.

SHIM — PRESSURE WASHER — RELEASE LEVER ROLLER — LINK PIN — PIVOT PIN — BACK PLATE SPRING — CENTER PLATE — FRONT PLATE — STUD — DRIVEN DISC — PRESSURE PLATE — RELEASE LEVER — WASHER RETAINER — LEVER LINK — BACK PLATE — SNAP RING

This exploded view shows an Allis-Chalmers clutch typical of that used on most overhead-valve engines. *AGCO Corporation*

TRANSMISSION INSPECTION AND REPAIR

As was stated earlier, transmissions used in tractors built in the 1920s, 1930s, and beyond were generally heavy-duty enough that they don't present any major problems, even after sitting for several years. Still, it is a good idea to at least open up the transmission to check out the gears and clean them up.

Several restorers say they like to drain any fluid they find in the transmission case and replace it with diesel fuel. Keep in mind that after sitting for several years, the fluid can be about as thick as tar. While you're draining the transmission, keep an eye out for pieces of metal or fine shavings that can tip you off to problems. Many times, there will be a magnet built into the drain plug to help catch these things.

Now, drive the tractor around the yard for several minutes to circulate the diesel around the transmission case, coating and rinsing all the gears. If the tractor can't be driven but can be towed, that would be your next-best option.

If you can't use gear action to do the work, though, you'll need to clean every part you can reach with cleaner and a stiff brush.

Next, inspect all the bearings, shafts, and seals for damage. Rotate the gears with your fingers as you go through the cleaning and inspection process. At the same time, check for looseness and rough action. If it wobbles or shakes, it's probably going to need repair.

Keep in mind, too, that transmissions built in the early part of the twentieth century were not synchronized like they are today. So if farmers didn't wait until the tractor stopped before shifting, they had a tendency to round off the gears. This was particularly the case with the "road gear" in many late 1930s and 1940s tractors. Consequently, you may find a gear or two that needs replacement due to ground teeth.

The main cause of noisy transmissions is damaged teeth on one or more of the gears. Sometimes even the slightest indentation of a gear will cause a distinct noise. Quite often, the damaged teeth can be smoothed up with a grinding stone passed back and forth over the damaged area. If this doesn't work, you'll need to find a replacement gear.

Unfortunately, the biggest challenge with transmission repair may not be the removal and replacement of a defective gear or bearing, but finding the necessary part in the first place—or finding it at a reasonable price. One option is to check at swap meets and salvage yards. Armed with all the measurements, you might also be able to find similar gears from another tractor model within the same brand. Another option, if you're faced with a transmission that needs extensive repair is to buy a rebuilt transmission or a used transmission that's in better shape from a salvage yard.

While inspecting or rebuilding the transmission, it's also important to pay particular attention to all transmission bearings. It should go without saying that any bearings and seals that look bad should be replaced.

CLUTCH INSPECTION AND REBUILDING

Once you've finished with the transmission—either having cleaned it and verified its condition, or replaced the appropriate gears and bearings—it's time to move on to the clutch. Essentially, these two components work together anyway.

The first step in transmission overhaul is cleaning up the gears and shifting mechanism. You should then inspect the gears for missing teeth.

Whether the transmission is inline with the engine or horizontal, like this John Deere two-cylinder, the next step is checking the bearings and seals.

Overhauling a clutch is never an easy job. But it's one of the most important, partly due to the safety issues. Obviously, you want the tractor to stop when you push in on the clutch and apply the brake. But if you have a tractor on which the clutch has rusted to the shaft, it's also possible for the tractor to move when the engine is started, even if the transmission is in neutral.

While some of the early tractors, including steam tractors, had positive-engagement clutches, the move toward internal-combustion engines necessitated the use of a friction clutch that could be slipped as the drive was engaged.

With the exception of John Deere two-cylinder tractors, which used an external, twin-disc clutch, most vintage tractors used a plate clutch that was attached to the engine flywheel. That means the tractor needs to be split at the bell housing or the engine removed for clutch replacement or inspection.

If you drove the tractor before you purchased it or started restoration, you should already have an idea

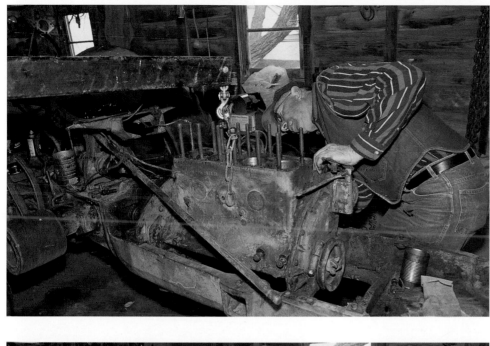

To access the clutch in most vintage tractors, you'll either need to pull the engine or split the tractor on models that use the engine and transmission as a structural support.

You can tell a lot about the transmission by simply shifting it into each gear and twisting or rocking the input shaft, as demonstrated by Stan Stamm, a farmer and tractor restorer from Washington, Kansas.

whether the clutch needs attention. Usually the trouble is obvious and falls into one of three categories:

- The clutch slips, chatters, or grabs when engaged
- It spins or drags when disengaged
- You experience clutch noises or clutch pedal pulsations

If the clutch slips, chatters, or grabs when engaged, or drags when disengaged, the first thing you should do before tearing into the clutch itself is see if the clutch linkage is improperly adjusted. In some cases, free travel of the clutch pedal is the only adjustment necessary for proper operation of the clutch—assuming your tractor is equipped with a foot clutch. Free travel is the distance the clutch pedal can be pushed before resistance is met. Refer to the repair manual for your tractor for this dimension.

On tractors with a hand clutch, there should be a definite feel of over-center action when pushing forward on the hand lever. A slight pressure should be felt in the

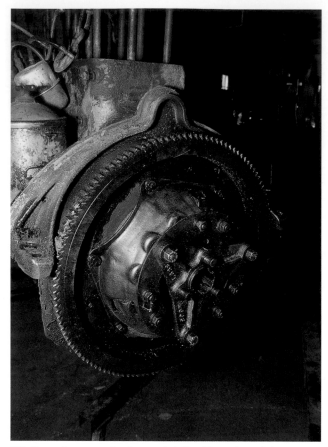

With the engine removed and supported, Stan Stamm is ready to rebuild the clutch on a vintage Co-op tractor, which was actually built by Cockshutt.

The chip in this throwout bearing from a Farmall Cub makes the need for a replacement rather obvious.

TORQUE AMPLIFIERS AND POWER-SHIFT TRANSMISSIONS

While it's true that most transmissions used on vintage tractors were limited to only four or five gears, some manufacturers began incorporating planetary gear systems for even more versatility. Among them was Ford, which introduced its ten-speed Select-O-Speed planetary transmission in 1959. Basically, the Select-O-Speed was a power-shift transmission that allowed the operator to shift from one speed range to the next without interrupting engine power.

International Harvester had its own version in the Torque Amplifier, which saw use as early as the Model M and W6. Models equipped with the Torque Amplifier were appropriately designated the MTA and W6TA. Later models, such as the 460 and 560, included a Torque Amplifier as standard equipment.

Basically, torque amplification is provided by a planetary gear reduction unit located between the engine clutch and transmission. The unit is controlled by a hand-operated, single-plate, spring-loaded clutch. When the clutch is engaged, engine power is delivered to both the primary sun gear and a planet carrier. This causes the planet carrier to rotate as a unit and

the system is in direct drive. When the clutch is disengaged, engine power is transmitted through the primary sun gear to a larger portion of the compound planet gears. As a result, an overall gear reduction of 1.482:1 is obtained when the torque amplification clutch is disengaged. Best of all, the reduction could be obtained without clutching and without interrupting engine power.

With the Ford Select-O-Speed, four planetary gear sets were used to provide ten forward and two reverse speeds. Speed, or gear, changes were made through a series of externally contracting brake/clutch units that stopped or released different segments of the planetary gear sets.

Due to the complexity of these types of units, it is often beyond the capability of most restorers to make repairs. Consequently, you may want to have the transmission serviced by the local equipment dealer or a qualified mechanic. If you choose to attempt it yourself, make sure you're equipped with a detailed service manual.

John Deere two-cylinder tractors incorporate the clutch with the belt pulley. The clutch is adjusted by evenly tightening each of the three nuts on the adjusting disc.

hand lever, then a definite release of pressure as the clutch goes into engagement.

It's worth noting, too, that the clutch linkage on some tractors, such as the Ford N Series, can be adjusted externally at or near the pedal linkage, while others, such as some of the International Harvester tractors, require you to make the adjustments through a hand hole cover in the clutch housing.

Beyond clutch linkage adjustment, the cause of most problems are generally found in the clutch housing where clutch components are either worn, damaged, or soaked with oil, which is causing the clutch facing to slip. Most often, the culprit is pressure springs that are weak or broken, or the friction disc facings are worn. Hence, clutch restoration generally consists of cleaning and checking all parts for wear, replacing bushings in the sleeve, if necessary, and replacing the clutch lining.

Although the clutch lining is attached with rivets on the majority of vintage tractors, some tractors use a drive plate to which the friction disc is bonded. If available, your best bet is to replace the entire clutch plate with a remanufactured part. If you're working with an older tractor, though, you may have to have a machine shop reline the existing plates by riveting new linings in place.

CLUTCH THROW-OUT BEARING

Another potential problem spot is the throw-out bearing, which compresses the springs to release pressure on the plates when the clutch is pushed in. Characteristics associated with a defective throw-out bearing include squealing when the clutch is released and rough

The John Deere clutch is engaged and disengaged by a set of clutch dogs that engage or release the spring pressure on the facings and clutch plates.

John Deere recommends replacing any clutch facings that are worn, badly glazed, or oil soaked.

If you're in the process of restoring a vintage John Deere two-cylinder tractor, forget everything you may have read in the previous pages on clutch restoration. Deere was unique in the fact that the clutch was external from the transmission and flywheel. In fact, it's on the opposite side of the tractor from the flywheel, where it was incorporated with the belt pulley.

To adjust the clutch, you need only remove the belt-pulley dust cover and the cotter pin from each of three clutch-adjustment bolts. Then, with the clutch in the engaged position, tighten the nuts evenly a little at a time and to the same tension. Check the tightness of the clutch after each adjustment by disengaging and re-engaging the clutch. When the adjustment is correct, the clutch lever will produce a distinct snap when engaged. Your tractor service manual should also provide you with a figure on how many pounds of pressure it takes to lock the clutch in the engaged position.

In practice, the clutch is engaged and disengaged by a set of clutch dogs that engages or releases the spring pressure on the facings and clutch plates. At the same time, the clutch lever actuates a drum brake each time the clutch is disengaged. Consequently, restoration consists of inspecting all clutch and fork bearings and replacing any clutch facings that are worn, badly glazed, or oil soaked. You should also replace any facing that bends easily. A facing that is in good condition should be rigid.

You'll also need to check to make sure the springs meet the specifications listed in your repair manual and ensure that springs are not rusted or distorted. In many cases, new fork bearings and/or new clutch facing plates are all that are needed to restore the two-cylinder clutch to operating condition.

---

actuation. Replace the throw-out bearing if there is any hint of roughness, looseness, or discoloration.

POWER TAKEOFF REPAIR

Although the first rear power takeoff appeared as early as 1918, the PTO never played a big role until a few decades later. Until rear-mounted PTO-driven implements began appearing in earnest, most farmers continued to use the belt pulley as their main power source.

Early PTO systems were also a pain to use with certain implements, since they were driven from the transmission. That meant the tractor had to be moving or in neutral with the clutch engaged for the PTO to operate. Many farmers can still remember mowing hay fields with a transmission-driven PTO. If the sicklebar started to plug, or you had to stop in the middle of the field, you could almost count on getting it plugged even worse, because the minute you stopped, so did the sickle. Stacking hay with a front-end loader powered by a hydraulic pump on the transmission-driven PTO was an adventure, too. You either had to have your timing down so you raised the loader as you approached the stack, or you pulled up to the stack, put the tractor in neutral, raised the loader to the appropriate height, and put the tractor back in gear to drive forward and dump.

Things changed, though, when Cockshutt introduced the first commercially available tractor with a live PTO in 1947. The live, or independent, PTO utilized its own clutch within the transmission, which meant the PTO could continue to operate in relation to the engine speed rather than slow or stop its function as the tractor slowed or stopped. Within a few years, all tractors had a live PTO.

It's important to check and adjust the pulley brake—replacing the brake pad if necessary—as part of a John Deere clutch restoration.

It's rather obvious that the broken clutch dog on this John Deere clutch/belt pulley will need to be replaced as part of the restoration.

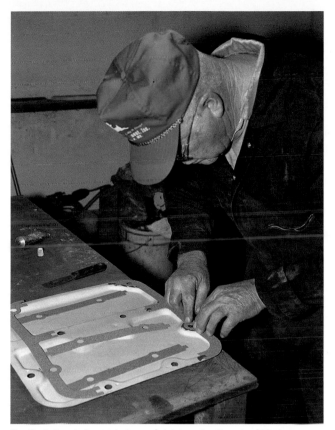

The final steps in transmission and clutch restoration should include installing a new gasket on the transmission cover.

Unfortunately, many Cockshutt tractors suffered the consequences, according to Jeff Gravert, a Cockshutt tractor enthusiast from Central City, Nebraska. Because the live PTO dramatically improved front-end loader operation, a number of Cockshutt tractors were equipped with loaders and asked to carry more than the tractor was designed to handle. As a result, Gravert says he always keeps a few extra cast-iron tractor frames on hand to replace those that have been cracked.

Whether your tractor is equipped with a transmission-drive PTO or an independent-drive system, you should check its condition as part of transmission inspection and repair. The most common problem tends to be seal leakage. Other ailments can include clutch problems with live PTO systems and worn gears and bearings. Due to the different variations used by tractor manufacturers, overhaul procedures are best explained in your tractor repair manual.

One tip worth passing on, though, comes from Eugene Mohr, who notes that leaks around the PTO shaft outlet can often be sealed with the use of plumbers cord, available at almost any hardware store.

POWER TAKEOFF DRIVESHAFT

The power takeoff on early tractors was geared directly to the drivetrain. Hence, when you pushed in on the clutch, the PTO stopped.

Chapter 7
Final Drive and Brakes

Your first thought may be that the final drive and brakes have little in common and really don't go together in one chapter. But when you consider that the role of the brakes on a tractor is to stop one or both rear wheels, you can begin to see how the two fit together.

In general, there are two points of application with the brakes used on most vintage farm tractors. What's more, that braking point has a lot to do with the type of final drive you find on the tractor. For example, most models that used bull gears to drive the axles have brake housings located on the sides of the transmission/final drive case. Generally, these are expanding-drum brakes on a splined shaft that engage the bull gears. So, in effect,

the brakes aren't stopping the axles or the wheels, but rather the bull gears that drive the axles.

In contrast, tractors that utilize a pinion shaft and ring gear in combination with a spider gear set don't have a braking point on the gear sets themselves. Hence, the brakes are located on the drive axles or in the wheel hubs.

DIFFERENTIALS AND FINAL DRIVES

Although there are a number of different types of final drives, you can count on all of them having one thing in common: They were generally built tough enough to take all the torque the engine and transmission could generate, and then some. As a result, the final drive on

In most cases, the final drive doesn't require anything more than a good cleaning and inspection of the gears.

SIDE GEAR

THRUST WASHER

PINION & BUSHING

THRUST WASHER

CARRIER SHIM

RIVET

OIL SEAL

BEARING CUP

BEARING CONE

LOCKING PIN

PIN CASE RING GEAR BUSHING

SHIM

The differential on most tractors includes the pinion, ring gear, and side gears.

most vintage tractors needs little attention other than replacing bearings and seals and changing the fluid.

With the exception of John Deere two-cylinder tractors, which utilized a horizontal transmission, you'll find that most tractors incorporated a hypoid- or bevel-gear type differential to transfer engine torque from the transmission to the axles. Composed of a bevel pinion and shaft, bevel ring gear, and a set of pinion and side gears, the differential provides a means of turning the power flow 90 degrees and dividing the power between the two rear wheels. The differential also provides further gear reduction beyond the choices provided by the transmission for additional torque to the rear wheels.

Since the proper gear mesh is important, most tractor manufacturers recommend that if you replace the ring gear, you should also replace the bevel pinion gear, so you maintain a matched set.

Beyond the differential, tractor manufacturers used various types of final drives. Some, like the Ford N Series, take care of all gear reduction in the transmission and differential and connect the axle shaft directly to the wheel hub. Others, like the Allis-Chalmers WD and WD-45, utilized another gear set at the wheel end of the axle. In addition to providing further gear reduction, which is the function of the bull gears on other tractors, the final drive gear set and housing raised the tractor for additional ground clearance.

Ironically, you'll find that some tractors still used chains as the final drive. Most notable were the John Deere D and GP models and some older McCormick-Deering and International models. While the chains aren't likely to need replacement due to their rugged construction, they may need adjustment. You'll notice, though, that Deere didn't use any type of idler. Instead, the axle housing incorporated a concentric casting which was attached to the rear end/transmission housing by a series of mounting clamps. To tighten the chains, loosen the clamps from the inside of the housing and rotate the axle housing.

Minneapolis-Moline and a few other manufacturers also used drive chains as part of the final drive system on certain high-clearance cane tractors.

DIFFERENTIAL AND FINAL DRIVE INSPECTION AND REPAIR

Inspecting and rebuilding the differential and final drive is not too much different from working on the transmission. Basically, it means draining the old fluid, if it is different than that in the transmission, cleaning the gears, and checking for worn bearings and seals and missing gear teeth. Naturally, every manufacturer seems to use a different configuration, so you'll need to refer to your tractor service manual for adjustment procedures and end play or backlash tolerances.

Eccentric-shaped housings, held in place by clamping brackets around the circumference, allow the drive chains on this John Deere Model D to be tightened or loosened.

The grease built up on the inside of the drive wheel is an easy-to-read sign that this tractor will require new drive axle seals.

On a number of tractor models, the gear mesh and backlash of the main drive bevel gears are controlled by shims on the shaft. In those cases, the repair manual generally recommends that tooth contact and backlash be checked and adjusted, if necessary, whenever the transmission is overhauled; it is imperative, however, when a new pinion or ring gear, or both, are installed. Of course, some tractors, such as the Ford and Ford-Ferguson models, have no adjustment at all for the drive pinion.

If shim adjustment is in order, the first step is to arrange the shims to provide the desired backlash between the main drive bevel pinion and ring gear as specified in your tractor service manual. The next step is to adjust the shims to provide proper tooth contact or mesh pattern of the bevel gears.

To do this, paint the bevel pinion teeth with a substance called Prussian blue or with another called red lead. Then, rotate the ring gear in the normal direction of operation under no load and observe the contact pattern on the teeth surfaces. The areas of heaviest contact will be indicated by the absence of the coating. In other words, the paint will be removed from the points of high tooth contact.

Ideally, the contact area should be uniform from the top edge of the active profile to the lower edge where it breaks to an undercut. Don't expect to see much contact beyond the toe, or narrowest end of the tooth, though. The teeth are ground in such a way that they deform under heavy load, allowing the contact area to increase and move toward the heel, thereby increasing the load-carrying capacity of the gear.

If the heavy contact is concentrated high on the toe or near the outer edge of the tooth, the pinion generally needs to be moved toward the front of the tractor by adding a shim behind the pinion bearing cage. If, on the other hand, the heavy contact is concentrated low on the pinion tooth, you'll need to remove a shim from the pinion bearing cage. Refer to your manual for proper adjustment procedures.

Once you've obtained the ideal tooth contact, you'll need to recheck the backlash obtained in the first step to make sure it is still within the specifications.

One tip offered by restorers is that if you find bull gears with excessive wear, you can often swap them side for side. In effect, you're positioning the gears so that what was the gear lash in the forward direction is now the gear lash for reverse and vice versa. In some cases, this can also work for other gears in the differential.

AXLE SHAFTS

Like all other components in the final drive, the rear axles on most farm tractors were built tough. They still will need attention, though.

One of the most common problems restorers encounter is an oil leak where the axle exits the rear axle carrier. This is most commonly caused by a seal failure. With few exceptions, most tractors use at least two seals at the end of the axle housing. Of course, if the seal failed, there's a chance that the bearing needs replacing, as well. To check the bearings, raise the axle and, with the wheel off the axle and the transmission in neutral, check for excessive axle shaft end play by attempting to move the axle in and out and up and down.

Another potential problem is that the defective seal may have a groove worn into the axle. Not only will this contribute to the leak, but it will make it impossible to repair with a new seal. Hence, it's important to check the axle, just as you would any shaft on which a seal is being

With few exceptions, most tractors use at least two seals at the end of the axle housing.

replaced. If you can feel the groove with your fingernail, it needs to be repaired.

While some shafts can be repaired with a Speedi-Sleeve, which is basically a thin collar that slips over the original shaft to create a new surface, a drive axle will generally require the second option. That is filling the groove with a metal-filled epoxy, such as J-B Weld. Two or three thin coats are usually better than one heavy one. Once it has cured, simply sand it to a smooth and symmetrical surface, finishing it off with extra-fine sandpaper or emery cloth.

Even if the seals aren't bad, it's a good idea to replace them as part of the restoration process.

BRAKE RESTORATION

Let's be honest: The brake system is not the place to cut corners. You might be able to get by without overhauling the transmission or opening up the rear end, but you'll want to give the brakes the attention they deserve. This isn't just for your safety, but for the safety of those around you. If you take your tractor to any shows at all, you're going to need to unload it off a truck or trailer. And this is not the place to have your brakes fail to hold. Consider, too, how you would feel if you lost control of your tractor in a parade, with people lining both sides of the street. Fortunately, brake restoration is not a difficult job.

Although you'll still find a number of vintage farm tractors with only one brake, which was primarily used for parking or holding the tractor in place while it was being used as a belt pulley power source, most tractors have a brake for each rear wheel. You're also likely to find one of three types of brakes in use. They include externally contracting band brakes, internally expanding drum brakes, and disc brakes. As was mentioned earlier, the brakes may also be located on the side of the final drive housing, within the axle housing, or on the wheel hub itself.

Before you begin, remember that brake springs can fly off unexpectedly and in who-knows-what direction if they are not handled properly. Always wear safety glasses when attempting any work on the brakes. Since you will

If damaged or worn seals have cut a groove in the axle shaft, you'll need to pull the axle and repair it with a sleeve or durable epoxy.

A number of tractors, including this Farmall Cub, utilize an enclosed gear set at the wheel end of the axle to provide further gear reduction, while increasing ground clearance.

While some tractor designs employed brakes on the axles or wheel hubs, others, like this Minneapolis-Moline, utilized externally mounted brake housings that applied braking pressure to the final-drive bull gears.

If you're lucky, you may be able to bring the brakes back to life by simply roughing up the brake shoes with sandpaper, or using a torch to dry out oil-soaked shoes. In this case, though, the job called for new shoes and a thorough clean-up.

If a brake kit is no longer available for your tractor model, any automotive shop that does brake work should be able to rivet new linings in place on your brake shoes.

no doubt be lifting the rear of the tractor off the ground, you should also double-check to make sure it is secure from rolling or tipping.

While it's important that you start brake troubleshooting by checking all brake adjustment points, it's also important to examine the brake linings or pads, as well. If brake linings aren't badly worn or oil soaked, you may be able to bring them back to life by simply roughing them up with sandpaper. Other restorers have used a torch to dry out oil-soaked brake shoes that have sufficient wear left on them.

You should also make sure the brake drum or brake disc is clean and free of rust. But again, a piece of emery cloth or sandpaper will fill the bill.

If you do find that the brake shoes or linings have become oil soaked or worn too far, it should be fairly easy to find replacement pads, linings, or shoes. If a brake kit is no longer available, any automotive shop that does brake work should be able to rivet new linings in place on your brake shoes. The same shop should also be able to turn any problem brake drums on a lathe, removing any grooves or out-of-round spots.

Of course, there are always those unusual mechanisms that vary from the norm. One example is the disc brake system used on many late-model Farmall tractors. This system employs a pair of actuating discs connected by springs that are held apart by steel balls in ramp-shaped grooves. When the brake pedal is depressed, the two actuating discs are rotated slightly in opposite directions.

This causes the balls between the actuator discs to roll to the shallow end of the grooves, which forces the brake lining discs to come in contact with the stationary braking surfaces. With this system, it's obviously important to check both the disc ramp and balls for wear or rust that could prevent the balls from rolling smoothly. If the steel balls can't be polished to an effective state, they should be replaced. Finally, replace or restore the disc brake lining and make sure the contact surfaces are smooth and free of rust.

Now, it's simply a matter of following the instructions in your repair manual to correctly adjust both brakes for equal pressure when depressed.

BRAKE ADJUSTMENT

Whether the brake's pads or discs have been renewed, touched up, or approved in the current condition, it

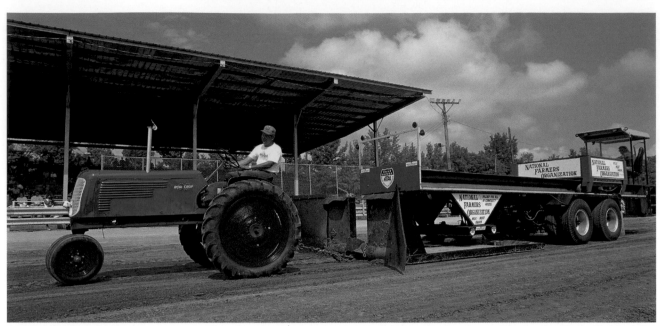

You'll need your brakes as soon as you start working with your tractor, whether it's in the field, in a parade, or in an antique tractor pull, as with this nicely restored Oliver Model 60 Row Crop.

Foot brakes that are adjacent to each other, or can be locked together, need to be adjusted to a comparable setting with an equal amount of free travel. This will prevent the tractor from pulling to one side when both brakes are applied in an emergency.

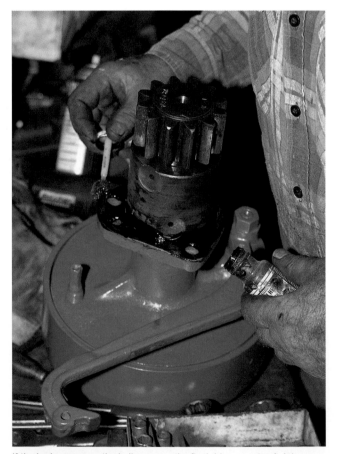

If the brake engages the bull gears on the final drive, or extends into any other oil-enclosed housing, make sure you install a new gasket during assembly.

The brake pedal is incorporated as part of the brake unit on this John Deere model.

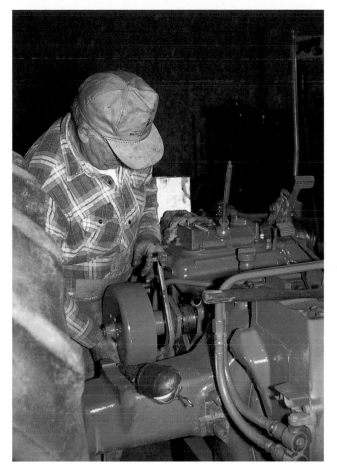

After the brakes have been refurbished and reinstalled, adjust the brakes to the point the rear wheels begin to drag and back them off slightly.

is important that the brakes be adjusted. Moreover, foot brakes that are adjacent to each other, or can be locked together, need to be adjusted to a comparable setting with an equal amount of free travel. Otherwise, one brake may be applied while the other just drags. This isn't a problem, of course, with hand brakes or on tractors where the left and right brake are operated by the corresponding feet.

The easiest way to adjust the brakes in most all cases is to raise the rear wheel off the ground and tighten the brake until you can no longer rotate the wheel by hand; then back it off until the rear wheel turns with only a slight drag. Naturally, the adjustment process will vary depending upon the brake configuration. Quite often the adjustment instructions will also tell you to depress the brake pedal approximately 2 inches and adjust the brake until the lining contacts the drum as a starting point.

At the very least, you should end up with around 3/4 inch of pedal free play before the brakes start to contact the drum.

Chapter 8
Front Axle and Steering

Over the years, the front axles on farm tractors basically went full circle—no pun intended. Going back as far as steam engines and tractor development, most farm tractors were originally equipped with wide-front axles only. The exceptions were some kerosene and gasoline tractors built in the early 1900s that came with a tricycle front end, such as the Allis-Chalmers Model 10/18, built from 1914 to 1921. As the first tractor to carry the Allis-Chalmers name, it featured an unusual three-wheel configuration, with the single front wheel offset to run ahead of the right rear wheel.

Of course, there were all kinds of configurations in those early days. The Albaugh-Dover Square Turn tractor, for instance, didn't use a steering axle at all. Instead, it featured a special transmission that allowed one of the two drive wheels, which were positioned at the front of the tractor, to go forward while the other went backward. A single rear wheel, which worked in conjunction with the powered front wheels, helped steer the tractor through "square turns." Still other tractors featured a three-wheel configuration with a single rear drive wheel in the back and two front tires on a wide axle for steering.

By the 1920s, however, most manufacturers had settled on a four-wheel configuration with two rear drive wheels and two wheels in the front on a wide axle. Ironically, that only lasted about ten years, though. By the 1930s, most manufacturers had gone back to a tricycle configuration as standard equipment on certain models and as an option on others. The trend started in 1924, when International Harvester introduced an "all-purpose," or tricycle-type, front end on the McCormick-Deering Farmall. By the time World War II ended and many veterans were going back to the farm, some dealers had a hard time selling a tractor with a wide front end.

You need only look at the history of tractor use, though, to understand the transition. When the first tractors came out, their primary role was plowing and providing power to belt-driven implements. Cultivation was still done by a team of horses.

But as tractors began to take on other roles and became multiple-use machines, farmers started demanding tractors that would turn around in a shorter amount of space. This was particularly important to row-crop farmers. Hence, tricycle front ends practically dominated the tractor market in corn country. To accommodate the needs of tractor owners, many companies even offered a choice of single- or dual-wheel tricycle front ends. Not only did the tricycle front end fit between corn rows of the time, and turn shorter at the ends of the field, but most farmers also liked the visibility the narrow front axle offered when using a front-mounted cultivator.

By reversing the front wheels on a dual-wheel tricycle, a farmer could also guide the tractor right down the top of the lister ridges in areas where bedders and listers were widely used. A lister was a type of planter that was

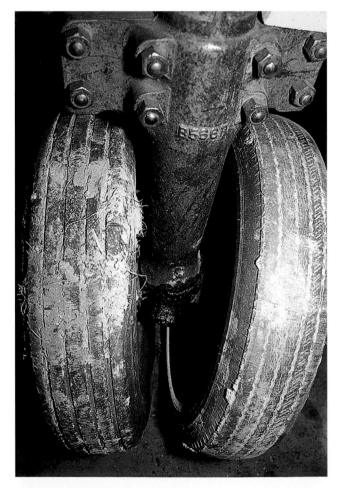

By the end of 1929, the tricycle-type tractor accounted for 40,000 units out of 229,000 produced by forty-seven tractor manufacturers.

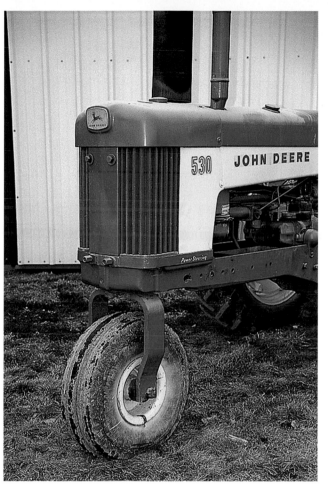

Although several tractor companies produced tricycle models with a single front wheel, these models still tend to be rarer than ones with dual tricycle wheels.

Until 1924, when McCormick-Deering introduced the first "all-purpose" or tricycle-type tractor, most gasoline and kerosene tractors such as this Fordson had a wide front axle. *Hans Halberstadt*

especially popular in semi-arid areas. Unlike today's corn planters, listers used a dual moldboard to cut a trench and build a ridge between each crop row. The corn or grain sorghum was then planted in the bottom of the furrow, where the soil was moist and young plants would be protected from the wind by the ridges.

After the crop emerged, cultivation brought soil from the ridges back into the row to cover small weeds and help retain moisture in the furrow bottom. By the time harvest rolled around, two or three cultivations had brought the field back to near-level conditions. But as it stated in the Minneapolis-Moline Model U operators manual, "It is impossible to keep any pneumatic-tired tractor on top of a ridge and pull a load at the same time." The manual went on to advise, "Set the rear wheels so the rear tires are slightly over the outside of each ridge and with the front wheels set to straddle the center ridge."

In the meantime, tractor manufacturers used their tricycle designs to incorporate other functions. Examples include two-row corn pickers that mounted on the tractor with reasonable ease, once the proper wheel tread setting had been established and various mounting brackets had been added. Once mounted, the center snout or row divider was positioned directly ahead of the tricycle front end. Farther south, cotton farmers could mount a two-row cotton stripper on their narrow-front tractor in much the same manner.

Allis-Chalmers even designed a bale loader that mounted on the frame of a narrow-front Model C, CA, WC, WD, or WD45. No wonder tricycle front ends were so popular through the middle of the twentieth century. Unfortunately, tractors with a narrow front axle also proved to be more dangerous, especially if they were top heavy or turned too fast on sloping terrain.

Tractor manufacturers used a variety of steering mechanisms to turn the front wheels. This Co-op tractor used a gear housing nestled in the frame below the radiator, while others, like John Deeres, utilized a gear set at the top of a tall pedestal.

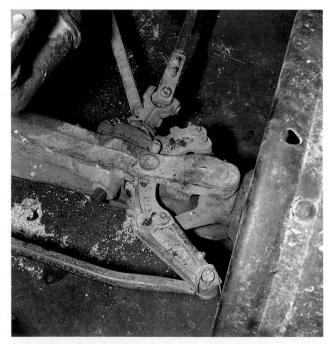

Some of the earliest tractors, like this John Deere Model D, simply used a gear on the end of the steering shaft to rotate a geared arm on the axle.

Times were changing, too. As equipment got bigger and the turning radius improved on standard tractors, farmers found they didn't have to turn such tight corners. They also discovered that they could guide the tires on a wide-front axle between the rows as easily as they could keep dual tricycle wheels in a single row width. Besides, rows were getting narrower.

When tricycle configurations became popular, most farmers were still using 36- or 40-inch rows, mainly because they were using some of the same equipment they had used with horses. And the rows were precisely that width so a horse could walk down between the rows. As soon as horses disappeared from the fields, though, there was no reason that rows couldn't be narrower.

FRONT AXLE REPAIR

Like a lot of things on a vintage tractor slated for restoration, the life it led before you acquired it has a lot to do with its condition and the repairs that it is going to need. The condition of the steering gear and front axle is a textbook example. A tractor that spent

STEERING CONFIGURATIONS

Although the steering mechanisms on most vintage farm tractors are relatively simple, there was a great deal of variation between brands and models. The challenge for most manufacturers was coming up with the best combination of comfort and steering-shaft routing. On many John Deere two-cylinder tractors, for example, the steering shaft was routed across the top of the hood, or through the hood and above the engine, to a gear head at the top of the steering pedestal.

Other tractors, like the Ford 8N, had the gearbox closer to the steering wheel and utilized a set of sector gears and pitman arms to turn the wheels. There were even a few unusual configurations, like the Case RC, VC, and S models, which utilized an offset steering arm, affectionately referred to as the "chicken roost," that connected the steering gearbox to the front axle bolster.

Regardless of the configuration, most were of the worm-and-gear type or cam-and-lever category. Hence, restoration will primarily consist of replacing worn parts, bearings, bushings, and seals, and making the appropriate adjustments. In some cases, such as on the Farmall M and H, the steering gear assembly is non-adjustable, particularly on worm-and-gear types. If free play is excessive, the only option is to replace the appropriate gears or replace the gearbox with a used or rebuilt unit.

In other cases, such as those systems that use a cam lever on a shaft, it's possible to adjust free play and backlash by adding shims between the steering column and steering gear housing.

In most cases, the bolster and horizontal axle are available as individual units, which makes it easier and less expensive to replace a damaged axle.

FELT SEALS

This cutaway shows a typical arrangement of the bearings and seals on a front axle spindle.

Quite often, the kingpin or pivot shaft, on which the wide front axle member pivots, is the first thing that wears out or needs replacement.

It would be a costly endeavor to replace the steering gear housing on this Farmall Cub, considering that the housing, forward frame section, and radiator base are all cast as one unit.

most of its days in large wheat fields in western Kansas, for example, isn't going to have near the wear on the knuckle bushings and axle pivot pin as a row-crop model that spent every working hour crossing corn furrows and turning around on end rows. This is just one more reason to find out all you can about the tractor before you make a purchase or calculate repair costs.

That said, the only satisfactory way to overhaul the front-axle assembly on a wide-front tractor is to remove it from the tractor and make a complete check of all bearings and bushings. That includes the center pivot pin, steering arms, ball seats on tie rods, knuckles, and wheels. It's important to note that on some tractors, the knuckle post bushings are pre-sized to provide a specified amount of clearance for the knuckle post, while other models require that a steering knuckle bushing be pressed into place and then reamed or honed to provide the suggested minimum clearance for the knuckles.

On models with a tricycle-type front end, inspection primarily consists of checking and replacing wheel bearings and seals. In fact, on most models, it's possible to remove the axle assembly or bolster assembly from the bolster,

making repair or replacement of the axle even easier. Depending upon the amount of free play in the bolster, it may also be necessary to replace bushings, bearings, and seals in the upper or lower sections of the bolster.

As a final note, some John Deere Model A, B, and G two-cylinder tractors were equipped with an optional tricycle-type front end called the Roll-O-Matic. This unique narrow-front assembly was intended to help smooth out rough fields by moving the front wheels in opposite directions when a bump or ditch was encountered. This was done by gearing the two wheels together in such a manner that when one wheel went up, the other wheel was forced down by an equal distance.

In general, overhaul of the Roll-O-Matic system is not much different than the conventional knuckle-mounted dual front wheels except that there is an extra bushing, retainer, and seal where the Roll-O-Matic knuckle attached to the pedestal extension. It's also important that the knuckle units on the Roll-O-Matic assembly are installed so the timing marks on the gears are in register. The center housing should also be packed with wheel-bearing grease before the final knuckle is reinstalled.

Not only has Nebraska restorer Lyle Wacker cleaned all the components on this industrial Case axle, but he has replaced all the bushings and seals.

Before installing new bearings, seals, and felt washers on the axles, make sure the spindle is clean and free of nicks and scoring. A piece of fine emery cloth can be used to remove any rough spots or rust.

In the majority of cases, new bearings and seals are all that are needed to restore the axle to like-new condition.

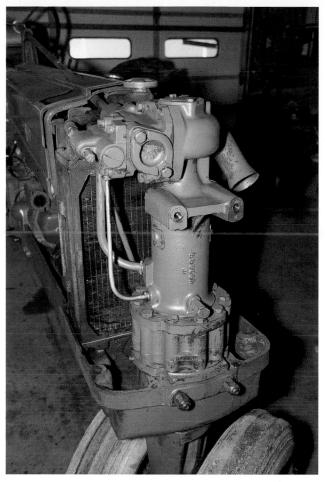

John Deere two-cylinder tractors have all the components of the power steering system, except for the pump, incorporated into the steering pedestal.

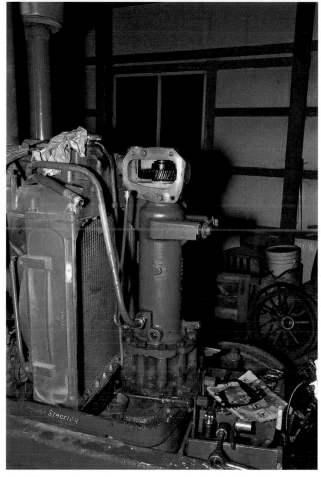

One of the steps in steering system restoration is checking for free play in the bolster on narrow-front models. Desired end play on this John Deere model is controlled by shims under the gear.

STEERING WHEEL REPAIR

Unless a tractor has been protected from the elements for most of its life, there's a pretty good chance the steering wheel is going to be severely cracked. Fortunately, there are several solutions available to you. Should you prefer to have the steering wheel professionally repaired, there are several companies that specialize in refurbishing plastic- or wood-rimmed steering wheels. Minn-Kota, is one of the most notable; it can take your old wheel and mold new plastic around the steel rim, complete with the original grooves, ribs, or finger ridges.

Should you choose to repair a cracked steering wheel yourself, there are a couple of options practiced by restorers. One professional restorer uses Fiberstrand body filler to fill all the cracks and crevices. Another uses a body filler such as Evercoat polyester glazing material and follows that with a coat of fast-fill primer. With either product, the steering wheel must be sanded smooth after the material hardens and then painted.

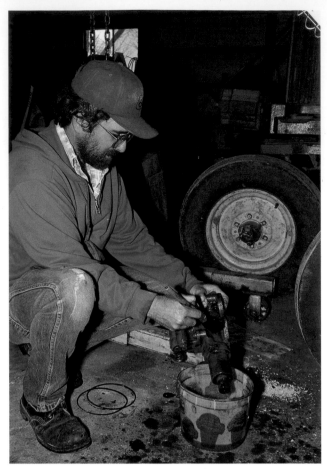

Just as it is with so many other components on a vintage tractor, cleanliness is next to godliness when it comes to restoring steering components.

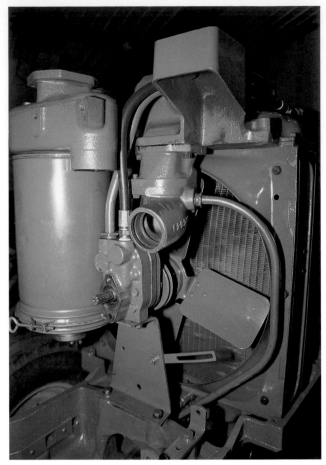

Offered as an option on some models, John Deere's Roll-O-Matic tricycle front axle was intended to help smooth out rough fields by moving the front wheels in opposite directions when a bump or ditch was encountered.

Power steering pump maintenance should be handled in the same manner as hydraulic system inspection and repair.

For a professional look, you might consider sending the steering wheel to one of several companies that specialize in refurbishing plastic- or wood-rimmed steering wheels.

As the steering wheel is the part of the tractor you come into contact with most frequently, you'll appreciate a quality restoration of the wheel every time you take the controls. This early Ford-Ferguson 9N was restored by Palmer Fossum of Northfield, Minnesota. *Chester Peterson Jr.*

Chapter 9
Hydraulic System

Depending upon the vintage of your tractor, this may or may not be a chapter you even need to worry about. After all, hydraulic systems weren't found on many early tractors. John Deere was the first to offer any kind of lift mechanism on a tractor when it introduced a mechanical power lift on its Model GP in 1928. However, it wasn't until the late 1930s, when the Ford 9N combined the Ferguson hydraulic-lift system with the three-point hitch that hydraulic force was used to raise and lower implements and attachments.

BASIC PRINCIPLES

Before we look at troubleshooting and repairing the hydraulic system, let's look at some of the basics associated with hydraulic systems. First of all, hydraulic fluid is just like any other liquid—it has no shape of its own and acquires the shape of the container. Because of this, oil in the hydraulic system will flow in any direction and into any pump or cylinder, regardless of the size or shape.

Like any fluid, it is also practically incompressible. As a result, when force is applied to hydraulic fluid, it transfers force to the work site. Hydraulic fluid has one other characteristic, though. It has the ability to provide substantial increases in work force, meaning that one pound of pressure on the piston in a small pump is converted to several pounds on a larger cylinder or piston. If you use a hydraulic bottle jack to lift your tractor, you already know how this works.

Now, let's look at the application of this principle on your tractor. Instead of pressure being supplied by a jack handle and piston, it comes from a hydraulic pump. From there, it flows through a valve, which directs its path to the appropriate point, and finally to a hydraulic cylinder on the three-point hitch, power steering, or remote.

Most hydraulic pumps used on farm tractors today are one of three types: a gear, vane, or piston pump. However, you're most likely to run into a gear pump, since it is the most common type of pump used in both hydraulic and power-steering systems on early tractors. One exception is a unique system developed by Allis-Chalmers and first used on the Model WD. It used a series of four pistons, driven by four cam lobes on the main driveshaft between the engine and transmission clutches, to generate up to

First used on the Model WD, Allis-Chalmers employed a unique hydraulic pump that used a series of four pistons, driven by cam lobes on the main driveshaft, to generate pressure. *AGCO Corporation*

Harry Ferguson's innovative three-point hitch with the hydraulic-lift system used hydraulic force to raise and lower implements and attachments on the revolutionary Ford-Ferguson 9N of 1939. *Chester Peterson Jr.*

3,500 psi pressure. At the end of the piston stroke, the pump unloaded to a standby pressure of 1,200 psi for a Traction-Booster draft control with mounted and semi-mounted implements.

TROUBLESHOOTING

Like many other systems on the tractor, you should have an idea whether the hydraulic system actually works and how well it works from your initial test drive, assuming that the tractor was in running condition when you acquired it. If the tractor has power steering, did it work? Did the three-point hitch system raise and lower properly?

Depending upon the age of your vintage tractor, you're probably lucky to have either one. If anything, you may just have a single remote outlet for attaching a set of hydraulic hoses. Other tractors, like the Farmall C, had a hydraulically actuated lift ahead of the operator's platform for raising and lowering a cultivator.

If your tests indicate a weakness in the system, the first thing you should do is check the fluid level in the reservoir and make sure it is filled to the proper level with the recommended grade and type of fluid. Improper fluid can not only cause low or erratic pressure, but it can eventually deteriorate seals and packing, particularly if it contains incompatible ingredients.

Next, check for any problems with the hoses, including kinking or leaks. Keep in mind that hydraulic pressure escaping under high pressure through a pinhole leak can actually penetrate the skin, leading to gangrene poisoning if not treated quickly. Hence, you should never check for leaks with your bare hands, or even with leather gloves. Instead, use a piece of cardboard or wood passed over any suspected areas to check for escaping fluid.

If you have access to a pressure gauge or know someone who can assist, you can also check the pressure in the system to see if the problem is in the pump or in one of the valves. The I&T Service Manual for the International Harvester MTA and W6TA, for example, suggests inserting a 1/2-inch pipe tee and shut-off valve in series with the pump discharge hose. A pressure gauge, capable of registering at least 1,500 psi, is then installed

At the very least, the hydraulic system on this Minneapolis-Moline model is going to need new hoses.

It appears, from evidence of torch welding on the back of the pump, that the previous owner of this Farmall Cub had problems with pump leakage.

in the tee. By slowly closing the shut-off valve for a few seconds only, you can then check to see if the problem lies in the pump or if it can be attributed to some other source, such as a leaky relief valve or a leak in the reservoir.

If the problem is traced back to the pump, you have the choice of either locating a replacement pump or trying to rebuild the pump yourself, realizing the need for absolute cleanliness.

HYDRAULIC SEALS

It almost goes without saying that due to the high pressure within the system, no hydraulic circuit can operate without the proper seals to hold the fluid under pressure. Seals also serve the purpose of keeping dirt and water out of the system.

In general, hydraulic seals fall into one of two categories—static seals that seal fixed parts and dynamic seals that seal moving parts. Static seals include gaskets, O-rings, and packings used around valves, between fittings, and between pump sections. Dynamic seals, in contrast, include shaft and rod seals on hydraulic cylinder pistons and piston rods.

As for seal types, they can include O-rings, U- and V-packings, spring-loaded lip seals, cup and flange

The scoring on the inner surface of this power steering gear pump body calls for a replacement of both the body and the gears.

The single remote cylinder valve housing on this John Deere two-cylinder model is located where it is easy to check pressures and fittings.

HYDRAULIC SYSTEM CONTAMINATION

The two biggest enemies of a hydraulic system are dirt and water. If these two contaminants were kept out of the system by the previous owner, you may not have any problems with the hydraulic system. But if they managed to work their way into the system, you may have some repairs ahead of you.

Just as in the engine, dirt can score the insides of cylinders, spool valves, and pumps. Water, meanwhile, will break down the inhibitors in the hydraulic oil, causing it to emulsify and lose its lubricating ability—again, leading to scoring of cylinder walls and breakdown of internal seals. Unfortunately, the tolerances in many hydraulic pumps and spools are even tighter than those in an engine.

One of the main ways dirt enters a system is through the air breather in the reservoir. The air breather is designed to let air move in and out of the reservoir in response to changes in the fluid level. It is also supposed to screen out dust by trapping it between layers of oil-saturated filter material. Unfortunately,

many farmers failed to clean the filter or check for cracks or leaks that permitted dirty air to penetrate the system.

Keep in mind, however, that many older tractors do not have a special reservoir or cooler for the hydraulic system, but simply use the same oil that lubricates the transmission and differential.

Another way dirt can get into the system is through the careless handling of the hoses, particularly if a broken or damaged hose is replaced. This should be a hint to practice cleanliness when making hydraulic repairs or inspections.

Dirt isn't the only enemy, though. Sludge, which is formed by the chemical reaction of hydraulic fluid to excessive temperature changes or condensation, can also cause havoc. If enough sludge builds up on the pump's internal parts, it will eventually plug the pump. To add insult to injury, a restriction on the inlet side of the pump can starve it of fluid, and heat and friction will cause the pump parts to seize.

packings, mechanical seals, metallic seals, and compression packings and gaskets. Troubleshooting, naturally, consists of looking for leaks. However, even though the perfect seal should prevent all leakage, this is not always practical or desirable. In dynamic uses, for instance, a slight amount of leakage is needed to provide lubrication to moving parts.

On the other hand, internal leakage, either from static seals or excessive leakage from dynamic seals, is hard to detect. Often, excessive leakage from an internal seal must be indicated by other means, such as pressure testing.

As a general rule, it's usually best to replace all seals that are disturbed during repair of the hydraulic system—assuming they are available. As is the case with the engine, transmission, and most other major components, it's a lot cheaper to replace a few seals or gaskets during restoration than to come back later and do a repair job to correct leaks.

It may sound a little extreme, but you should also give seals the same care during handling and replacement as precision bearings. This means keeping them protected in their containers and storing them in a cool, dry place free of dirt until you're ready to use them.

Following installation, static O-rings used as gaskets should be tightened a second time after the unit has been warmed up and cycled a few times, to make sure they seal properly.

Dynamic O-rings, on the other hand, should be cycled or moved back and forth (as on a hydraulic cylinder) several times to allow the ring to rotate and assume a neutral position. In the process of rotating, the O-ring should allow a very small amount of fluid to pass. This is normal, since it permits a lubricating film of oil to pass between the O-ring and the shaft.

Most hydraulic pumps utilize either a gear pump, in which two meshing gears operate, or a rotor assembly as illustrated above.

When rebuilding any type of hydraulic pump, it's a good idea to replace all bushings and seals.

When you start working with implements, a bulldozer blade, or other tractor-mounted tools, you'll want your hydraulic system on good working order. This 1952 Allis-Chalmers Model WD is fitted with a #33 corn picker. Owner: Duane Eilts. *Ralph W. Sanders*

Chapter 10
Electrical System

Earlier, we talked about how fuel was one of the two important ingredients in the proper operation of any engine. The other—unless you are restoring a diesel engine—is ignition. Even then, it's not likely you're going to be restoring a tractor that doesn't have an electrical system. Without a starter of some kind, you're simply not going to get a diesel engine started. Even if it is equipped with a pony engine, instead of an electrical starter, a diesel tractor still needs an electrical circuit to provide ignition to the gasoline-powered starter engine.

The first thing you need to know about the electrical system is that there were two kinds of ignition systems used on vintage farm tractors. We're all familiar with the distributor, which is the type of ignition system used on current gasoline engines. However, many early tractors had

no electrical system, which is a necessity on a distributor-equipped model. Hence, they used a magneto.

Although many tractors with a magneto are equipped with a battery, the battery is not a necessary component for ignition. Its primary function is to operate the starter, lights, and any other accessories on the tractor. In fact, most tractors that use a magneto also include an engine crank, which is usually stored somewhere on the frame, and a crank lug on the front of the engine—even if it has a starter—for starting the engine without battery power.

MAGNETO SYSTEMS

In the event you're restoring an older tractor without a battery or any other electrical components, let's start with the magneto. You can always move on to other

Since they required no electrical power, a magneto was used on almost all early model tractors to provide spark to the cylinders.

As tractors got more advanced, such as this 1944 Minneapolis-Moline Model R with its enclosed cab, they were outfitted with full electrical systems, including electric starters, lights, and more. The M-M R's sibling, the top-of-the-line UDLX, even boasted a cigar lighter! The Model R was restored by the late Roger Mohr of Vail, Iowa. *Chester Peterson Jr.*

sections in this chapter if your tractor has a more complete electrical system.

In essence, the magneto operates like a generator, coil, and distributor wrapped up in one unit. Assuming yours is an impulse-type magneto, which covers all but the very earliest units, the magneto works much like a miniature spring-driven generator. As the drive cog is rotated, the magneto drive wraps up a spring that is positioned between the drive link and magneto rotor. At the appropriate moment, the spring is released and the rotor is quickly rotated within a magnetic field to generate a charge of electricity—hence, the clicking sound associated with magneto operation. Of course, the distributor portion of the magneto determines which of the cylinders receives the spark.

Due to the complexity of the spring-drive system and the internal workings of a magneto, it's best to have any adjustment or rebuilding done by a professional shop. However, there are some things you can check and/or replace.

You'll also need to make sure the magneto is reinstalled properly. This is especially important, since the magneto

must initiate the spark before the piston reaches the top of the compression stroke.

On the other hand, the impulse coupling is designed to retard the timing during slow engine revolution, such as when it is being started. The result is a stronger spark for starting the engine and a reduced chance of kick-back, which can occur when the spark reaches the cylinder before the piston has reached the top of the cylinder. If you do not hear the click, your magneto may have a broken impulse coupler.

It is possible for a tractor to start with a defective impulse coupler, but to do so, the starter must be able to crank the engine at fairly high rpm to overcome its effects. Your options for fixing this are to buy a new magneto or send the magneto to one of the businesses that specialize in restoration.

MAGNETO INSPECTION AND SERVICE

While there are a couple of ways to check for electrical output, one of the easiest for a novice is to attach a spark plug, via a piece of electrical wiring, to the coil output terminal. Then ground the spark plug to the base of the

Unlike modern electrical systems, the magneto operates like a generator, coil, and distributor wrapped up in one unit. The magneto is generally operated off the governor shaft.

magneto and test for a spark while rotating the driven lug. A word of warning, though: keep your hand clear of the coil and coil output terminal. If it's working properly the coil can put out nearly 30,000 volts, which you will obviously feel.

Most auto parts stores carry a spark tester that makes testing even easier. Basically, a spark tester looks like a spark plug with a large alligator clip. Hook the device to a plug wire and connect the clip to ground. When the tractor is cranked, the tester will flash if you have sufficient spark.

The presence of a spark won't be a guarantee that the magneto is putting out enough current, but it can give you an idea of how well the unit is working and if the spark is hot enough for ignition. If there isn't any spark, you at least know you're wasting your energy.

The other testing alternative is connecting a special multimeter that records and stores readings in excess of 30,000 volts.

If you do choose to disassemble the magneto and try to service it on your own, the first thing you should do is inspect all the gaskets and insulators that isolate the generating components from the body of the unit. This especially applies to any bolts that protrude through the magneto body. Any voltage leakage can ground out the unit and make it ineffective.

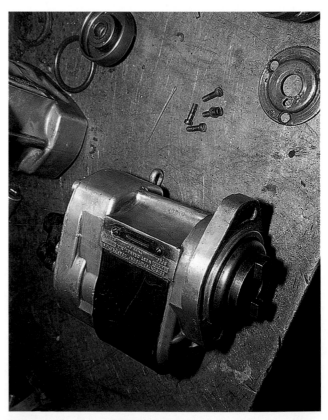

This photo of an Edison-Splitdorf magneto clearly shows the horseshoe magnet (black area of the unit) that generates the magnetic field around the armature.

The two pawls (arms) on the driven end of the magneto swing out of the way at higher engine speeds to keep them from tripping the impulse assembly.

Just as with a distributor overhaul, it is a good idea to replace the magneto rotor tower and rotor if the parts are still available.

You'll also want to clean all dirt and grime out of the unit, using a combination of compressed air and electrical parts cleaner. Finally, inspect and replace, if necessary, any seals or bearings that appear to be faulty. While you have the unit apart, it's also a good idea to have someone recharge the large, horseshoe-shaped magnet that generates the magnetic field around the armature.

Before putting everything back together, apply a light coat of oil to all drive parts and bushings. Be careful not to over-apply the oil, though. Lastly, replace any tune-up components for which you can find parts. This includes the condenser, points, rotor tower, and rotor cap. It's easier and cheaper to replace them now than struggle with problems later on.

TIMING THE MAGNETO

There are two phases to magneto timing. The first step is to get the magneto roughly timed. The second is to get it dialed in.

The rough-timing process begins with aligning the cap. There is a gear on the magneto shaft that will drive a gear on a rotor (similar to a distributor ignition). These gears must mesh at the proper point. On the FMJ-style magnetos, there are two teeth with bevels on the magneto side and a tooth with a timing mark on the cap side. The marked tooth meshes between the bevel teeth.

The intent of this process—in case all the marks are gone—is to get the points to open and close at the correct times to provide voltage to the appropriate plug wire. Knowing this, it is possible to guess the meshing

in the case of missing markings. Once the cap is aligned, it can be screwed back on.

Lining Up the Engine

To begin the timing process, the engine should be at the top of the compression stroke of the No. 1 piston. On most inline engines, this is the front cylinder; on two-cylinder John Deere engines, it is the left cylinder as viewed from the driver's seat.

There were many ways that top dead center (TDC) was marked on engines. Unfortunately, the timing marks are often missing on old machines. Still, there are some ways you can tell when the cylinder is in the proper position. One is to install a small fitting that has the same thread as the spark plug on one side and a nipple for a hose on the other end. This is screwed into the No. 1 spark plug hole and a hose is attached to the other side. Some people simply place their finger over the spark plug hole or place a tissue over the hole for a visual indicator.

Now, crank the engine until air begins to rush out the hose or begins pushing the tissue aside. When the air starts coming out, it means you are headed into the compression stroke. Then, slowly continue turning the engine until the No. 1 piston reaches its highest point. If your engine has a TDC mark, you can stop when the TDC mark reaches the index pin. John Deere two-cylinder tractors have an index mark on the flywheel.

If there is no other way to determine TDC, you can always insert a long, thin plastic rod in the spark plug

Considering the complexity of a tractor magneto, many restorers choose to have it professionally cleaned and overhauled.

When overhauling a magneto, it's important to clean all dirt and grime out of the unit, using a combination of compressed air and electrical parts cleaner.

hole so you can feel the piston move to the top of the stroke. Just be sure the rod is long enough that there's no possible way it can drop into the cylinder; you don't want to have to remove the head to retrieve it. Also, be careful not to disturb any carbon on the top of an old piston, since it could get stuck in an exhaust valve when you finally start the engine.

Bolting On the Magneto

At this point, you'll need to turn the magneto-driven lug in the direction it was designed to operate until the rotor is positioned over the No. 1 plug wire terminal. When correctly positioned, the dogs or slots on the magneto should line up with the corresponding dogs or slots on the engine and slide right in. Loosely bolt the magneto to the engine so that it can still be turned but is held in place.

Then, connect the grounding wire. Be sure your grounding/kill switch is in the off position. You may not have a ground wire if your magneto is one that requires you to get off the tractor and ground it manually to kill the engine. In this case, it is a good idea to make a wire to ground it temporarily or the engine may start or seriously backfire unexpectedly during the final timing.

At this point, the plug wires should be connected in the order specified in your manual. The firing order and direction of magneto rotation are the keys to hooking up the rest of the wires. The Allis-Chalmers WD, WC, WF, B, C, CA, and IB, for example, use 1-2-4-3, while the Farmall Cub, Allis-Chalmers G, and Massey-Harris Pony use 1-3-4-2. If no manual is available for your tractor,

Be careful when tightening the magneto on its mounting bracket or you may end up looking for a rebuilt unit.

Carefully check the cover and rotor tower for cracks or defects. Any voltage leakage can ground out the unit and make it ineffective.

you can determine this by watching the order in which the intake valves open: the rocker arm will go down when the valve opens. Unfortunately, determining the firing order in this manner involves removal of the valve cover.

Final Timing

By the time you've reached this step, you have the engine "rough timed." But don't try to start it this way. In this state, the tractor can backfire and run pretty rough. If you are using a hand-crank, it can rapidly spin backward and cause serious injury. So, before you go any farther, make sure the magneto is grounded (it is turned off or a safety wire is hooked up between the ground lug and a good ground on the tractor).

Once that's done, rotate the body of the magneto in the opposite direction of normal rotation. In most cases, this will be counterclockwise. Slowly turn the engine through its strokes until you have the No. 1 piston at the top of its compression stroke again. Now, gently rotate the magneto clockwise until you hear the pronounced click of the impulse coupler. This indicates that the magneto is right at the point where it will fire the No. 1 piston. Tighten up the bolts, remove your temporary safety ground wire, and try starting the engine.

If you are hand-cranking the engine, be sure you follow the hand-cranking safety precautions in your manual, since you are trying to start an untested engine; there are several factors beyond magneto timing that go into backfires. Or, you may have made a mistake. This isn't a time to be careless.

DISTRIBUTOR INSPECTION AND REPAIR

Since the distributor doesn't actually produce electricity, as the magneto does, but only serves to distribute the spark to the appropriate cylinder, service and rebuilding is much easier. Unless you plan to replace the spark plug wires, start distributor restoration by grasping the spark plug and coil wires and gently twisting the boot as you remove them from the cap. It's also a good idea to label the wires with tape and a marker so they can be reinstalled in the correct position.

If you plan to do much work on the distributor or engine, you may want to go ahead and remove the whole distributor at this time and clamp it in a vise where it will be easier to work on. Getting it reinstalled and timed correctly isn't that much different than reinstalling a magneto. However, to save some time later, make a note of which plug wire tower serves the No. 1 cylinder and make a mark on the side of the distributor housing that corresponds with this tower.

Now, pull the cap off and note where the rotor firing prong is positioned. Slowly rotate the engine so the rotor prong lines up with the mark on the house. Note, too, which direction the rotor turns.

With the engine timed to No. 1, you can now remove the mounting bolt and fork that retains the distributor in the engine housing. You'll note that the rotor shaft will rotate slightly as you remove the distributor due to the taper on the drive gear. You'll just need to remember to compensate when you reinstall it later. It's a good idea to reconfirm the proper timing anyway.

The first step in inspection and restoration is to check the inside and outside of the distributor cap and individual cap towers for cracks, burned spots, and

Rebuilding a distributor is not nearly as difficult as overhauling a magneto since a distributor doesn't generate its own electricity.

corrosion. If there is any doubt about the condition, it's best to just replace the cap.

Before you throw the cap in the trash, though, check for carbon tracking around the plug towers and around the cap base. Defective spark plugs or spark plug wires can cause sparks to travel from the tower to the nearest ground, which is usually the mounting clip. The evidence is a small carbon trail that resembles a tiny tree root.

You should also take a look at the inside of the cap for carbon tracking that can indicate past problems with cross-firing, backfiring, or missing. In this case, the lines will usually connect from one post to the next.

Once you have inspected and cleaned all parts at the top end of the distributor, it's time to take a look at the bottom end. Start by checking for any free play or wobble in the driveshaft. Generally, there are two bushings or seals on the shaft: one at the top and one at the bottom. If either one is badly worn, it should be replaced as part of the rebuild. To access the bushings, remove the drive gear, which is usually held on by a pin through the shaft and gear. This will allow the entire shaft to slide out of the housing.

Next, remove the points and condenser. Beneath the mounting plate you'll find a spark advance system of springs and counterweights. Replace any springs that are broken or weak and make sure the weights aren't rusted and that they move freely. The springs must be replaced

Final timing involves carefully rotating the magneto by hand until it has been correctly positioned, and tightening the mounting bolts.

Note the cylinder firing order molded into the engine block. This will help you later when reinstalling the distributor and timing the engine.

Check the inside and outside of the distributor cap and individual cap towers for cracks, burned spots, and corrosion. If there is any doubt about the condition, replace the cap.

A quality distributor rebuild should include new points, condenser, rotor, and spark plugs.

A set of marks on the flywheel serve as a guide when reinstalling the magneto or distributor and timing the engine.

As was the case with the magneto, you'll need to make sure final adjustments have been made before tightening the brackets that hold the distributor in place.

FORD FRONT-MOUNT DISTRIBUTOR

Ford tractor models built between 1939 and 1950 are unique in that they have a front-mounted distributor and coil, which requires that the timing be done before the distributor is reinstalled, rather than after. To set the timing, place a straight-edged ruler on the wide side of the shaft. Rotate the shaft until the straight edge is 1/4 inch away from the outside edge of the smallest distributor mounting hole. This will also be the mounting hole nearest the timing plate. At this distance, the distributor points should start to open. If they don't, loosen the timing plate lock screw and turn to advance or retard the timing. Keep making adjustments until you obtain the proper 1/4-inch setting. As you adjust, eliminate backlash by turning the shaft backwards and bring the shaft forward to measure your setting. This 1/4-inch setting will get you static timing at top dead center.

When reinstalling the front-mounted distributor, keep in mind that the slot in the end of the camshaft (front of motor) is offset. Consequently, the tang on the distributor can only mate easily to the slot on the engine camshaft one way. Mounted correctly, it will slide on easily without force and fit flush to the motor. If the tang is 180 degrees off, the distributor will have to be forced on. This should be a warning, because if you tighten down the mounting bolts at this point, you will break the casting on the distributor.

in pairs and by springs of identical size. In the meantime, clean all pieces in solvent before reassembling.

Although some restorers like to reuse the points, touching them up with a file before they're reinstalled, a quality rebuild should include new points, condenser, rotor, cap, and spark plugs.

Setting the Point Gap

You will need to adjust the gap between the points. To do this, rotate the shaft to a point where the cam lobe separates the points, creating a gap. Now, using a wire-type feeler gauge, adjust the points to match the specifications in your service manual and tighten the mounting screws.

Be sure you remove any oil film from the feeler gauge before inserting it between the points. Oil on the contact points can cause the points to burn or become pitted. Finish off point adjustment by lubricating the rubbing block with a small amount of high-temperature grease.

At this point, you can install a new rotor, line up the casing marks, and reinstall the distributor in the housing. If you've compensated for the gear taper during installation, the mark on the distributor casing should line up with the rotor tang. If not, it shouldn't be off by more than one tooth.

If the distributor is completely off, though, there's no need to panic. Most service manuals include a detailed procedure for timing the engine. You can also retime the engine by placing your finger or a tissue over the No. 1 spark plug hole, just as you would when timing a magneto. Then crank the engine until the No. 1 cylinder begins compression. Continue turning the engine until the timing mark on the flywheel lines up with the timing mark or indicator pin.

Now, turn the drive shaft on the distributor until the rotor lines up with the terminal for the No. 1 spark plug. Hopefully, you marked the distributor casing earlier, making this an easy task. Offset the rotor a little to compensate for the gear mesh and slide it in. Some engines will have a tang at the bottom of the distributor driveshaft that runs the oil pump. Make sure this tang engages the pump shaft. If it doesn't, put a little downward pressure on the shaft and rotate the engine a quarter or half turn. It should drop into position. Don't tighten the bolts yet, though.

Install a new distributor cap and spark plug wires, and finish the timing process with the ignition on. To do so, slowly turn the distributor in the direction of normal rotation, and watch for the exact moment that a spark occurs at the plug. If you missed it, back the distributor

up and try it again. The engine should now be timed properly. Tighten the distributor mounting bolt(s). If you have one available, you may still want to check everything with a timing light.

COILS

Perhaps the easiest way to check the coil is to gently pull the wire that runs from the coil to the distributor and hold it about 1/8 inch from the engine block or a good ground. A strong spark should jump the gap when the engine is turned over. The coil should also be clean and dry. If you're not confident that it is in good condition, consider replacing it.

GENERATORS AND VOLTAGE REGULATORS

If you ever did any experiments with electricity or with a generator in high school science class, you may already have an idea how the generator on your tractor works. But if not, don't despair. It's not that complicated.

By the simplest explanation, one way electricity can be created is by moving a conductor through a magnetic field. So if you look at this principle in terms of a generator, the armature, which serves as the conductor, is moved,

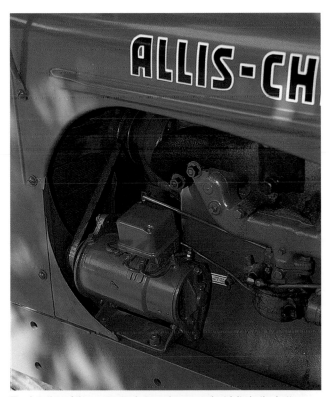

The function of the generator is to replace any electricity in the battery that has been used elsewhere in the electrical circuit. Hence, generators weren't needed until the advent of lights and electric starters on tractors.

As long as the field coils are not damaged or shorted out, a generator can usually be rebuilt for minimal cost.

or in this case spun, inside two or more magnets. But think back again to science class. Remember the time you wrapped electrical wire around a nail and attached it to a battery? You created an electromagnet. The generator on your tractor just uses a larger version.

So now you can envision the field coils as electromagnets attached to the generator case. As the armature spins within this magnetic field, electricity moves through the armature to where it is allowed to flow though the brushes.

The wire that makes up the coils actually begins at the F terminal of the generator, winds its way around the case and terminates either at a third brush on a three-brush generator, or is connected to the wire going to the output brush or A terminal on a two-brush generator. On most tractors, the generator cases uses two coils, although some generators use four coils for high-output applications. You're not likely to run into one of these four-coil units, though, since they weren't used until the 1980s, and by that time, most tractors used alternators.

The magnets are actually a two-piece arrangement that consists of a coil of wire that fits around a pole shoe made of a special kind of metal. As the armature spins within the

magnetic field, it begins to generate electricity—some of which is used to charge the battery or run electric lights, while the rest goes back into the field coils to make the magnetic field even stronger. Naturally, this calls for some sort of control, which becomes the role of the regulator. Its job is to control the generator by manipulating the ground connection of the field coils.

Among the most important components, though, are the brushes, which serve to gather the electricity that is being produced. The brushes ride on the commutator and allow the generated electricity to travel to the voltage regulator, and ultimately the battery or other load, and back into the field coils.

As a result, the primary problem areas on a generator are the brushes, commuter, and bushings. Generally, brushes should be replaced if they are worn more than half way. Quite often, the bushings and bearings that support the main shaft will also be worn and require replacement.

To perform any of these repairs, however, it will be necessary to disassemble, clean, and inspect the generator. Don't try to remove the field coils unless it is absolutely necessary. If you take them out, it will be difficult to get them back in without the proper tools. There are only

Any rebuild of a generator usually includes putting the armature on a lathe and turning the commutator or at least polishing it with a piece of emery cloth.

The brushes on generators and starters alike should be replaced if they are worn more than half-way.

two things that can go wrong anyway—either the wires have lost their insulation somewhere and are touching ground (such as the generator casing), or they have broken and have created an open circuit.

Considering the cost and availability of rebuilt generators, most restorers will tell you it's seldom worth your time to try to repair a generator yourself. Moreover, most communities have a machine shop or automotive shop that can test and rebuild your generator to factory specifications.

The same could be said about the voltage regulator. If there is doubt about whether it is working properly, your best bet is to take it to a shop that specializes in starter and generator rebuilds and let them test it. If it can be

repaired, they'll be able to take care of it, and if not, they should be able to suggest the correct replacement.

STARTERS

Not every antique tractor is going to have a starter. Even when electric starters became available, they were only an option on many models.

In essence, the starter is much like the generator, only it operates in the opposite manner. Instead of generating electricity, it takes electricity and uses it to turn a drive sprocket. However, like the generator, it contains an armature, coils, brushes, and commutator that can wear or short out in much the same manner. Hence, overhaul consists of inspecting the brushes for good contact with the commutator and making sure the latter is reasonably

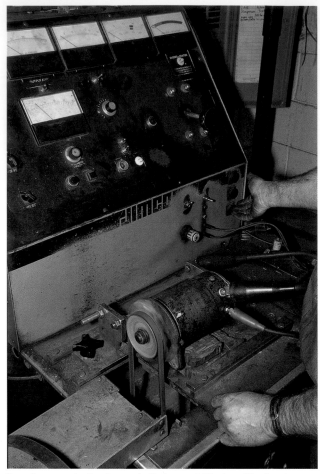

Once the generator has been rebuilt at a reputable shop, it's placed on a test stand to ensure that it will work like new.

clean and smooth. If it is not, it will need to be turned down on a lathe.

Just as you did with the generator, you'll also need to check for worn, dirty, or damaged bearings. Again, it may be easier and less costly in the long run to have these things done by a shop that specializes in starter and generator repairs or trade it for a rebuilt unit.

Before you pull the starter off the tractor, though, you need to realize that some tractors have a neutral start interlock switch that prevents the tractor from being started if the tractor is in gear. If the interlock switch is faulty, you may be wasting your time on the starter itself.

The problem may also be related to the battery or loose or corroded connections. To omit these possibilities, connect a fully charged battery to the starter using a set of jumper cables. If there is a significant difference in the way the starter turns over, check the battery; then inspect, clean, and tighten all starter relay connections as well as the battery ground on the frame and engine.

If the starter still does not crank with the jumper cables, plan on removing and replacing or repairing the starter.

CONVERTING TO 12-VOLT ELECTRICS

If you intend to use your restored tractor as a working machine rather than a parade or show tractor, you may want to consider converting the charging and electrical system to 12 volts by replacing the generator and 6-volt battery with an alternator. Modern alternators not only improve an older tractor's charging system, but they cost far less than a new generator. As a result, problems associated with inadequate voltage may be cured for about the same cost as refurbishing the 6-volt system.

When asked about converting a Farmall tractor to a 12-volt electrical system, T. W. Cook, a Farmall enthusiast from Georgetown, Texas, generally answers, "Why? These tractors were designed to start perfectly well on six volts and will today if you have proper cables and a good battery."

He says the problems can often be traced to the battery cables, noting that many tractors he's seen have had the cables replaced with thin 12-volt cables.

"If you have these," he says, "you need to throw them away and replace them with big 2-gauge or larger cables."

If you do convert to a 12-volt system, John Brillman of the Brillman Company, which sells wiring harnesses and bulk wire, says it's important to install the correct wiring for the system. "It depends on how they've done it," he relates. "In many cases, it's possible to rebuild the generator for 12 volts, in which case, the wiring harness layout will be identical. However, if they upgrade the system to use an alternator, it's a totally different layout."

Before you begin any kind of conversion, though, you need to make sure your system is a negative-ground charging system. It will also be necessary to install a 12-volt battery, making any changes that are required to fit the battery in the battery case or tray. Finally, you'll need to remove the previous charging system, including the associated voltage regulator. You may want to save these parts, just in case you want to go back and do a classic restoration sometime in the future.

In the meantime, it may be helpful to locate a wiring diagram. Note any wires from instruments or parts other than the generator/alternator and be ready to replace their function either by routing them differently or by adding jumpers.

Mechanical mounting of the alternator is generally a case-by-case issue. If you're fortunate, you may only need to use a longer bolt for the mounting lugs and a piece of pipe for a spacer. You may also need to change

It takes more than a heavy-duty starter to turn over a diesel engine—it also takes a lot of power. That's why many diesel tractors use two 12-volt batteries wired in series.

Judging from the looks of the starter on this Ferguson tractor, a starter cleanup and overhaul may be in order.

the drive pulley to match the speed capability of the alternator. Most tractors don't run fast enough to get the full potential out of the alternator.

Finally, you'll need to change the coil or install a resistor to limit the output voltage to a level the system can handle. If there is any doubt about whether the starter, lights, or other components can handle the alteration, check with your local tractor service technician or with knowledgeable tractor club members.

WIRING

Unless your tractor has been treated with tender loving care for the past fifty to seventy-five years, it's doubtful that you will get by without replacing at least part of the wiring. At the very least, you will want to replace the spark plug wires as part of the engine rebuild.

However, replacing crimped, spliced, and inferior wiring on the rest of the tractor not only improves the looks of your restored tractor, but can be a safety feature. Wiring with cracked insulation and wires on which the old, cotton braiding has dry rotted can ground out electrical components—and at the worst, create a fire hazard.

The first step in wiring restoration is locating a wiring diagram. Hopefully, this will be included in your service and repair manual. If not, you'll have to trace the wiring from the power source, or the battery, to each switch and component. Don't put too much stock in what you find, though. Previous owners may have replaced the original wiring with a different gauge of wire, the incorrect type of wire, or they may have even taken short cuts with the routing.

Whether you're overhauling a starter or generator, it's worth the time and money to put in new bearings.

If you intend to use your restored tractor strictly as a work tractor, you might want to install an alternator and convert the electrical system to 12 volts.

If there is any doubt, talk to other tractor owners or try to find a well-restored model like your own and take notes. As a general rule, you should use at least 10-gauge wiring for circuits that carry a heavy load, such as those from the generator. Switches and other components can be wired with 14-gauge wire. Remember, the larger the gauge number, the smaller the wire diameter.

Typically, if you find sections of wiring that are badly deteriorated, it's usually bad throughout. Rarely will you find a good section and bad section. Quite often, you'll find that the insulation on the original wiring, which sometimes consisted of nothing more than waxed paper, has deteriorated to the point it's only being held together by the cotton braid. When that happens, there's not much

to keep electric current from jumping through the cotton to a nearby frame rail or component.

So now you need to decide whether you want to locate a wiring diagram and rewire the tractor on your own, or purchase a pre-assembled wiring harness. It's obviously less expensive to buy the wire and all the connectors, but you also have to consider your experience and the amount of time you have available.

Your purchase will also depend on whether you're restoring the tractor as a working machine or an accurate restoration. If the plan is to rebuild it as a work tractor, you can easily substitute modern PVC-coated, automotive-type wiring in the correct gauge and crimp-style connections. However, if you're going for accuracy, you'll want to locate the appropriate gauge of lacquer-coated, cotton-covered wiring, which was used on most tractors built before the mid-1950s.

The wiring harnesses stocked by most restoration supply companies have all the terminals soldered in place and sealed and all wires are numbered and color-coded to correspond with an installation guide that's included. All reproduction harnesses are also made up of the appropriate-gauge wire covered by PVC, which, in turn, is covered with cloth loom, cloth braid, nylon braid or tape to match the factory original—giving you the best of both worlds.

The main thing to watch for when replacing wiring or installing a new wiring harness is to make sure the ground points are free of paint. Unlike the original manufacturer, most restorers paint all the parts and then assemble the tractor. So make sure you don't paint over your grounds or else clean the paint from those areas before you do any rewiring.

SPARK PLUG WIRES

Contrary to their rugged appearance, spark plug wires are quite sensitive. That's because most secondary wires consist of a soft-copper-core wire surrounded by stainless steel or carbon-impregnated thread mixed with an elastomer-type conductor. The outside covering of a heavy layer of insulation prevents the 12,000 to 25,000 volts from bleeding out when the wire is carrying current.

Consequently, the resistance-type wires do not handle sharp bending or jerking and can break internally, ruining the wire. Excessive exposure to oil and antifreeze can chemically break down the coating, as well.

Perhaps the most damaging effect, though, is caused when someone pulls on the wires to remove them from the spark plugs. This can separate the conducting material, causing internal arcing.

Consequently, it's important that you keep spark plug wires clean and separated from each other with any wire clips that are integral to the routing. To remove wires from the plugs during service or restoration, grasp the rubber boot, not the wires. Keep in mind, too, that secondary wires, including the coil wire and spark plug wires, can appear in good condition, yet be faulty.

According to Curtis Von Fange, a tractor enthusiast from Indiana, they can be the cause of irritating engine "poofs" that simply can't be located or can make an engine run erratic and backfire. If there is any doubt about the condition of the wires, it's generally best to replace them.

However, one way to check their condition is to measure the wire resistance using an ohmmeter. In general, the wires should register around 8,000 to 12,000 ohms per foot. This will also test the wire for continuity, ensuring that there are no breaks in the copper-wire core.

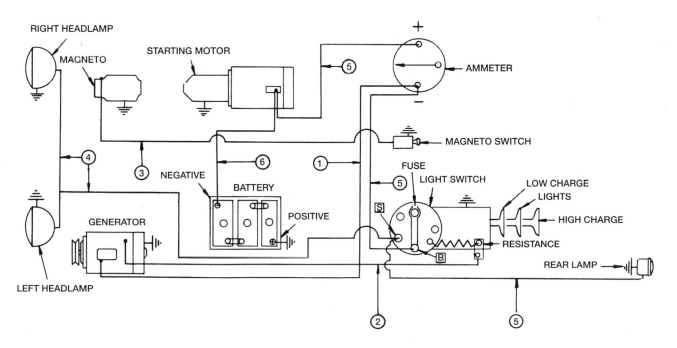

A wiring diagram can be a tremendous help when rewiring a tractor or tracing electrical problems. *AGCO Corporation*

LIGHTS

Depending upon the age of your tractor, you may not even have to concern yourself with refurbishing the lights. That's because lights on tractors didn't become standard equipment until the 1940s. Still, they can be a real challenge if you have a tractor equipped with such "modern" amenities.

Unfortunately, electric lights need some kind of work on nearly every complete tractor restoration. Moreover, the simplicity and cost of repair are going to depend on the age of the tractor and whether it uses bulb-type lights or sealed-beam lights. While Ford was the first to use sealed-beam headlights in 1939, it wasn't until 1954 that most of the other tractor companies joined the sealed-beam bandwagon.

Fortunately, pre-sealed-beam lights are fairly easy to repair or replace. On a pre-sealed-beam light, if it's completely shot or in really bad shape, it's usually easiest and most cost-effective to just replace the whole light with a new assembly. Even if the housing is in good shape—without any dents, which aren't uncommon on free-standing lights—replacing all the components will still cost you more than a whole new light.

In most every case, the reflector will also be rusted or tarnished and the gasket between the lens and housing will be dried out and brittle. With the exception of some Allis-Chalmers and Ford models, which have the wiring inside the post, most lights had the wiring attached externally, which leads to other problems.

Dan Steiner, president of Steiner Tractor Parts, explains that in most cases, the terminal was made out of Bakelite, which was an early form of plastic. "Over the course of time, those were prone to decay. So the terminal, along with the reflector and gasket are generally the minimum that will need to be replaced."

As part of the renewal process, most restorers start disassembling the light, then cleaning it inside and out. Most lights have a retaining ring around the front of the light that, once removed, allows the entire light to be disassembled. Once it's been taken apart, one restorer likes to bead blast the light housing to a smooth finish—although he admits paint stripper can have the same effect.

Unless the light fixtures are a totally different color, the outer shell can then be painted at the same time you're painting other tractor components. As for the reflector, you can follow Steiner's suggestion and replace it with a new one, which generally costs in the range of $10 to $15. Or as a less costly option, simply spray paint it with chrome-colored or galvanizing-effect spray paint.

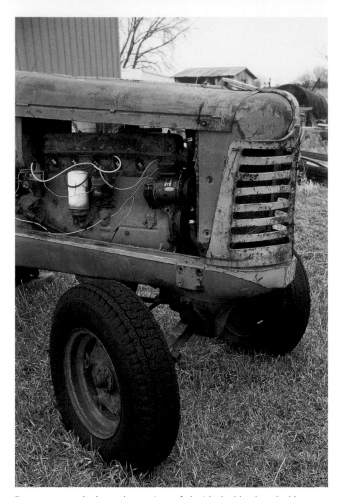

It appears somebody used every type of electrical wiring imaginable on this vintage Oliver—and none of it is stock.

It depends, of course, on how much you plan to use the lights. Reflective paint will obviously not give off the amount of light that a new reflector will provide.

Should you have any trouble finding a replacement gasket for reassembly—or choose to go a cheaper route there, as well—you might want to use a tip provided by Jeff Gravert, a tractor restorer from Central City, Nebraska. He says a good substitute for the gasket that fits between the lens and the reflector is a strip of caulking that comes in rolls and pulls off like a piece of cord. The caulk also helps hold the lens in place, while you reattach the headlight ring.

Unfortunately, when it comes to sealed-beam headlights, Steiner says they often pose a lot greater challenge during restoration than their incandescent counterpart. The problem, he says, is there are so many different types of sealed-beam bulbs that were used over the years.

"The issue with sealed-beam light is there is a lot of variation between them," he says. "We carry the most common sealed-beam bulbs, as well as the most common sealed-beam lamps. What we don't have are the oddballs—and there were a lot of oddballs."

The variation, he explains, not only involved size, but the connections, tabs molded into the beam to hold them in place, etc. Fortunately, most sealed-beams have a four-digit number on the back of the bulb that can be used for reference.

"Some of the numbers are interchangeable, if the only difference is the amperage, rather than shape or voltage," he continues. "But if you can find the number, that's the best place to start, whether you're buying a sealed-beam bulb from us or another vendor."

You may find, too, that equipped with the number, you can locate a less expensive bulb from an aftermarket supplier than you can from the John Deere or Case–IH dealer, assuming they still carry the appropriate bulb.

Should you need to replace the whole light due to damage, or find that doing so is the least expensive option, you can expect to pay somewhere between $35 and $75 for a new headlight or taillight assembly. Finally, if you find you have an "oddball" sealed-beam light for which a replacement is simply unavailable, you basically have three options—restore it for appearance only as a non-working light; find a replacement light assembly that as closely as possible resembles the original light; or modify the light internally to accept a different type of bulb within the housing.

For those who insist on originality, no matter how much a replacement assembly resembles the factory

Whether it is readily visible or not, many restorers prefer to use the older-style, cotton-coated wiring for a true restoration.

original, your best option is to visit swap meets and salvage yards and search for used original lights or do a similar search on the Internet.

Whether you replace the bulb or the whole assembly, though, be sure you purchase a component for the appropriate voltage. That also applies to tractors that were originally operated on a 6-volt system and have since been converted to 12 volts. If you're going back

Although the original wiring on this Farmall appears to be in good condition, the fact that the wiring harness is coming unraveled obviously detracts from the appearance.

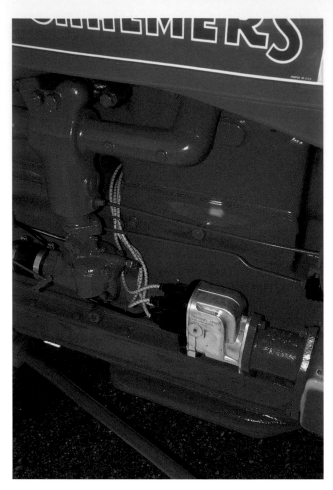

The use of lacquer-coated cotton-braided wiring, which was common on tractors built before the mid-1950s, really sets off this Allis-Chalmers engine.

Estel Theis is as meticulous about the lights as he is about any other tractor component. Having been cleaned, painted, and fitted with a new rubber seal, this light is ready for reassembly.

to 6 volts, you may not have a problem. But going the other way can be costly.

If you put a 12-volt light on a 6-volt system, it's just not going to light up as bright as it should, Steiner explains. "But if you put a 6-volt bulb on a 12-volt system, it might light up for about a second, but you're going to blow the bulb. That's bad enough with an incandescent bulb, but when you blow up a sealed-beam, you're talking anywhere from $15 to $50. But even if you go the other way and are restoring a converted 12-volt system back to the original 6-volt system during a tractor restoration, it's generally best to change out the bulbs."

Finally, no light is going to work correctly if the wiring is frayed and grounding out. So make sure the wiring throughout the system has been checked and repaired or the entire wiring assembly has been replaced. Furthermore, each light must have a good ground to function. Pre-sealed-beam lights are usually grounded

through the reflector to the housing and then through the post.

GAUGES

Gauges used to be a real challenge for the tractor restorer trying to obtain an authentic look. Fortunately, there are a lot more options today, as suppliers have introduced reproduction gauges that look just like the original.

If you're lucky, though, you may find that you can get the old gauge cleaned up and working properly and save some money in the process. The first step with any gauge that doesn't seem to work is to make sure the needle isn't stuck. If you tap the gauge while the engine is running and it moves or attempts to move, you at least know the problem is in the gauge.

Gauge Replacement

If it becomes necessary to replace the gauge, you have several options. Stewart-Warner (S-W), for one, has

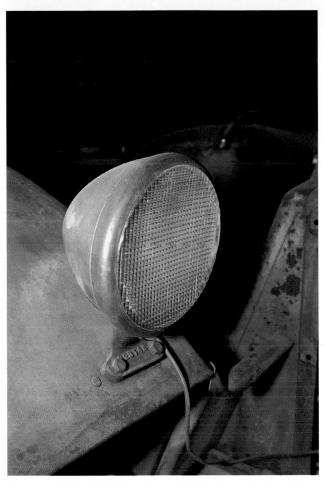

The owner of this old John Deere two-cylinder tractor was lucky to find a model on which both lights were complete and unbroken.

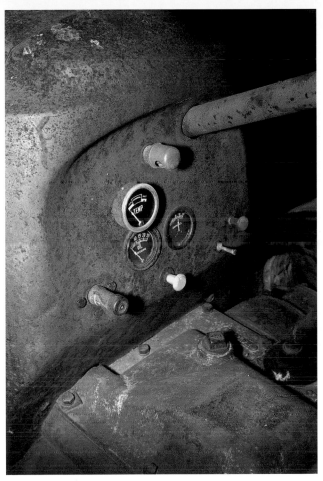

Despite the rust on the rest of the tractor, the gauges on this vintage model appear to be reusable with a little attention.

always stocked gauges that work fine for many older tractors. Many of them even look a lot like the original, except they have the S-W logo at the bottom of the gauge face. In fact, if you're not terribly concerned about authenticity or if you're restoring a tractor as a work unit, you can still replace any gauge that is no longer working with an off-the-shelf model.

However, until the last ten to twenty years, it was nearly impossible to find gauges like the original that had the "Case," "A-C," or "I-H" logo on the gauge face. Even John Deere two-cylinder enthusiasts couldn't find gauges with the authentic look that included a white gauge face and the words "John Deere" on the face. The choices were limited to S-W gauges or the current John Deere gauges with a black faceplate.

Times have changed, though, to the point that replica gauges are not only readily available for all major tractor brands, but they're also cost-effective to replace. An Internet search, or the ads in some of the tractor magazines

will direct you to a number of vendors, but they include Antique Gauges, Inc., Steiner Tractor, Restoration Supply, and a myriad of specialty shops like N-Complete (Ford gauges), and Farmallparts.com.

AGCO carries an inventory of vintage parts, including certain gauges for older Oliver, Minneapolis-Moline, Massey-Harris, Massey Ferguson, and Allis-Chalmers tractors.

"When it comes to the ammeter, oil, temperature and fuel gauges, you can typically buy a replacement gauge for less money than you can rebuild it," says Dan Steiner, president of Steiner Tractor Parts. "Plus, with the exception of tachometers, there aren't that many guys out there who restore gauges."

If you're looking for an authentic John Deere two-cylinder or new generation tractor gauge, though, you can always contact EverGreen Restoration in Spooner, Wisconsin. They can either restore the gauge you send to them or sell you a gauge that has all the details of the

TROUBLESHOOTING GAUGES

Electric Gauges

- With electric gauges, locate the two wires that attach to the rear and make sure the contacts are good or use a voltmeter to check power to the gauge.

- Check to make sure the wiring isn't shorted out at some point along its length.

- Check for a fuse in the electrical circuit and make sure it hasn't blown. The fuse may be in-line in the wiring harness.

- Locate the sending unit to the problem gauge. Then, with the ignition key turned on, use an ohmmeter to check for power to the sender or have someone watch the gauge while you wiggle the wires that attach to the sending unit and the ground. If the gauge doesn't move, disconnect the wires and touch them together. If it still doesn't move, you'll need to replace the gauge.

Mechanical Gauges

- Make sure the drive cable is working properly. Cables often bind within the sheath, especially if it has been kinked.

- Clean the cable and housing with a spray electrical cleaner; then lubricate the cable before replacing it in the housing.

Water Temperature Gauge

- Remove the bulb assembly from the engine, being careful not to kink the tube.

- Place the bulb in hot or boiling water and watch for the gauge to register "hot."

- Now, substitute cold water. If the gauge doesn't follow to read cool, the assembly must be replaced, since the gauge and tubing/bulb can't be repaired separately.

Oil Pressure Gauge

- If the oil pressure gauge fails to register, shut off the engine immediately, assuming that the gauge could be correct, until you find the real issue.

- Disconnect the tiny oil line from the fitting on the engine block and restart the engine to see if oil comes out of the hole in a steady flow. If so, reconnect the tube to the engine and disconnect it at the gauge, examining it along the way to make sure it isn't kinked.

- Finally, check to make sure the metering hole on the back of the gauge isn't blocked. By this point you should know if the problem is in the engine, the tubing or the gauge.

---

original—because it is essentially an original with a new decal face.

You'll also find a number of individuals on the web and through tractor magazine ads who restore and rebuild tractor tachometers. Again, you'll need to compare the cost of repair and shipping both directions to that of purchasing a new reproduction.

The only disadvantage of buying a reproduction tachometer is that the manufacturer doesn't have any way of adjusting the number of hours on the hour meter. Hence, the tractor owner will be starting over at "zero"hours. So if the number of hours on the tractor is important for sentimental reasons or if you want to keep a running log of the hours on the engine, they may want to have the tachometer rebuilt. Remember, though, the hour meter only records hours at PTO speed, which means that the hours spent idling or at low speed can be misleading.

Gauge Restoration

If a gauge is available from no other source, however, there's still the salvage yard. Depending on the reason the tractor ended up there, it may have a gauge that's in better shape than the one on your tractor. If the face plate is in relatively good shape, it's easy enough to refurbish the rest of the gauge.

First, you'll need to carefully remove the bezel ring that holds the glass in place. On some gauges, you may have to bend up the lip around the edge of the gauge to do so. Now, it's just a matter of cleaning it up, making sure the mechanisms work properly, and repainting it.

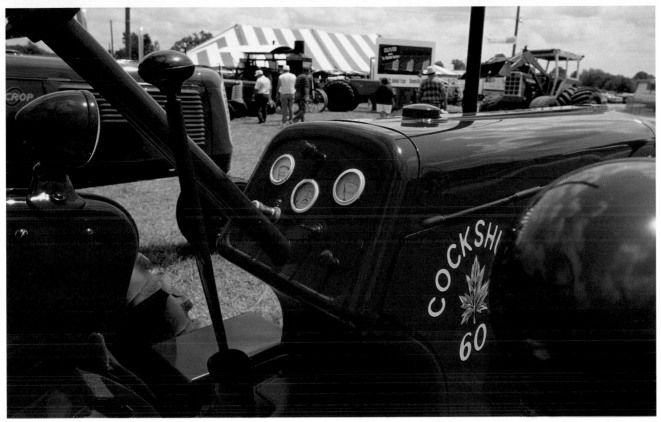

Since you'll often be looking at the gauges as you operate your restored tractor, you'll appreciate the effort and cost you put into a quality restoration of the gauges, as on this Cockshutt Model 60.

New gauges, complete with the Oliver name, really set off the dash on this Row Crop 88 restoration.

The black-faced gauges on this John Deere two-cylinder tractor are not original. For an accurate restoration, they should be white—but white-faced gauges are only available from reproduction parts suppliers and usually at a premium price. If you're restoring a work tractor, you can still get the black gauges from any John Deere dealer.

Chapter 11
Fuel System

It goes without saying that every engine needs at least three ingredients to operate—spark, fuel, and air. We covered the electrical system already; now it's time to examine the requirements for fuel and air.

There can be a wide variation in the amount of work a fuel system is going to need, depending upon the age of the tractor and whether it was running at the time you bought it. If you had a chance to drive it before the purchase, or before you started tearing it down, you should have a good idea about how smoothly it was running.

On the other hand, if you're restoring a treasure that has been sitting in the weeds or an old barn for the last twenty years, chances are there's a lot of rust, varnish, water, and who knows what else in the system.

FUEL TANK

Let's start with a basic fact: You can rebuild the carburetor, clean or replace the fuel lines, and change the fuel filter, but all that does little good if the fuel tank was the source of contamination. So the first step in fuel system overhaul should be to clean the tank and reseal the interior if necessary.

Everyone seems to have their own story about how to clean a fuel tank. Some have been known to stick the sandblast nozzle in the fill opening and move it around to hit all sides with silica sand or glass beads. The risk, of course, is that you might just blow a hole through any weak spot in the tank. Plus, you'll need to get all the sand out of the tank.

A more common option is to fill the tank about one-third full of water and add a few handfuls of 1/2-inch nuts, shingle nails, or pebbles. The key is to provide a slight abrasive action to clean up the inside. A word of caution is in order, though, particularly if you want to avoid frustrations later on. Check to see if the filler neck extends into the tank to act as a baffle that keeps fuel from splashing back out. If it does and you add a non-metallic abrasive like pebbles or even brass nuts, you may have a hard time getting all the material out of the tank. It will be a little like trying to shake pennies out of the slot in a piggy bank. That's part of the reason most professional restorers seem to prefer nuts and bolts. At least you can use a magnet to fish out the stragglers.

The next step is to agitate the tank rather vigorously with this mixture sealed inside. One restorer claims the best way to agitate the mixture, assuming you do some farming, is to strap the tank to a tractor wheel with bungee cords and let it rotate while you do a day's field work. In lieu of hauling it around in the field, another restorer says he does the same thing, but simply blocks the front wheels on a tractor, locks the brakes, and jacks up one rear wheel to which the tank is strapped. Then, he lets the tractor idle in gear for four or five hours, letting the tractor wheel work much like a rock tumbler.

Yet another restorer says he simply secures the tank in the back of his pickup and hauls it around for about a month while he's working on other parts of the tractor. If you're going to use that method, though, it helps if you live on country roads. Anyway, you get the picture. You need to agitate the tank vigorously enough and long enough to scour all the rust and residue out of the tank.

If the tank is in really bad shape, you might want to start by adding a lye-based cleaner to the initial mixture for the first fifteen or twenty minutes and then switch to a water-and-abrasive mixture. Once the tank has agitated for a sufficient period of time, remove the abrasive and rinse the tank with clean water. You may have to repeat the rinsing process several times until you get clean water coming back out of the tank.

A vital step in fuel system overhaul is cleaning the tank and, if necessary, resealing the interior with a quality tank sealer.

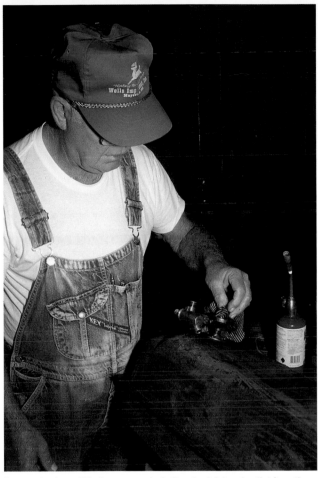
Be sure to clean all fuel passages, including the inlet and outlet from the sediment bowl.

If you find that the fuel tank leaks, you have a couple of choices, but one of them should not be trying to solder it yourself, regardless of what kind of instructions your friends have given you—like filling the tank with exhaust gas from your car's exhaust pipe, which supposedly makes it safer.

Shops that weld automobile gasoline tanks usually steam clean the inside for an hour or more to ensure that no residual gasoline is emitted from the pores in the metal during heating. Even then, welding a gas tank can be a dangerous proposition. That's why many professionals also fill the tank with an inert gas or liquid before heating the tank.

One thing you can try on your own, though, is patching the hole with an epoxy, assuming the patch will be hidden beneath the tractor sheet metal. Several restorers have reported success with materials marketed as Magic Metal, J-B Weld, and other "gas tank menders" sold in automotive stores. The key is getting the surface clean with a good parts cleaner prior to mixing and applying the epoxy.

Once the tank has been repaired or proven to be free of leaks, it still makes good sense to coat the interior with a fuel tank sealer. Most sealers recommend that you first etch the tank with phosphoric acid or an acid metal-prep solution to stabilize any remaining rust prior to adding the sealer. Be sure to leave the gas tank lid off, though, when rinsing the tank with acid, since the reaction with the metal creates a gas. Then, rinse the tank several times with clean water and air dry the tank with a warm air source to prevent any further rust.

As soon as the tank interior has adequately dried, pour in enough sealer to cover all sides of the tank interior. Refer to the instructions that come with the sealer, but in most cases, they will tell you to allow several days for the material to cure before adding fuel. While you're waiting, you can finish up the fuel delivery system by cleaning the sediment bowl assembly and replacing all gaskets and screens.

FUEL HOSE INSPECTION

They may look fine right now, but the few minutes it takes to inspect the fuel lines and fuel filter could save you a lot of headaches later. Start by inspecting any rubber fuel hoses for kinking, pinching at tight bends, and internal swelling. Also, make sure fuel lines are not running near an exhaust manifold or pipe, which could lead to a vaporizing problem on hot days. If the fuel turns into a gas in the line, it can cause the fuel circuit to vapor lock and stop delivering fuel to the carburetor.

Finally, make sure fuel is flowing freely to and from the fuel filter. A partially plugged fuel filter can lean out the fuel mixture and cause backfiring, spitting, and misfiring. Unfortunately, when the engine dies, back pressure from expanding vapor can push debris from the filter back into the fuel tank, thereby hiding the problem. The engine will start up and run like normal until debris once again finds its way back into the filter element.

CARBURETOR REPAIR

To your benefit as a tractor restorer, the carburetor on most vintage farm tractors is not as complex as it would appear. To begin with, there was no such thing as a fuel pump on most early tractors. The fuel tank was simply mounted above the engine, and the fuel was fed to the carburetor by gravity. The carburetor itself is equally simple. In most cases, the only adjustments are the idle or low-speed adjustment and the high-speed or full-load adjustment that regulates the flow of fuel to the jets.

Having been thoroughly cleaned and coated with a primer, this fuel tank is ready for a final coat of paint and reassembly on the tractor.

If you plan any engine work that involves starting and running the engine while the fuel tank is removed, you'll need to rig up some sort of temporary fuel supply.

Internally, about the only adjustment that is ever needed is to bend the float stem to change the fuel level in the bowl. Of course, some service manuals will tell you to never bend the float arm, but rather change the float valve level by using thicker or thinner washers under the float valve or filing a washer to the correct thickness. Either way, the float setting is important because the fuel level in the bowl plays a critical role in low- and high-speed adjustment.

In principle, the float bowl acts as a reservoir to hold a supply of fuel for the carburetor. However, it's important that the depth of fuel in the bowl remains consistent, since this regulates fuel flow to the carburetor itself. As fuel flows into the bowl by gravity, the brass float raises on a

hinge and pushes the needle valve into a seat to shut off the fuel flow. In effect, it works in much the same way as the float and valve in the toilet tank in your bathroom.

If the fuel level in the bowl is too low, the engine does not respond readily when accelerated and it will be difficult to maintain carburetor adjustments. If the fuel level in the bowl is too high, it can cause excessive fuel consumption and crankcase dilution. Plus, it can cause the carburetor to leak. Again, it will be difficult to maintain carburetor adjustments.

CARBURETOR REBUILDING

The first step in rebuilding a carburetor is to remove it from the tractor and get it cleaned up. Start by closing the valve on the fuel tank, if this hasn't already been done, or if the fuel tank hasn't already been removed, and disconnect the fuel line from the carburetor. You'll also need to disconnect any choke cables and governor linkage on most carburetors.

Now, remove the carburetor from the intake manifold and air cleaner and move it to a clean workbench or an area where you can disassemble it without losing pieces. Remember that until you empty the bowl, the carburetor still contains a small amount of gasoline. So treat it as you would a flammable substance until you've had a chance to clean it out. If the carburetor is equipped with a drain plug or a drain valve, you can try draining the fuel that way, if it's not rusted in place.

You'll want to begin by removing the top half of the carburetor and dumping the gasoline that is still in the bowl in a safe place. Next, carefully disassemble the carburetor, inspecting all parts for wear as you go. Before you remove the idle-mixture and main-jet adjusting needles, though, carefully tighten each against the bottom of the seat, noting how many turns it takes to do so. When reassembling the carburetor, you can again tighten the needles to the seat and back off the recorded number of turns. That will at least give you a starting point to dialing in the carburetor.

Be sure you make notes if you have any doubts about how it goes back together—including the orientation of any gaskets you remove. Many of the parts will be replaced while installing a carburetor rebuild kit, but don't throw anything away until you know you have the proper replacement part. Some kits are applicable to more than one carburetor, so there may be parts you don't need—and that means you need to be able to match the parts you do need!

Next, soak the two halves of the carburetor, along with the components you've removed, in a new container

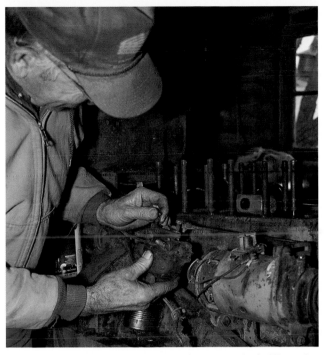

To remove the carburetor, it's necessary to first remove the fuel line and all throttle and choke linkages. Then, unbolt it from the intake manifold.

of carburetor cleaner for at least twelve hours or for the amount of time recommended on the label. Many carburetor cleaner solutions come with a parts bucket, so use it to turn and move the components from time to time.

Some restorers have also used a small sandblasting unit and glass beads to scour the two halves of the unit once all the parts have been removed. You need to use care, though—and never use sand. Otherwise, you can quickly ruin the brass jets that remain in place.

You'll also need to clean these brass jets, either by removing them with a screwdriver or cleaning the passageway with a sturdy piece of nylon fishing line and an air hose, directing the air in the opposite direction of the fuel flow. Some jets are pressed into place and can't be removed without destroying them, which means you need to know ahead of time whether a replacement is available. If a jet is removable, though, make sure you have a screwdriver that fits the slot securely. Brass parts are easy to strip or damage.

The fuel jet must be clean and unobstructed for the carburetor to operator properly.

CARBURETOR REASSEMBLY

Once the carburetor has been thoroughly cleaned, it's time to put it all back together and make the necessary adjustments. Hopefully, you were able to find a kit for your carburetor that contained all the appropriate parts. Should you own that rare exception, though, don't give up hope yet.

Jeff Gravert says one of the tricks he has learned is to look at other options and ask questions of other restorers. As an example, he's found that the throttle shaft bushings from certain Briggs & Stratton engines can be used in a pinch to repair the carburetors on Cockshutt tractors. While the inside of the bushing is too large for the shaft, the outside bushing diameter is the perfect size to fit in the throttle-shaft bore. Gravert then uses a drill bit to carefully enlarge the inside bushing diameter to match that of the throttle shaft.

It's important, however, that such worn parts be replaced. If the throttle-shaft bushings or seals, for example, are worn to the point they are letting air leak into the carburetor, it's going to affect the gas-air mixture. In the process of reassembling the carburetor, you also need to make sure all gaskets are properly oriented, too. Otherwise, you may block a vital orifice or passageway.

Also, when checking the float height, be sure the gasket has been positioned on the top half of the carburetor.

The measurement specified in your service manual or kit instructions is almost always taken from the surface of the gasket to the top surface of the float (which will be the bottom side if you have the upper half of the carburetor inverted during measurement).

Finally, when reinstalling the main-jet and idle-speed mixture screws, be sure to screw them all the way in and then back them out the number of turns recorded during disassembly.

DIESEL SYSTEMS

According to historical accounts, Rudolf Diesel, the man who designed and built the first diesel engine, was almost killed when one of his first prototypes exploded. Fortunately, Diesel went on to perfect his design and turn it into what is today the most popular form of farm power in history.

Despite the shaky start, diesel engines used in modern farm tractors are relatively safe. However, they also operate in an entirely different manner than do gasoline engines. Because diesel fuel—also referred to at times as No. 2 fuel oil and distillate—is heavier and doesn't vaporize nearly as easily as gasoline, there is neither a carburetor nor spark plugs on a diesel engine.

Instead, diesel fuel is injected directly into the cylinder at pressures of up to 2,500 psi. In fact, some of today's

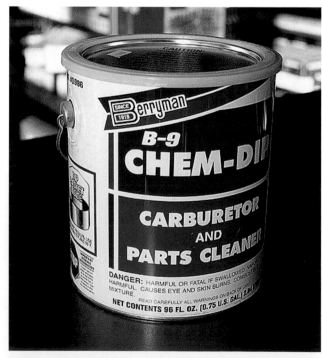

Soaking the disassembled carburetor in a bucket of cleaner should be the first step in the overhaul process.

If the tiny holes in this jet become plugged, it can dramatically affect the air-fuel mixture.

APPROX. 5/16 INCHES

Your tractor repair manual should provide the specified float level dimension, which controls fuel level in the bowl.

diesel engines utilize pumps producing up to 5,000 psi pressure at the injector. It is this high injection pressure, combined with cylinder compression, that creates the heat needed to ignite the fuel. Obviously, this means that the injector pump needs to force the precise amount of fuel into each cylinder, via an injector, at exactly the right time. That's why the injection pump is generally geared to the crankshaft.

That's also the reason injection-pump testing and rebuilding is best left to a professional who has the knowledge and the equipment to work on it. Roy Ritter, a Missouri-based tractor restorer who has been working on John Deere two-cylinder diesel pumps for nearly fifty years, says one thing you can do, though, is make sure the injector is the correct size for the tractor model and engine. As an example, he notes that every John Deere injector has a number stamped on the end. It may take a magnifying glass to read it, but it's there. Moreover, every John Deere diesel engine has a certain tip number specified.

"You wouldn't believe how often I receive a pump and injector set that has the wrong injector tips installed," he says. "Or one injector will have one tip number and the second one will have another number. Once I've installed the right tips for their particular tractor model and cleaned the injectors, it's usually just a matter of getting the pump adjusted to deliver the correct pressure and volume."

OIL-BATH AIR FILTERS

For many of us, an air filter is a square or round element composed of aluminum screen and folded, paperlike material that traps dirt particles as air flows to the carburetor. Once it gets dirty or has been in place a certain length of time, it's tossed and replaced with a new one.

While some vintage tractors may have that type of filter, it's more likely that the engine on your tractor has an oil-bath air filter. After all, replaceable air filters didn't become a feature on farm tractors until the 1960s.

So, assuming an oil-bath air filter is a new concept to many people, let's first look at how it works. As you probably noticed, the filter itself looks like it is made out of a pile of metal shavings. What's more, there's a cup at the bottom filled with oil. When you start the engine, a certain amount of oil is sucked out of the oil cup or pan and onto the metal shavings, which then act to filter the air that flows through it.

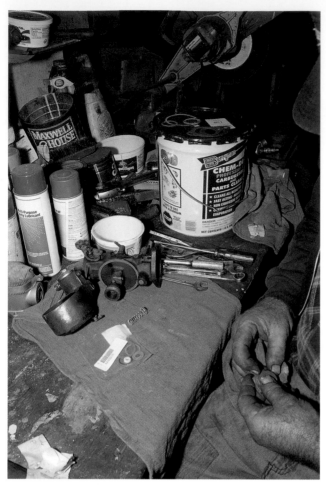

Most carburetors are not as complicated as they might appear. If you don't think you can handle installation of a carburetor kit, though, there are plenty of businesses that offer rebuilding services.

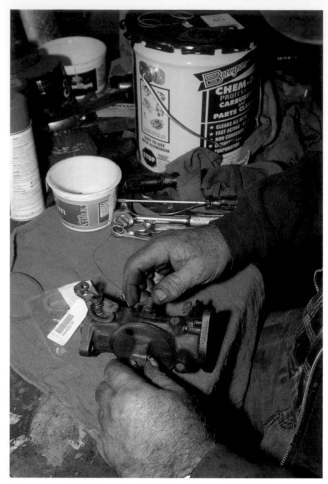

When reassembling the carburetor, it's best to reset all adjusting screws and needles to their original settings as a starting point.

CHECKING BOWL LEVEL

Depending upon the carburetor brand and configuration, one way to check the fuel level in the carburetor bowl is to connect a short piece of hose to the carburetor drain cock. Into the other end of the hose, insert a piece of glass tubing, such as that used in chemistry labs. You might even be able to find what you need from a medicine dropper. The idea is to use the glass tube as a sight gauge.

Now, open the drain valve while holding the glass portion of your gauge next to the carburetor bowl. The correct fuel level should be at the upper mark cast on the side of the carburetor bowl, assuming the carburetor on your tractor has such a mark. If the level is too high, it is an indication that the float needle valve is leaking, the float arm has become bent, or the float itself is leaking.

Another method of checking the fuel and float level—and one you should use if you are doing any other carburetor repair—is to remove the bowl from the throttle casting. Turn the throttle casting upside down and measure the distance between the float and the milled surface of the casting. This distance should match that specified in the operator's manual or your service and repair manual. A typical measurement for a Marvel-Schebler carburetor, used on a number of tractors in the 1940s and 1950s, is 5/16 inch, but check the manual to see what your specific model recommends.

If the dimension is not correct, carefully adjust the float arm in the appropriate direction until the correct measurement is obtained.

Naturally, the filter canister is designed to be just the right height and size so that the engine can pull oil up into the screen along with the air, without pulling it into the carburetor and engine. If you notice, too, incoming air is drawn into the filter through a center pipe that leads to the bottom of the canister. As a result, any heavy dirt particles should fall directly into the oil cup. Lighter particles, of course, should be trapped on the oil-soaked filter surface as the air moves upward through the outer portion of the canister toward the carburetor.

Now that you understand how it works, it should also be easier to visualize the potential problems. The first comes with using the wrong weight oil. If you add oil that is too light, it can be drawn beyond the filter and into the engine. Using oil that is too heavy will have the opposite effect: Not enough oil will be drawn up into the filter element and much of the air-cleaning surface will go unused.

As inconvenient as it may sound, oil-bath air filters were also designed to be cleaned and refilled daily when in use. In really dusty conditions, a farmer sometimes had to service the air cleaner a couple times a day. Naturally, the air cleaner is going to work best when the oil is at the recommended level. However, letting the oil cup fill up with sludge can be even more detrimental. Simply adding more oil to the cup, in fact, can make it worse. When the particles-to-oil ratio gets to a certain level, the dirt will begin to hang onto the cleaning surfaces. Eventually, instead of just clean air being sucked into the intake, chunks of dirt and sludge are going with it. So it's important to dump the old oil and wipe the oil cup out on a regular basis, as well.

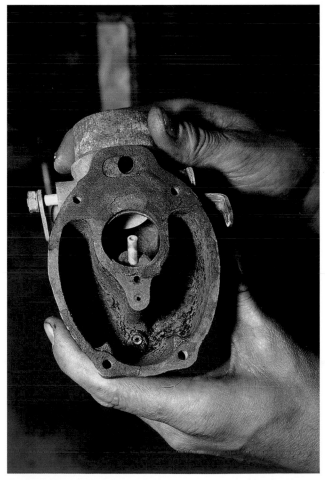

The fuel bowl on this carburetor is in serious need of cleaning due to a buildup of rust from years of sitting empty.

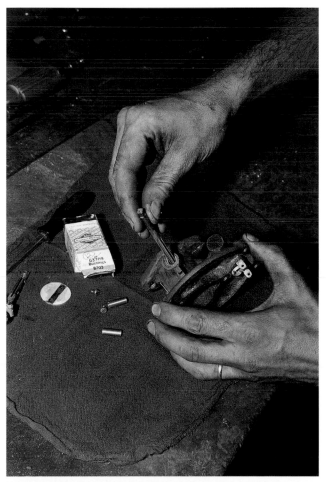

Not being able to find bushings to fit the carburetor for a vintage Cockshutt model, Jeff Gravert substituted a pair of throttle shaft bushings from a Briggs & Stratton engine. Although the outer diameter of his substitute bushings was a perfect fit, Gravert still had to drill out the inside diameter of the bushings to accept the throttle shaft.

Finally, you'll recall that the air cleaner was designed to be just the right size to match engine air intake. Otherwise, too much or too little oil is drawn into the filter canister. That means that any replacement air filter needs to be similar in size and design, if not identical to the original. By the same token, if you make dramatic changes in the engine that are going to affect air intake, you will need to make comparable changes in the air-cleaning system.

When it comes to repairing an oil-bath air cleaner, your biggest enemy will likely be rust, particularly if the oil in the bottom pan has long been replaced with water. Although some restorers have had success rebuilding small holes with epoxy or J-B Weld, about the only option when you're faced with a rusted-out canister is to locate a replacement.

MANIFOLD INSPECTION AND REPAIR

Just as an air leak in the carburetor can affect how smoothly your tractor runs, so can a crack in the intake manifold. Unfortunately, finding a replacement for a cracked intake or exhaust manifold on certain tractors can be a difficult challenge. So what are your options if you can't find a replacement?

One is to have a local welder or machine shop make the repair. Unfortunately, most intake and exhaust manifolds are made out of one of four types of cast-iron material—white, gray, malleable, or ductile iron. To properly weld it, the material must be properly prepared, preheated, and welded with the appropriate method. However, the type of material must first be identified, which involves one or more of the following tests: chemical analysis, a grinding test that identifies the types of sparks a grinding wheel gives off when in contact with the material, and a ring test that helps identify the material by the type of ringing sound it gives off when struck with a hammer.

Should you decide to try arc welding a cracked manifold yourself, it's important to use a high-content nickel/cast rod or a nickel/cadmium rod with a cast-iron-

Once the throttle shaft bushings have been replaced or cleaned, make sure the valve moves freely and without binding.

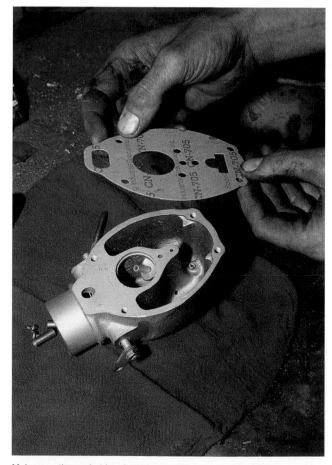

Make sure the gasket is oriented correctly when reassembling the carburetor. Otherwise, you may be blocking off a vital orifice or passageway.

Be sure to replace any damaged hoses that connect the carburetor to the air intake. Air leaks can negatively affect the air-fuel mixture.

friendly flux. Also, try to preheat the manifold with a torch. If preheating is not possible, strike an arc and weld only an inch or so of the crack. Then stop and let the heat spread to other parts of the material. If you try to lay a long bead of weld on a cold manifold, it could easily warp and cause a sudden stress crack somewhere else.

One option to arc welding, however, is brazing the manifold using a brass rod melted into a prepared groove on the manifold crack. Start by locating the crack and grinding a groove along its length with a grinder. Extend the groove a half inch or so beyond the crack. Then, use a coarse file to remove the grinder marks from the groove. This helps remove any graphite particles that could prevent the brazing material from adhering to the iron.

As for the brazing material, it's best to select a brass rod that is high in copper content with some nickel added. Also, select a torch tip that has a high-heat output with low gas pressure. As with arc welding, it's also helpful to preheat the material to be welded so it won't crack under isolated heat stress. Once brazing has been completed, try to cool the manifold slowly, using a bed of sand, if available.

One last option when trying to repair a manifold is to prepare and use an epoxy, such as J-B Weld. This is a particularly viable option on an intake manifold that is in a relatively cool area of the engine and when the crack is not in a stress area. Just make sure the area is clean and free of grease and grit and has been prepared according to the directions on the epoxy package.

GOVERNOR OVERHAUL

While it doesn't come in contact with the fuel, the governor plays an important part in the fuel-delivery system and needs to be inspected as part of your overhaul. In general, the governor is a mechanism that uses a rotating mass applied against a spring to adjust the carburetor throttle shaft to regulate the engine speed around a set point established by the throttle lever position.

In almost all cases, the governor is driven by the timing gear or by a drive coming off the magneto or distributor drive shaft and interconnected with the hand throttle linkage and the carburetor throttle plate. The rotating mass, meanwhile, is usually a set of flyweights or cams

Some early kerosene-powered tractors utilized a water-injection system that drew water from the engine water jacket in a supposed effort to increase engine power. The other brass valve on the block is a compression-release petcock, which partially releases compression on the cylinder when hand starting the engine.

Having been professionally cleaned, overhauled, and returned with caps on the outlet ports, this diesel pump has been reinstalled and is ready to be connected.

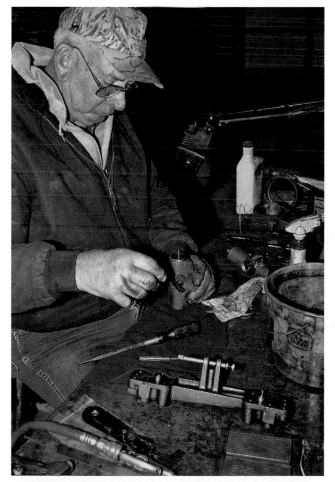

Roy Ritter, who retired after forty-five years of working as a John Deere mechanic, currently rebuilds John Deere two-cylinder injection pumps and injectors for restorers throughout North America.

with weights at the end. However, in some cases, such as the governor used on Ford 9N, 2N, and 8N tractors, a set of steel balls within a pair of races is used.

The first step in governor inspection is checking for any signs of malfunction. Symptoms can include the engine idling too fast or not idling down when the throttle lever is moved to the idle position; surging, over-revving, the engine not reaching the specified top speed; engine speed control that is erratic; and delayed reaction or sluggish response to changing load conditions or throttle movement.

Before removing the governor or attempting any disassembly, check the condition of any external springs, such as the one used on the Ford N Series governor. On most models, though, the governor spring will be enclosed in the governor housing. Also inspect all linkages and link rods for free movement and the absence of any bends or binding.

There is also a maximum-speed set screw on most governors that can be adjusted to increase or decrease the maximum-rpm setting. If the governor reaches the maximum-speed stop setting before the hand throttle is in the wide-open position, or if the governor fails to reach the maximum-speed stop before the hand throttle is wide open, it may also be necessary to adjust the connecting rod linkage between the governor and the carburetor. Refer to your service manual for the correct procedure for maximum-speed adjustment and linkage adjustment.

Your manual should also have a procedure for governor overhaul, although the basics include inspecting and

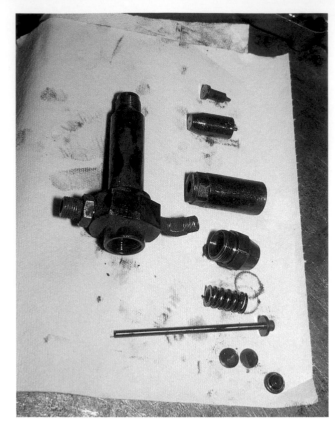

Because of the complex nature of a diesel injector, it's important that the injector tip and shims are a match for the tractor model and engine.

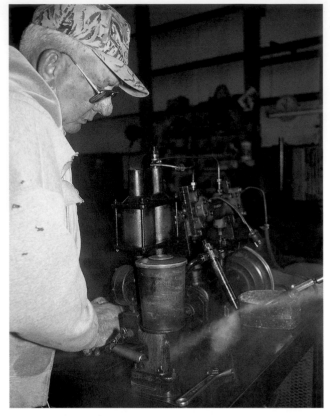

Ritter also pressurizes each injector to ensure the jets atomize the fuel, and to determine the "cracking" pressure.

After overhauling an injector pump, Roy Ritter places it on a test stand to make sure the output matches the engine specifications.

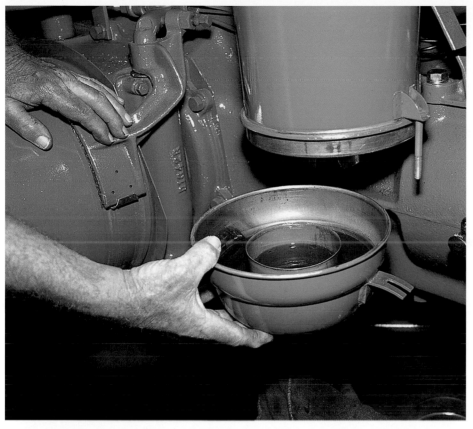

To work correctly, the oil-bath air cleaner cup must be filler to the recommended level with the correct weight of oil.

Because it was beyond repair, the combination intake/exhaust manifold on this Cletrac crawler had to be replaced.

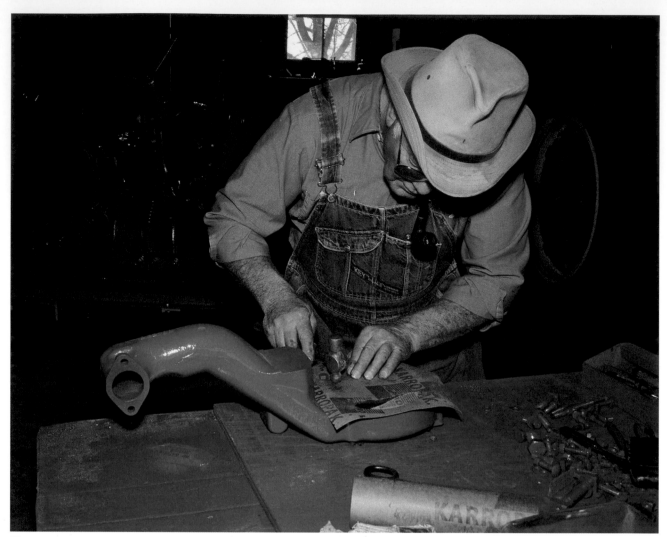

When an intake manifold gasket is no longer available, you have to settle for making your own.

replacing any defective bearings, seals, and drive gears. Also, ensure that the flyweights move freely, or in the case of governors that use flyballs, that the balls are free of flat spots, pits, and excessive wear. The inner surface of the cone race should also be smooth and even.

If you're not sure of your ability to rebuild the governor, you might consider sending it out to a shop that specializes in governor restoration. Considering the role it plays in controlling engine speed, you want to make sure it's done right.

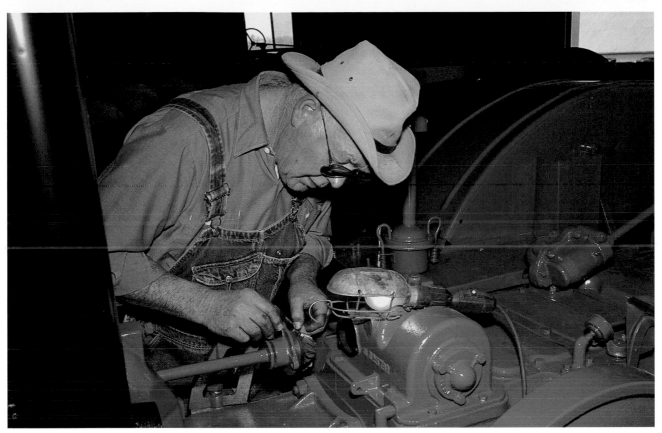

After years of exposure to the elements, the manifold material on some tractors simply cracks and disintegrates.

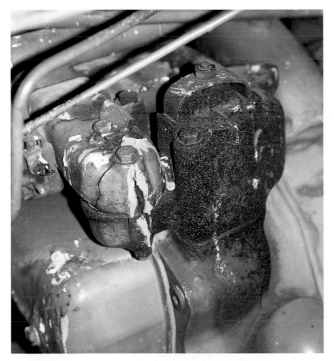

The governor mechanism on this John Deere Model D being restored by Ed Hoyt, also drives a shaft to the radiator fan.

Inspection of the governor should include making sure the flyweights move freely.

Chapter 12
Cooling System

You don't have to be a master mechanic to know that engines create a great deal of heat during operation. It's a natural byproduct of any system that burns fuel and converts thermal energy into mechanical energy. However, dissipating that heat has occasionally been a challenge, prompting tractor engineers to try a number of different ideas over the years.

In the early years, tractors simply boiled away the cooling liquid, which meant the reservoir had to be refilled every few hours. As tractor designs progressed, manufacturers experimented with both oil and air cooling. However, only a few companies—most notably Deutz, based in Germany—have stuck with air cooling.

Today, nearly every tractor on the market utilizes liquid cooling, which in effect uses air to cool the water as it flows through a radiator. Chances are, any tractor you are restoring will also be liquid cooled. However, it may or may not be comparable to today's liquid-cooling system, which normally includes a radiator, pressurized radiator cap, fan and fan belt, thermostat, and water pump.

Many early tractors, including many two-cylinder John Deere models, Fordsons, and some early Farmall tractors, used a simple thermo-siphon circulating system, which consisted of a radiator and two hoses that connected it to the engine block. Because hot water is lighter, it is forced upward from the engine, through a narrowing passage, to the radiator. Here, it sinks as it is cooled, only to exit at the bottom and return to the engine.

COOLING SYSTEM INSPECTION AND REPAIR

You've probably had an opportunity to evaluate the cooling system to some extent when you purchased the tractor or during the troubleshooting operation. Perhaps you even had a chance to start the engine and let it run long enough to see if there were any water leaks, problems with overheating, or traces of oil in the coolant.

Unfortunately, radiator cores tend to clog up with rust, lime, or other mineral deposits, and the fins plug up with weeds, seeds, and debris. In addition, the metal

Since Minneapolis-Moline used a separate block for every two cylinders, this four-cylinder engine requires two upper water pipes that converge at the radiator.

In order to raise the engine temperature to a level sufficient for kerosene ignition, many early model tractors were equipped with louvers in front of the radiator.

headers often corrode away after years of use, and the seams become moist with residual antifreeze.

Hence, it's best to start cooling-system inspection and restoration at the front of the tractor, the radiator. The first thing you should do is check the front and rear of the radiator for a buildup of bugs, seeds, weeds, and so on. A strong stream of water sprayed from the back side, or fan side, of the radiator will remove a lot of the debris.

Next, check for moisture around the radiator core and headers. These areas tend to rot out if the tractor has sat dry for a long period of time. If there is leakage, the area will be moist, and perhaps even smell sweet if there is antifreeze in the system. If the leakage is minor, you can sometimes take care of the problem by adding one or two cans of radiator "stop leak" material.

If there is substantial leakage, however, it's best to remove the radiator and have it professionally serviced. Considering that you may have to remove the radiator

anyway as part of the tractor or engine restoration process, you may want to consider taking the radiator to a professional, just to have it flushed, flow tested, and checked for integrity. The other option is to simply replace the radiator core as part of the restoration process.

RADIATOR CAPS

The next step in your cooling system check is to remove the radiator cap and inspect the bottom of the cap.

There are basically two types of radiator caps used on vintage tractors. The earliest type consisted of a simple cap that covered the radiator opening. In essence, its only purpose was to keep some of the steam in and the dirt out. Often, they just sat on top of the radiator opening and were held in place by a wire that snapped over the top. If this is the case, you only need to inspect the condition of the cap and make sure it is clean and not damaged.

If your tractor was built in the 1940s or later, however, it's probably equipped with a pressurized cooling system. As part of the system, the radiator cap was designed to raise the pressure in the cooling system so the coolant boils at a higher temperature. This, in effect, accomplished two purposes. First, each pound of pressure raises the boiling point by approximately 3 degrees Fahrenheit, allowing the engine to operate at a higher temperature. Second, since there is now a greater difference between the water and air temperature, the radiator can operate more efficiently.

If the system is equipped with a pressurized cap, check to make sure the bottom of the cap is clean and fits snugly into the filler neck. Check the rubber bottom for swelling, nicks, or cracks. Also check the brass filler neck for uniformity on the sealing surfaces. A warp or hairline crack will cause pressure to leak out when in use. Finally, make sure any replacement cap has the proper pressure relief rating. If the relief setting is too high, you run the risk of blowing hoses or the radiator core, especially if the core is weak in the first place.

FANS

The fans on most vintage tractors were pretty basic pieces of equipment. There were no such things as thermostatically controlled electrical fans, and fans weren't enclosed in shrouds that helped direct airflow. You simply had four or six blades on a belt-driven hub, which was positioned directly behind the radiator.

Hence, restoration consists of little more than checking the integrity of the blades to make sure the attachment rivets are tight and the blades haven't been bent, and checking the fan shaft bearings to make sure they're in good condition.

Ironically, the cooling systems in some older tractors were designed to do more than just cool the engine. Sometimes, they were used to increase the engine temperature. This was particularly important on tractors that operated on kerosene, since they had to run hotter than gasoline engines in order to properly vaporize the fuel.

In fact, most kerosene tractors include a small gasoline tank that was used for starting the engine. Once the engine and intake manifold were hot enough, the fuel system was switched over to kerosene. That meant the operator had to continually keep an eye on engine temperature—not just keeping it cool when necessary, but keeping it hot enough, too. To assist in this endeavor, the manufacturer equipped some models with shutters or curtains ahead of the radiator.

Many John Deere two-cylinder models, for example, were equipped with a set of vertical shutters that could be closed by a lever near the steering wheel. To get the tractor warmed up quickly, the operator simply closed the shutters and deprived the radiator of air circulation. However, there were times, such as when driving back to the farmstead from the field or when moving between fields, that it again became necessary to close the shutters to keep the engine temperature elevated and the engine running smoothly.

As part of your tractor research, you may find that other tractors used their own heat-control apparatus, like the cloth curtain that pulled up to cover the radiator on early unstyled Allis-Chalmers WC tractors.

Unfortunately, such temperature control devices can be hard to locate, particularly when it comes to radiator shutters. Over the years, dirt and chaff would naturally collect between the bottom of the shutters, radiator, and grille. As a result, the shutters on a lot of restoration-quality tractors have since rusted out as moisture collected in the residue and did its damage.

HOSES

On many tractor restorations, the biggest problem with the cooling system—and many times the only problem—is the condition of the hoses. Hoses that are hard, brittle, or cracked need to be replaced. Keep an eye out, too, for small patches of moisture on the hose surface. If you do discover any of these patches, gently knead the area while looking for a hairline crack or pinhole. Such areas tend to leak only when the tractor is at operating temperature and under pressure, making them difficult to locate. Unfortunately, they can shoot a hair-sized stream of hot water onto electrical components and cause misfiring, which can lead you to suspect the electrical system, rather than the cooling system.

Also, look for hoses that have swelled up because of oil contamination. They feel greasy and spongy when kneaded. Replace any hoses that are marginal. While you're at it, it's a good idea to change the hose clamps, too, since dirt and grit can keep them from being sufficiently tightened to seal water.

As a final note, you'll want to consider how the tractor is to be used before replacing the hoses and clamps with conventional equipment. If you're restoring the tractor as a show model, you'll want to find hoses that match the original rather than the type you find at automotive and equipment dealers today. Moreover, you probably don't want to use the type of hose clamps that tighten up with a screwdriver. More than likely, the original hoses were held in place by the old-style, spring-loaded, wire clamps.

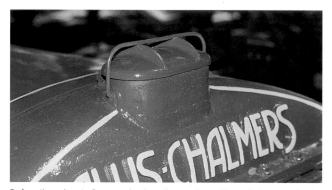

Before the advent of pressurized cooling systems, the radiator was simply equipped with a cap held in place with a wire clip.

Some radiators, especially those used on thermo-siphon cooling systems, can be split into three sections. This allows you to clean or even sandblast the upper and lower cast housings.

This radiator core, which was designed to bolt between an upper and lower casting is definitely in need of replacement.

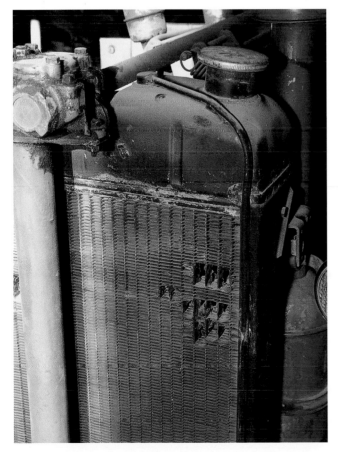

One of the important steps in cooling system restoration is checking the integrity of the radiator.

They may not work as well or hold as tight, but if you're going for an authentic look, you need to go all the way.

WATER PUMPS

Like a lot of the components used on older-model tractors, the water pump on most vintage models is relatively simple. In fact, most consisted of a pump housing, an impeller to move the water, a driveshaft, and a pulley that was driven by the same belt as the fan. Quite often, the water pump isn't even on a separate bracket. Instead, it's mounted to the engine block and the fan is simply attached to a hub on the end of the water pump shaft, combining both functions on a single drive.

Regardless of the configuration on your tractor, the most likely problem you'll encounter is a water leak or worn bearings. Unless the impeller blades or an internal divider have been completely attacked by rust, you can usually rebuild the unit with new seals and bearings. Even if an impeller blade is rusted pretty badly, you may be able to find somebody to rebuild it with a welder once you get it cleaned up.

Unfortunately, the shaft and bearings on many water pump units were not designed to be serviced separately. They could only be replaced as a unit, so unless the part is still available, you may be in for more of a challenge.

The first step in rebuilding the water pump is removing it from the tractor. The exception would be if the pump is working fine as indicated by the flow of water in the radiator, but is leaking water around a front shaft seal, a common problem. If this is the case, you might try a trick practiced by some restorers and force a short section of string-type packing around the shaft seal. If you don't already have some on hand, various diameters of the packing material can be found in the plumbing section of your local hardware store.

If coolant is leaking from the drain hole in the pump housing, though, it usually indicates a leaking internal seal, which will require disassembly.

If it becomes necessary to remove the water pump, you'll generally find a cover plate that must first be removed. The impeller may be screwed onto the shaft or it may be a press fit, so it's best to refer to your repair manual for details.

Before reassembly, though, it's important that you inspect the water pump shaft, assuming it is being reused, to be sure it is smooth and free of rust. Otherwise, it won't be long before you're replacing seals again. If necessary, use a piece of emery cloth to smooth the shaft where it fits against the seal.

While restoring this John Deere model, Estel Theis elected to replace the radiator core to ensure against future problems.

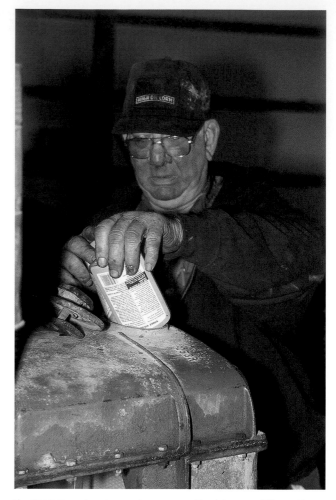

If water leakage is not excessive, you can often take care of the problem by adding one or two cans of radiator "stop leak" material.

A small amount of grease on the pump shaft will also prevent damage to the water seal as the pump is being reassembled, especially if the impeller has to be pressed or screwed back onto the shaft.

Finally, if the water pump is equipped with a drain hole behind the pump body, make sure it is kept free of dirt, grease, and paint so that any water that may leak past the seal can drain away and prevent problems.

THERMOSTATS

Assuming your tractor is new enough to have a water pump, you'll need to make sure the thermostat is operating correctly before you finish the restoration project and put the tractor into use. Obviously, you can tell a lot about its operation by looking into the top of the radiator with the cap removed. (It should go without saying to never open the radiator cap when the engine is hot.)

As soon as the water gets hot enough to open the thermostat, you should see water start to flow into the top of the radiator from the upper radiator hose. If this is not the case, you have a couple choices. You can test the thermostat by placing it in a pan of water on a stove and watching for the diaphragm to open as the water heats up and attains the temperature at which the thermostat should open. Or, considering the price of a new thermostat and the age of the tractor, you may just want to replace it with a new one. Either way, you'll need to remove the old thermostat, which is usually found in the upper radiator hose where it attaches to the engine, or in a fitting attached to the radiator.

Due to excessive rust, the pipe section of this cold water line was replaced during restoration. Note the lack of a water pump, since the thermo-siphon system relied only on the laws of physics.

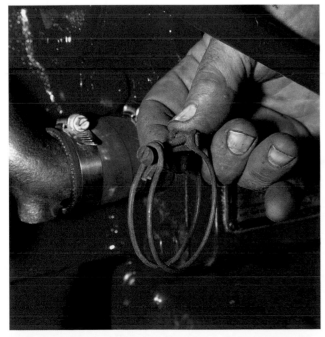

Tractor restorers who are striving for originality are always in search of the old-style wire clamps that were first used to clamp hoses in place.

The water pump on most John Deere two-cylinder tractors is located at the base of the radiator and is driven directly off the fan belt.

BELTS

Most vintage farm tractors only have one belt—or at most two—that normally runs the fan/water pump and the generator. However, you need to make sure it is in good condition and not slipping, or the whole cooling system can suffer the consequences.

To check the belt(s), twist it around in several spots so the bottom and one side are clearly visible. Look for signs of cracking; oil soaking; hard, glazed contact surface; splitting; or fraying. Replace any belt showing these symptoms.

Make sure you adjust for the proper belt tension, though. A belt that is too tight can cause premature wear on the bearings, while a belt that is too loose can slip, squeal, or cause other problems.

Some tractor models, like this Minneapolis-Moline, incorporate the water pump with other driven components. In this case, the water pump and distributor share a common driveshaft.

Unless the impeller blades or an internal divider have been destroyed by rust, you can usually rebuild a water pump with new seals and bearings.

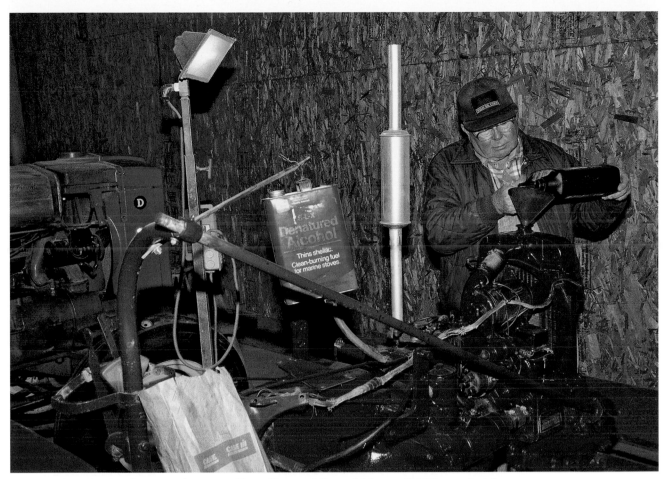

To preserve the restored cooling system, be sure to add an antifreeze solution containing a rust inhibitor as a final step.

Having a working cooling system will prove essential as soon as you start using your restored machine. The most visible part of the system is the radiator, so you'll want it looking its best, as on this 1928 Caterpillar Two Ton crawler. Owner: Robert Garwood.
Ralph W. Sanders

Cooling System **143**

Chapter 13
Tires, Rims, and Wheels

If you haven't yet discovered it, you will soon learn that tires, wheels, and rims can be a restorer's nightmare. Granted, you may be lucky and find that your tractor has the correct, factory-installed wheels—and that they are still in good condition. If you're even luckier, you'll find that all the tires are the proper size and the rubber is still in reasonable shape.

What you are just as likely to find are rear wheel rims that have been corroded by calcium chloride. Perhaps the tires have rotted away after years of sitting in a pasture, allowing the wheels contact with the ground. Naturally, rust quickly followed, eating away at the rim.

On the other hand, you may find that those tires and wheels that appear to be in good condition are not the original size or style. If you're planning to use the restored tractor as a work tractor, that may not matter to you. But if you plan to restore it as a show tractor, you'll want to find the correct components or listen to other collectors point out the inaccuracies.

Another thing you might run into is a tractor that originally had steel wheels, but they were converted to rubber tires sometime during the tractor's working life. Generally, the old-time, shade-tree mechanic cut the steel rims off the spoked wheels, then welded the spokes to drop rims designed for a rubber tire. Hence, you'll have to decide whether you want to keep the rubber tires or go back to the original steel wheels.

In a way, the desire to convert steel-wheeled tractors to rubber tires is ironic in and of itself, considering the history of tractor tires. Up until the mid-1930s, almost every tractor on the market had steel wheels equipped with cleats, lugs, and the like. It wasn't until 1932 that

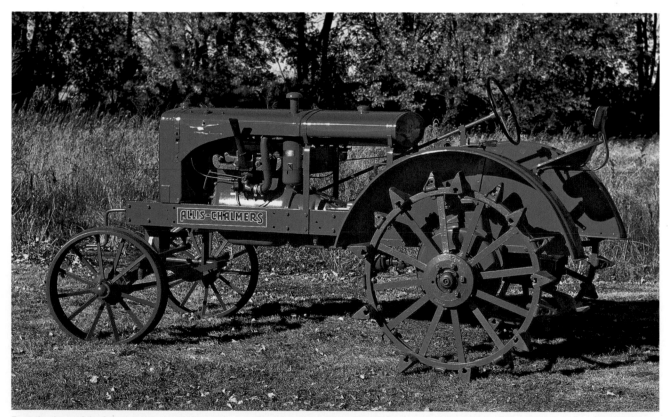

From the dawn of the farm tractor, all machines rode on steel wheels. It wasn't until Allis-Chalmers began experimenting with pneumatic rubber tires in 1932 on its Model U that change came. But acceptance of the rubber-tire revolution was slow, as shown by this unstyled 1938 Allis-Chalmers WC with steel skeleton wheels. *Chester Peterson Jr.*

Following World War II, almost every tractor sold was equipped with pneumatic rubber tires, as on this 1955 Minneapolis-Moline ZB. This Minne-Mo was restored by the late Roger Mohr. *Chester Peterson Jr.*

low-pressure pneumatic tires even made an appearance on a farm tractor. Allis-Chalmers initiated the concept when the company mounted a pair of 48x12 Firestone airplane tires on a Model U. By the end of the year, the company was offering the rubber tires as an option.

But farmers were slow to accept rubber tires, even though they offered a smoother ride and required substantially less horsepower to move the tractor. Consequently, the sales promotion manager at Allis-Chalmers came up with the idea of equipping Model U tractors with rubber tires and special high-speed fourth gears, and holding tractor races. Tractor races, along with plowing demonstrations, were held at state fairs and special events all over the country. The company also sponsored cross-country tractor runs and speed-record attempts, setting a record of 67.87 mph with a Model U on the Utah salt flats.

By 1934, all of the leading manufacturers were offering rubber tires, even though the country was in a depression and few tractors were being sold. Then, just as rubber tires were gaining widespread acceptance, the United States was thrust into World War II, putting rubber on the list of critical war materiel. As a result, steel wheels made a return, if only temporarily.

The bottom line is it is sometimes difficult to know what tires and wheels were standard or optional on your model and what components are correct.

REAR WHEEL REMOVAL

Some tractor models, including all Ford models built from 1939 through the 1960s, use a two-piece wheel that consists of a wheel and a rim center. The rim and center could be mounted in different configurations to adjust tread width. This configuration also makes it easier and more economical to replace a wheel. Even if the rim portion of the wheel is rusted out or damaged, the center portion is usually fine, which means simply replacing the wheel itself at a cost of around $100 to $150.

Before you remove the rear wheels, it's important that you check the tires for calcium chloride. The light weight of many early-model tractors meant that weight had to be added if the tractor was to pull loads that weren't attached to the three-point hitch. This was also important for counter balance when using a front-end loader. That usually meant adding calcium chloride to the rear tires, since it isn't often convenient to add rear wheel weights and cover the wheel bolts. Unfortunately, calcium chloride is extremely corrosive and can destroy the rim if it leaks inside the tire. One of the first places you'll notice this corrosion is around the valve stem.

To see if the tires are filled with a calcium chloride mixture, position the valve stem near the bottom and carefully let a little air out of the valve stem. If the tires are filled, you will see liquid come out. It's important that you handle the tires carefully until you know for sure. Tires filled with the mixture are very heavy and could easily cause injury if you were to remove the bolts and have one fall over on you.

If you intend to use the tractor as a work tractor once you've finished with restoration, and plan to put fluid back in the tire, keep in mind that tires should never be filled more than two-thirds full. Any more than that can contribute to instability on slopes and hillsides.

Most row-crop Farmall tractors are equipped with an adjustable rear axle that allows the wheels to be moved in or out for variable tread widths. If you're lucky and the tractor has been well cared for, you should be able to

When you find a tractor sitting on one or more rims, you'll need to carefully inspect the wheel for signs of rust or holes that might call for wheel replacement or a patch in the rim. And even if the front tires on this vintage John Deere weren't flat, they would need to be replaced, considering that car tires were never used as stock equipment.

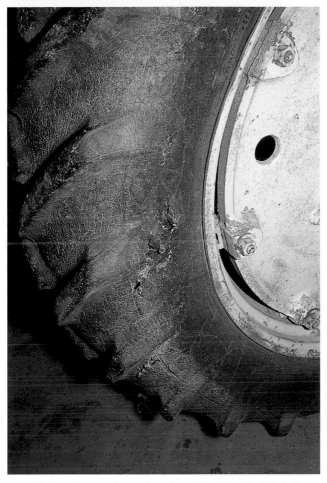

Although tire reliners can be used to salvage some tires, the hole in the sidewall on this rear tire has essentially ended its usable life.

In an effort to convert steel-wheeled tractors to rubber tires, shade-tree mechanics often welded tire rims to the old spokes and added a few extra braces.

slide the rear wheels on the axles, or even off the axles, in the intended manner.

Unfortunately, wheel hubs are like a lot of components on classic tractors. If they have sat long enough without being moved, there's a good chance they have solidly rusted into place. If this is the case, you'll need to start the removal process by saturating them on a regular basis with some type of penetrating oil.

If after trying to remove the hub in the traditional manner, it still doesn't budge, you may need to heat the hub with a torch to expand it. Don't expect a propane torch to do it, though. The hub will absorb a lot of heat, so an acetylene torch is usually more appropriate. Don't beat on the hub when it's hot. This will only deform the parts and make matters worse.

Once the wheel and hub have been removed, by whatever means necessary, you can clean and smooth the axle so that the wheel will slide effortlessly when reinstalled.

TIRE REPAIR AND RESTORATION

If you're only looking for a working tractor, any tires that fit the rim will generally be acceptable. The newer-style tires, with their 23-degree bar, or long-bar/short-bar design may even offer better traction than the 45-degree lug tires originally found on the tractor.

If your goal is to restore a vintage tractor to show condition, and you're after accuracy, you may be in for a challenge. Not only did the tire companies change their size standards, but they have also changed tire styles as more effective patterns were discovered.

Fortunately, there are several independent sources for the most sought-after sizes and types of tractor tires, including M. E. Miller, Gempler's, and Wallace W. Wade.

One option for repairing tires that are worn or slightly damaged, but still usable, is to install a set of tire reliners. These are made from old tires that have had the lugs ground down, making the reliner itself about 1/4

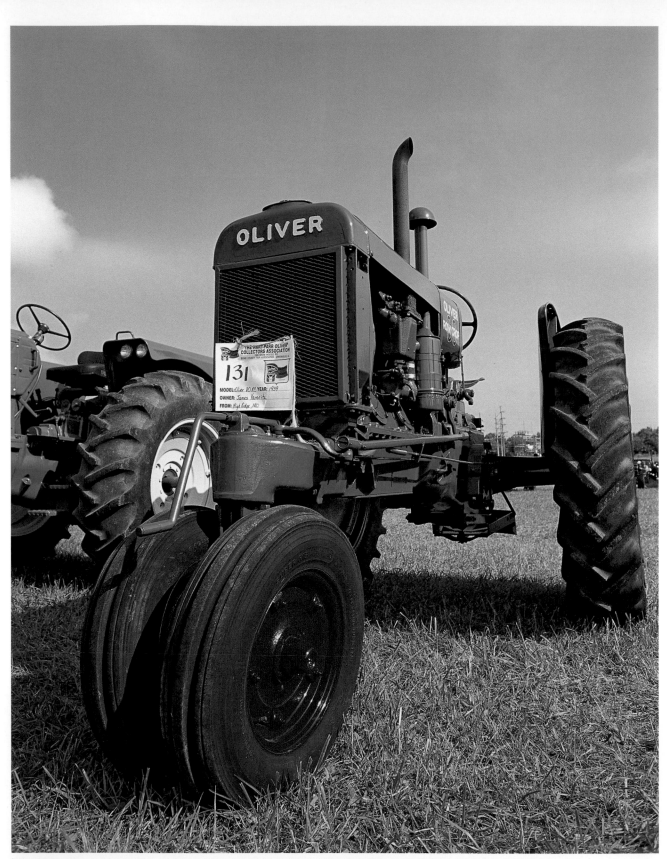

This vintage Oliver has been nicely restored and fitted with new "shoes" on the front. Unfortunately, finding tires that match the original is sometimes difficult.

One of the most important aspects of tire care is maintaining the correct amount of air pressure.

If you're restoring a work tractor, newer tires, with their 23-degree bars, generally offer better traction than the 45-degree lug tires originally found on the tractor.

In order to run steel-wheel tractors on the streets and in parades, some restorers have fitted the wheels with hard-rubber rims.

inch thick. Generally, they come in half-moon shapes so they can be easily inserted into the old tire, where they partially overlap. However, some companies also offer spot reliners. The inner tube is then inserted into the tire, where, once inflated, it holds the reliners in place.

Other tire repair products include rubber putty that can be used to repair cracks, gouges, weather checking, and other minor problems. Unfortunately, it can't be used to repair a hole.

Finally, various companies carry a concentrated black tire paint that can be used to revive the color in old, gray-looking tires. Simply mix it with paint thinner according to the directions on the label and apply it as you would paint.

WHEEL AND RIM RESTORATION

If you've been fortunate enough to find rims and wheels that are in relatively good shape, the restoration process may be as simple as sandblasting the appropriate parts and applying one or more coats of primer prior to painting.

Unfortunately, vintage wheels and rims didn't take kindly to age, especially if they were ballasted with calcium chloride. They didn't take well to rust, either. If one or more of the wheels are too far gone, your only choice will be to frequent the auctions, swap meets, salvage yards, and classified ads for a replacement.

If you're only dealing with a few rust holes, however, you should be able to take care of those by thoroughly cleaning the holes and filling them in with small beads of weld.

If you're good with a welder, you may even be able to repair larger rust areas by totally replacing the damaged area. The first step will be cutting out the corroded or rusted portion of the wheel. Quite often, this will be the outer edge of the rim, where it has rested on the ground. Next, you'll have to find a scrap wheel or rim that is identical in size and style from which you can cut a replacement piece. Make sure all edges have been ground smooth, clamp the splice into position, tack weld around the whole piece to keep it from warping, and carefully weld it into place. Once you've finished welding, grind all splices down until they are flush with the surrounding metal and prepare the wheel for painting.

If a rim is in very bad shape, though, the best bet is to search the salvage yards or swap meets for a new one.

It may be a challenge to find replacement tires with a tread pattern that matches this unique design. Fortunately, the tires are still in good shape.

Considering that wide tires with all-season tread were never used as stock equipment, this tractor will need new front tires to return it to original condition.

This is a good example of how tractor owners often cut away parts of the steel wheels and welded rims onto the wheels to accept rubber tires. Ever wonder why some steel wheels are so hard to find? In an effort to convert steel-wheeled tractors to rubber tires, shade-tree mechanics often welded tire rims to the old wheel or spokes, as was the case with the identical wheels on the right.

Neglect and years of exposure to calcium chloride as a rear wheel weight have obviously taken a toll on these wheels. The worst damage is almost always around the valve stem.

Most Ford wheels consisted of two parts. However, the original-style wheels that bolt directly to "top hat–wheels" used on early N Series tractors are becoming hard to find.

Chapter 14
Setting Up Shop for Bodywork and Painting

If you're serious about doing a first-class tractor restoration or paint job, the first thing you're going to need is a good set of basic tools to remove parts such as the shields, fuel tank, and radiator. Make sure you put the emphasis on good. Cheap tools are only going to lead to frustration as they break, strip, or worse, damage a tractor part. Look for a set of automotive-quality tools that come with a warranty, such as those offered by Sears (Craftsman), NAPA, and Snap-On.

BODYWORK TOOLS

If you're going to be doing any sheetmetal repair—and chances are you'll find it necessary—you'll need a few basic body repair tools. The truth is that it's pretty rare to find a tractor that doesn't have at least a few dents or ripples in the hood, grille, or one or both fenders.

In most cases, you can get by with a simple body hammer and dolly. Although body hammers and dollies both come in various sizes and shapes, the role of the hammer is to stretch and shape sheet metal, while the dolly acts as the anvil to keep it from moving too far.

Since most shops have a ball-peen hammer in their inventory, you might find that of value as the body hammer, too, since one end of the head is rounded and the other end is flat. The key is to hold the dolly on the back side of the dent or crease while striking the front side.

Another tool that may be valuable in certain situations is a dent puller, though these are generally used in areas where it is hard to gain access to the back side of a dent. In essence, this is a slide-hammer device that is attached to a hole drilled into a dented panel and used to pull it back into place. The drawback is that the holes you make to attach the slide hammer to the sheet metal have to be filled later with body putty. As a result, it's generally better to remove the panel, grille, or fender and simply use a hammer and dolly.

If the sheetmetal component is one that you can remove and relocate to a more solid location, you may even want to invest in some kind of an anvil. You don't have to run out and spend hundreds of dollars for a commercial shop anvil, though. For what you'll need most of the time, a 2- or 21/2-foot piece of railroad track rail will do. In fact, the rounded edge of the rail will work better than a real anvil for some sheetmetal repair and fabrication.

If you occasionally need a flat surface or a square end for bending, you can weld a piece of bar stock across

If you plan to remove the tires and wheels during the painting process—which generally works best—you'll need a set of jacks or some type of cribbing to hold up the frame.

If you plan to do your own painting, an air compressor with adequate capacity, an inline water filter, and plenty of hose will make the job a lot easier. You'll find compressed air equally helpful when cleaning parts and components.

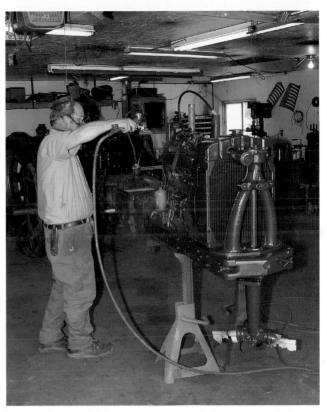

You'll need plenty of air hose to move around the tractor while painting. However, keep in mind that the greater the distance, the greater the air pressure loss. Most paint specialists recommend the hose have at least a 5/16-inch inside diameter to prevent excessive pressure loss.

one or both ends of the rail so it will stand upright when turned rail side down.

Grinders, Sanders, and Files

Depending on the amount of bodywork you have to do on the sheet metal before painting, you're going to need some type of grinder, sander, or both. A grinder can't generally be used for light sanding or buffing because it spins too fast. But if you get the right model, it can be used for an assortment of jobs—including grinding down welds where you've had to make a splice, cutting out rust areas, and smoothing rough spots. Equipped with a wire brush, it can also be used for rust or old paint removal. And by substituting a sanding disc for the grinding wheel, you can do some rough shaping.

Grinders basically come in two types: electric or air-driven. Both have advantages and disadvantages. Air tools are generally lighter weight and less bulky, but you need to have an adequate air compressor.

On the other hand, it's often easier to drag around an extension cord than a 1/2-inch hose. Also, electric

grinders come in different sizes, making them more adaptable to your needs.

Another thing to consider is that if your needs are limited, a good electric drill may be sufficient. You can find a wide assortment of tools to fit a 3/8-inch drill, including grinding discs, wire brushes, and sanding discs. Plus, you'll probably need a drill at some point anyway.

You won't be able to get along without a good sander, though. Again, several types are available, including both air- and electric-powered units. Both types can be found as disc sanders, orbital sanders, straight-line sanders, and belt sanders. Perhaps the most popular among those who do a lot of painting and bodywork are the air-powered dual-action (DA) sanders. Because of their dual action, which prevents scratches and swirls from forming, they work equally well for rapid shaping of body filler and fine finishing work.

Disc sanders also work well for feathering paint and body filler, and they can be useful for buffing when equipped with a buffing pad. But you need to watch out for swirls if they're used on a fine finish. The same goes for straight-line sanders, which work great for removing old paint and working large plastic-filled surfaces. They can, however, leave distinct scratch marks that will have to be sanded out before painting.

Finally, an orbital sander works great for smoothing body filler on both vertical and horizontal planes, particularly since orbital sanders generally have a large sanding pad; however, these still won't leave the smooth, swirl-free finish that a DA sander is capable of producing.

Unfortunately, you'll probably need a few tools powered by elbow grease and a little wrist action, as well. Among these are a metal file to clean and shape sheetmetal panels and a Surform or "cheese grater" file for shaping body filler. The latter isn't used on metal, but instead it has an open-tooth design that allows it to shave off filler material before it hardens. It's possible you already have one of these because they're also used to shape wood.

Last but not least, you may want to keep one or more sanding blocks on hand for hand sanding tight spots. One thing I have found to be very handy are the small, wet sanding blocks that are made from a sponge rubber. Since the sanding grit is adhered to the rubber

face on four of the six sides, they easily shape to the surface contour. Plus, when the grit gets clogged, they can simply be rinsed in a bucket of water, squeezed out, and reused again and again.

AIR COMPRESSOR

While an air-powered sander can be a valuable asset when removing stubborn rust and paint, air-powered tools aren't quite as necessary as the air compressor itself. Its most obvious use, of course, is to power the paint sprayer; however, an air hose and nozzle are also invaluable for blowing dust and dirt out of crevices and away from parts while you're cleaning surfaces. If you're doing a full tractor restoration, you'll want to use it to blow out fuel lines, water passages, and the like. It will also come in handy when you get to engine repairs.

Most commercial body shops use a compressor with at least 10 horsepower. For the average tractor restorer, however, a compressor rated at 5 horsepower or greater is generally sufficient. The goal is to have a compressor that can build up a reserve of compressed air in the tank and then shut off for a few minutes to cool down.

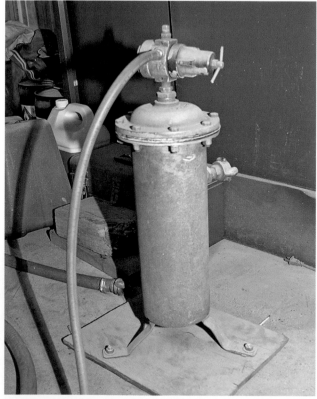

Regardless of what type of compressor you use, you'll need some type of air filter, since raw air contains small but harmful quantities of water, oil, dirt, and other contaminants that can affect the quality of the sprayed finish.

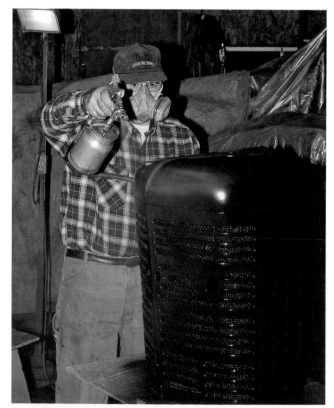

It's important to have a quality paint gun that you feel comfortable using. That's why a lot of tractor hobbyists continue to use a conventional siphon-type paint gun.

Your local paint supplier will have a variety of paint guns available, including complete kits that have everything you need but the air hose.

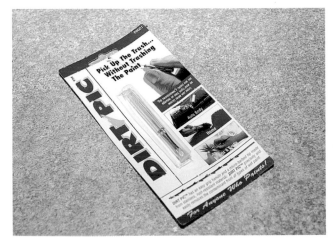

One of the newest types of applicators is the HVLP, or high-volume, low-pressure paint gun, which helps conserve paint and reduce vaporization.

If the compressor works too hard and doesn't have a chance to shut off, the friction generated will increase the air temperature, which, in turn, leads to condensation in the air lines. And moisture in the air supply doesn't go well with acrylic- and urethane-based paints.

You'll need to consider the volume of the air tank on the compressor, too. Generally, this goes hand in hand with the horsepower level of the compressor and is set accordingly by the manufacturer. If the tank doesn't have enough capacity and the pump can't keep up, you're going to be painting a few minutes, stopping to let the air supply build in the tank, then painting a few more minutes, and then waiting again.

The best way to determine the volume you'll need in the air compressor is to find out the cubic feet per minute (cfm) of air required by your spray gun and consult the application guide sheet for the paint product you intend to use. You might, therefore, want to shop for a paint sprayer before you look for a compressor.

Air Pressure

The final criterion concerning the compressor is air pressure. The gauge may say one thing, but you need to make sure the air pressure at the paint gun meets the minimum psi rating specified on the product label or in the product's application guide.

Even if the pump has the capacity to produce the appropriate amount of pressure, it can easily be lost if the air has to travel too far through too small of a hose. In general, most paint specialists recommend the hose have at least a 5/16-inch inside diameter. Even then, 60 pounds of pressure can drop by 6 pounds over 25 feet of 5/16-inch hose length. In comparison, the same 60 pounds of pressure can drop by 19 pounds when traveling through 25 feet of 1/4-inch hose.

For HVLP spray guns, it pays to go larger, which means that 3/8-inch hose is generally recommended. Regardless of the size of the hose, you need to select the ideal compromise. In other words, you want enough hose to be able to freely move around the tractor, but not so much that it results in a loss of air pressure over the required distance.

Air Filter

No matter what type of compressor you own or purchase, you need to realize that raw air contains small but harmful quantities of water, oil, dirt, and other contaminants that can affect the quality of the sprayed finish. This may not have been a problem if you only used the compressor in the past to power air tools or inflate tires, but it's different when you use a paint sprayer. Air filters filter out these contaminants before they get on your paint job. Air entering the filter is swirled to remove moisture that collects in the baffled quiet zone. Accumulated liquid is then carried away through either a manual or automatic drain.

Most paint gun and air tool suppliers will have a variety of filters and filter systems that will work for your application and budget.

PAINT GUNS

Since this book is about painting tractors, perhaps the most important piece of equipment you'll need is the paint gun. Before you decide to purchase one, you'll need to do a little research and evaluate your needs. Some restorers still use a siphon-type gun that siphons the paint out of a canister or cup and draws it into the airstream; however, a growing number of serious tractor restorers have switched to an HVLP (high-volume low-pressure) unit, even though the gun costs about twice as much as a siphon unit. Regardless of the type, the role of the paint gun is to use air pressure to atomize a sprayable material like primer or paint onto a prepared surface. In the paragraphs that follow is some more information on your options.

Conventional Spray Guns

Although they have pretty much been abandoned by the automotive world, conventional spray guns are still used with great success by a number of people who paint tractors. Obviously, a conventional siphon-type gun is going to be your lowest-priced option. The greatest drawback is that they typically require 60 pounds of air pressure or more to work properly.

That means the paint is also hitting the surface at a much higher pressure and more of the product is being atomized into the air. Consequently, by some estimates, as much as 65 to 70 percent of the paint can be wasted as overspray. In addition, the greater amount of air pressure is more likely to stir up dirt and debris that can land back on the fresh paint coat. If you're one who prefers a conventional gun, however, don't worry. Some of the reputable companies known for their HVLP guns, such as DeVilbiss and Sharpe, still make a very good siphon gun, too.

Some of the newer HVLP guns even offer the option of using them with a canister as a siphon gun or with a paint pot as a pressure-feed gun.

High-Volume Low-Pressure (HVLP) Spray Guns

Basically, a high-volume low-pressure spray gun is just what the name implies. It works by increasing the volume of paint passing through the nozzle, yet it requires substantially less pressure at the nozzle. That doesn't mean it requires less air pressure from the air compressor, though. The important thing is it uses less pressure to propel the paint from the gun, which means less waste. Consequently, if you plan to do a lot of painting, you may want to consider an HVLP gun, knowing that the savings in quality paint can offset the cost difference in two or three uses.

An HVLP gun is also better for the environment, not to mention friendlier to your shop or work area, since the amount of overspray is substantially reduced.

HVLP guns can be divided into two primary categories: pressure feed and gravity feed. Since the use of pressure-feed guns is pretty much limited to body shops

and professional painters, your most likely choice will be a gravity-feed gun, although there are a few companies that market a siphon HVLP gun. This type of gun has the paint cup mounted above the air nozzle so paint feeds directly into the airstream by gravity. This design further contributes to the need for less air pressure, although you may need to refill the cup more often than you would a siphon-gun canister.

Additional Paint Gun Considerations

No matter what kind of paint gun you buy, it's important that you get a quality unit. The old adage that you get what you pay for is still true in this case. A cheap gun is likely to produce cheap-looking results. Consequently, it's generally best to purchase the gun at a reputable paint supplier or auto supply store. You not only stand a better chance of getting a quality gun, but the sales staff can explain the gun's operation and the best way to care for it. Plus, they can do a better job of matching the gun to the type of paint you plan to use and the type of surface you're painting.

Jim Deardorff, owner of Superior Coatings in Chillicothe, Missouri, also advises restoration enthusiasts to check into the price of replacement parts. A reasonably priced spray gun may not be that good of a deal if the replacement nozzles are exceptionally expensive, or, at the very least, if they are just as costly as they are for a higher-quality gun.

Finally, you'll want a gun that is fairly easy to clean and take care of, since it's important to clean the gun after each use. Paint guns require very small air and material passageways in order to atomize the paint. As a result, the guns can easily clog if paint is allowed to dry in small orifices or if debris infiltrates the passageways.

Although the manual that came with your paint gun should provide the best procedure for cleaning the unit, you should know that cleaning it basically involves rinsing the paint cup with solvent to remove the bulk of the paint

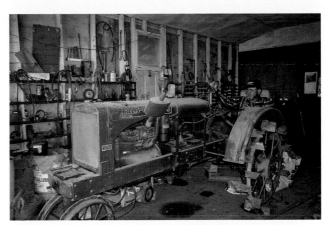
While your work area doesn't have to be anything fancy, it does help to have a place where you can keep the tractor indoors while it is being disassembled, especially when it comes time to paint the tractor.

or primer, then filling the cup with the prescribed amount of solvent and spraying it through the unit. Quite often a second round of solvent is recommended to ensure that the gun has been thoroughly cleared and only clear solvent comes out the nozzle.

You may also want to acquire a spray gun cleaning kit that includes the appropriate brushes for cleaning the housing, air caps, and other ports. Just be sure you don't use any sharp objects or a piece of wire to try to clean any ports or nozzles. It takes a precision instrument to take 30 to 40 pounds of air pressure and use it to push a one-millimeter drop of paint through a nozzle into an 8-inch pattern. If you damage the nozzle, you've damaged the gun's ability to do its job. And don't soak the whole gun in solvent thinking that "if a little is good, a lot is better." The solvent can loosen debris on the outside and allow it to enter passages it wouldn't have gotten to on its own.

Finish up by blowing clean air through the gun to remove any remaining solvent from the passageways and wiping down the gun with a clean cloth that's been dampened with a small amount of solvent.

BODYWORK AND PAINT AREA

If you're doing a complete tractor restoration, chances are you already have a shop or garage available. That doesn't mean you have to do all the work inside, though. In fact, it might be a good idea to move outside when stripping paint or using a wire brush to remove rust and grime. Thanks to the fresh air, you won't be exposed to as many fumes or dust particles. It would be best, however, if you can work on a concrete pad, so it's easier to clean up the residue and debris.

You'll find that your paint dealer has plenty of accessories for painting, too, including this Dirt Pic for removing stray contaminants from wet paint.

Next, get some large plastic sheets or painter's drop cloths to cover tools, workbenches, storage shelves, etc. Keeping things covered will save you a lot of cleanup later.

Jim Seward, a tractor painter from Iowa, says he likes to make a "paint booth" around the project with a drop cloth or plastic sheeting. The plastic not only keeps paint from drifting away from the area, but the plastic holds enough static electricity to attract dust and spray that could negatively affect the paint coat.

Some painters also recommend that you wet down the floor prior to doing any painting, including the application of primer. Naturally, it helps if the floor is clean to begin with so you don't end up with mud. The idea is that it minimizes the risk of stirring up dust that can end up embedded in the paint; however, you certainly don't want to overdo it if you do wet down the floor. For one thing, it increases the electrocution hazard of working with electrical devices. It can also increase the humidity in the work area, which can create new problems.

Next, take a look at your lighting. It certainly helps to have good lighting while performing other work, like engine repair or bodywork, but it's even more important when painting. You need to be able to see how the spray is going on and whether an area has been sufficiently covered, which will help avoid touch-ups later. One of the easiest solutions is to set up a 4-foot fluorescent light fixture like those commonly available at hardware and home improvement stores. You might even be able to build a unit that can be moved around the tractor as you paint.

Finally, you really should have some sort of storage area or cabinet that can be locked or secured. Paint and the other chemical products that you will be using can be very dangerous. If they're not toxic, they're at least flammable and should be kept out of the hands of anyone not intent on using them properly.

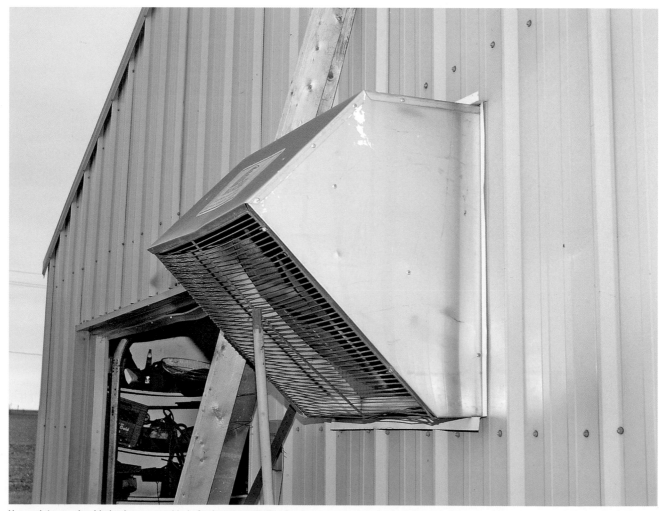

Your paint area should also have some kind of exhaust ventilation fan or a way to move fresh air through the area without introducing dust and debris.

A respirator approved for use with organic mists is one of the most important pieces of equipment to have on hand when painting a tractor. Remember, too, that not only are paint fumes hazardous to your health, but they are flammable.

SAFETY EQUIPMENT

Selecting the right paint and equipment for tractor restoration and painting is one thing. Gathering the right equipment to protect yourself while performing a quality job is quite another. In the long run, the latter is really the most important. At the least, your protective equipment should include rubber gloves, protective clothing, and an approved respirator or mask.

To be safe, use a respirator approved for organic mists, which is the type labeled for use with pesticides. A charcoal-filter mask may be sufficient for enamel paint, but not for urethane coatings and acrylic enamels to which a hardener has been added. These contain chemicals known as isocyanates, which are especially toxic. Therefore, the use of urethane requires either a

fresh-air mask and painting suit, or a charcoal-filtered mask, hat, gloves, and a fully ventilated environment. That's because isocyanates are not only dangerous when inhaled, but they can be absorbed through body pores and the tear ducts in your eyes.

Don't just wear your mask when painting either. Granted, paint products are most dangerous when they have been atomized by the paint gun, but the paint dust you generate when you're sanding dried paint is just as bad. So keep a filtered mask on any time you're removing old paint or rust, shaping body filler, or sanding new paint.

Chapter 15
Paint Removal

Without a doubt, surface preparation is the single most important variable in determining the life of any paint coating, whether you're painting your house or a vintage tractor. Even the best paint you can buy won't adhere to an excessively dirty or greasy surface or if moisture and contaminants get behind the paint film. So the first step you'll need to take with any tractor is getting it clean.

You may have cleaned the tractor to some extent already as part of the disassembly process. If you bought the tractor at a sale, there's a good chance the previous owner even cleaned it up to make a good impression with prospective customers. Or you may have run it through the car wash on your way home.

Regardless of how much cleaning has been done to this point, though, the job has really just begun. The sheet metal will need to be thoroughly cleaned and degreased. And once the sheet metal has been removed, you're bound to find a lot more grease and grime than was originally evident.

The goal is to make sure every surface will hold the primer and paint you will be applying later. To handle tough, baked-on grease on the engine, frame, and powertrain, some restorers like to spray oven cleaner on the really greasy areas and let it soak before power washing the whole tractor. Others use a hand-pump sprayer to soak the tractor and engine with diesel fuel for several hours.

It is not recommended that you use gasoline or kerosene as a cleaner. The cleaners and degreasers available at any automotive store are both safer and more effective. In the meantime, you might even want to keep a putty

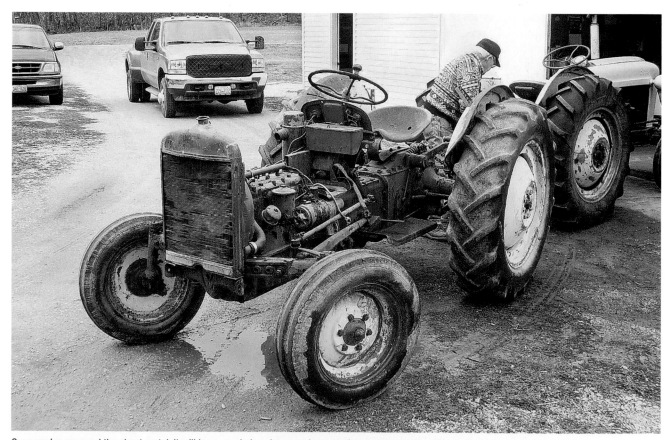

Once you've removed the sheet metal, it will become obvious how much grease has accumulated on the engine, frame, and transmission.

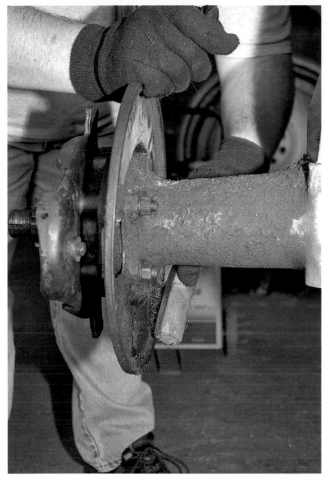

In the early stages of tractor cleanup, a putty knife and wire brush can be valuable tools for removing baked-on grease, particularly on cast-iron surfaces. In this case, cleaning up the tractor was combined with a brake replacement job.

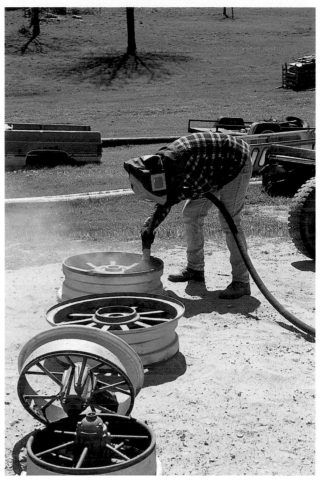

Sandblasting, or media blasting, is perhaps the quickest way to remove paint and rust from cast parts and heavy components, such as the wheels and frames.

knife, screwdriver, and wire brush handy while you're cleaning to dig at the really caked-on stuff.

Jim Deardorff, owner of Superior Coatings in Chillicothe, Missouri, insists that even if you plan on sandblasting the frame and drivetrain, it's important that you first remove as much grease as possible. Hitting it with a sandblaster, he insists, will only drive grease particles into the surface. That is especially true if you use too much pressure or the type of media that can pit or scratch the surface. If grease is driven into the pits or scratches instead of removed, it will only make it more difficult to apply a quality paint job. As a result, Deardorff uses a combination of stripper and media blasting on most cast-iron components.

Before he does that, though, he uses a hand sprayer to apply a coat of Dawn dishwashing detergent over the entire tractor and lets it soak overnight. It's not that

Deardorff specifically endorses Dawn, but it's the only detergent he has found that rinses clean without leaving any kind of film. Don't dilute it with water, he cautions, or it will foam too much. If he uses anything to thin the Dawn concentrate, Deardorff will add 10 percent to 20 percent of a product called Chlor*Wash, which is a multipurpose cleaner formulated to remove dirt and salts that can cause corrosion. In fact, Deardorff says Chlor*Wash also works well for cleaning restored tractors that have been exposed to exhaust fumes, salts, and dirt during tractor shows and events.

Once the detergent or combination has had 10 to 12 hours to soak, Deardorff uses a power washer and hot water to completely clean the project. If that isn't enough to remove the majority of the grease, he occasionally picks up the oven cleaner.

Jim Deardorff masks everything he wants to protect during media blasting with a layer of masking tape covered by a layer of duct tape.

If you plan to sandblast the tractor frame, don't forget to cover the serial number plate with several layers of duct tape to protect it from damage.

Although this John Deere two-cylinder tractor has extensive fire damage, the sheet metal appears to be in good condition.

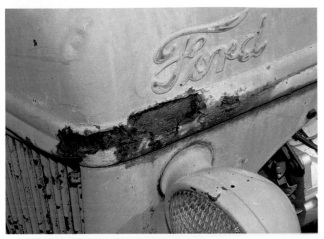

You'll find that some tractor hoods have a ridge on the underside that was originally meant to provide strength and rigidity. Unfortunately, ridges that fold inward easily collect moisture and dirt, which can cause the hood to rust from the inside out. By the time it gets to this point, as illustrated on a Ford 8N hood, it's often too late for body filler. You may want to save your time and effort and just purchase a replacement.

Because the grille on styled farm tractors is easily dented or gouged, it is often damaged beyond simple repair. Even the optional bumper failed to fully protect the grille on this Ford 9N. Replacement grilles are often available at a reasonable price.

CAST-IRON PREPARATION

In most cases, the easiest way to finish preparing steel and cast-iron components, once you've gotten most of the grease off, is to use a sandblaster or hire someone to sandblast the components for you. This includes the frame, wheels, transmission, and rear-end housing.

Before you start any sandblasting, it's vital that you go over the entire tractor, looking for holes that will let sand in and cause later damage. Many machines have passages to the brakes in the pinion housings. Be sure to pack these areas with heavy rags. Check, too, to see if any of the bolts you removed during disassembly left an open hole that will let sand into the clutch or shaft areas. If so, you'll want to put bolts back in these holes.

Unless you're planning to replace the spark plugs on a gasoline engine, it's a good idea to pull the good spark plugs and replace them with old plugs or dummies. At the very least, you'll want to remove the spark plug wires and cover the entire distributor to protect the distributor cap. The same goes for the coil. If the distributor body and shaft are to be painted, some restorers simply remove the cap and rotor and mask off the top of the distributor itself.

Watch out for the clutch inspection plate, as well. It won't seal well enough to keep sand out. Most water pumps also have a vent on the bottom side that will let sand up into the bearing and shaft area. Don't count on just trying to avoid these areas, because if there is a hole, sand will get in.

Don't rely on masking tape to adequately protect an area either. With enough pressure behind it, sand will go right through masking tape. Instead, some restorers rely on multiple layers of duct tape placed over any vulnerable components or openings.

Jim Deardorff says he likes to use masking tape covered by a layer of duct tape. Masking tape by itself isn't enough, he insists. On the other hand, media blasting material can tear up the plastic backing on the duct tape, making it very difficult to remove when you're finished. A layer of masking tape beneath it solves this problem.

Deardorff has another tip for those who find themselves masking off a hydraulic cylinder shaft prior to sandblasting or painting. While very few older tractors included hydraulic cylinders, you'll still find them on tractor loaders and on some of the three-point lift systems.

"If you have a cylinder shaft that you need to mask off, simply run a piece of heavy fishing line along the length of the shaft before wrapping it with tape," he says. "Then, when it comes time to remove the tape, you can just pull on the fishing line and 'unzip' the tape."

Media blasting makes quick work of paint removal on the wheels of this classic John Deere two-cylinder tractor.

The radiator can also pose a challenge when it comes to sandblasting the tractor frame. In most cases, the best bet is to simply remove it from the tractor. If there is any area on the frame that really needs cleaning, it's probably the area under the radiator anyway. That's where the rust, caked-on dirt, and grease are prone to collect in the first place. So if you don't remove the radiator, you're going to miss a vital area.

If by chance you don't remove the radiator prior to media blasting, you should at least cover the radiator core with several layers of cardboard and seal the seams with several layers of duct tape. That is unless you plan to replace the whole radiator core anyway.

Be sure you cover the serial number plate, as well. Depending upon the age of your tractor and the serial number, this can be a valuable component, especially if you're painting an older, vintage tractor. Wheels and cast parts can be sandblasted without much risk of damage. In fact, if you're dealing with spoke wheels, sandblasting may be the best way to get in and around the individual spokes.

The last method of removing paint, and the one you're probably going to have to employ as well, is

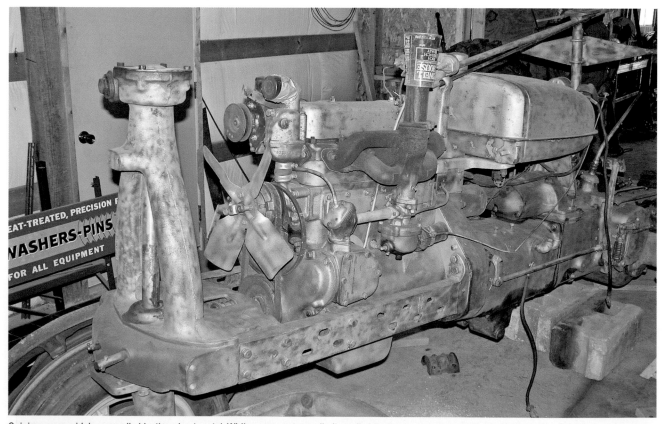

Opinions vary widely on media blasting sheet metal. While some restorers limit media blasting to cast parts such as wheels and engine blocks, others use fine silica sand to strip the paint on sheet metal, as well. If you use a sandblaster near engine parts, though, make sure every hole that could allow sand to enter the engine is plugged, including water-pump vents. Also remove electrical components such as the generator and starter.

If you have access to a cabinet-type sandblaster that uses glass beads, even small parts like the shell for a headlight can be sandblasted.

Jim Deardorff media blasts sheet metal by putting his own blend of Classic Blast material in a closed-top sandblast pot that uses a vacuum to pull the media into the chamber. That allows him to reduce the pressure to as little as 35 pounds and still clean fragile parts without damage. The key is using a large nozzle and holding it at an angle to strip away material quickly.

mechanical removal. Unfortunately, this method requires the most sweat and hard work. You'll find a wide range of items available at most hardware and automotive stores for this task, but you might want to start with the basics, including wire brushes and putty knives. A wire brush or a sander that fits on an electric drill can also come in handy when removing paint and grease from powertrain and frame components.

SHEET METAL

Thanks to the huge interest in antique tractor restoration, today's tractor restoration enthusiast has more choices than ever before. Due to the growing interest in the restoration hobby, vendors now offer hundreds of sheetmetal parts as aftermarket reproductions. Leaf through any issue of an *Antique Power, Red Power,* or *Green* magazine and you'll find ads for everything from complete bare-metal hoods to replacement fenders, dash panels, grilles, and PTO shields. If you're working on a vintage Ford tractor, N-Complete and Carpenter both offer reproductions of nearly any sheetmetal component you could ever need, including fenders, hoods, and nose pieces for 8N, 2N, and 9N models.

In addition, plenty of sheetmetal parts are available through salvage operations that specialize in vintage tractors. Finally, a number of businesses, including many tractor dealerships, sell what is commonly referred to as new-old stock (NOS). These are old parts that have never been used, but instead have been stored in a warehouse or stock room and have only recently been "discovered" and put into circulation to meet the growing demand from antique tractor enthusiasts. Unfortunately, due to the number of tractor brand mergers in recent years, these are becoming harder to find; however, there's still a

To demonstrate the gentle action of his Classic Blast material on sheet metal, Deardorff has been known to sandblast one-half of a soft drink can. His special blend is composed of aluminum oxide, ground black walnut shells, and his own blend of other materials, including garnet.

There's a definite difference between the silica sand used for media blasting and the Classic Blast mix (in left bucket), which uses ground walnut shells as a major component.

potential to find such parts within the John Deere, Case IH, and AGCO dealer networks.

SHEETMETAL PAINT REMOVAL

Due to the availability of so many new parts, some restorers like to replace any sheetmetal parts that are in questionable shape with reproduction components. For others, particularly those on a tight budget, it's more economical to strip and repair existing sheetmetal components, unless they are extremely rusted or wrinkled. Whatever route you take, it's important to get as much paint as possible off the sheet metal. At the very least, you'll want every bit of loose paint off the parts, but new paint and primer will always adhere best to bare metal.

MEDIA BLASTING SHEETMETAL

When it comes to using a sandblaster or media blaster to strip sheet metal, you'll find differing opinions. Some restorers sandblast all the sheet metal and every bit of the frame prior to a restoration project. Others wouldn't take a sandblast nozzle anywhere near the sheet metal, regardless of how much elbow grease it saved.

The key word here is "sandblasting." These days, it's more commonly referred to as media blasting, simply because there are a lot more media types than sand that can be used. That's particularly the case when you're media blasting sheet metal. Check out current media suppliers and you'll find a wide variety of media types, including aluminum oxide, garnet, glass beads, plastic beads, wheat starch, carbon dioxide pellets, and even dry ice.

Jim Seward, a tractor restorer from Wellman, Iowa, who also manages the body shop for a local General Motors dealership, is one who uses a sandblaster on everything. He insists sandblasting sheet metal is one of the quickest and most efficient methods available for removing paint and rust, providing it is done delicately. In response to people who say sandblasting will blow a hole through weak metal, he says, "If the metal is so weak that you're going to blow a hole through it, it needs to be repaired anyway."

For anything but the heaviest gauge steel, make sure you or the commercial operator use fine silica sand, glass beads, or plastic. Keep plenty of distance between the nozzle and the steel to avoid warping or stretching the part. Always keep the nozzle moving. If the metal gets too hot, it will end up having ripples that are virtually impossible to remove.

Jim Deardorff, who has stripped hundreds of cars and tractors in his career, says he has developed his own way to media blast sheet metal. A few years ago, he developed Classic Blast, a special blasting mix made up of aluminum oxide, ground black walnut shells, and his own blend of other materials, including some garnet. Using the product in a closed-top sandblast pot, which uses a vacuum to pull the media into the chamber, he says he can reduce the pressure to as little as 35 pounds and still clean fragile parts without damage. To prove it, he often demonstrates the effectiveness of his sandblast method by removing the paint from an aluminum pop can that's still filled with liquid.

Since the walnuts shells in the blend tend to polish the sheet metal as they assist in paint removal, Deardorff says the stripped surface is also less prone to rust than if other types of media are used. The walnut shells also soften the impact of the more aggressive material in the mix.

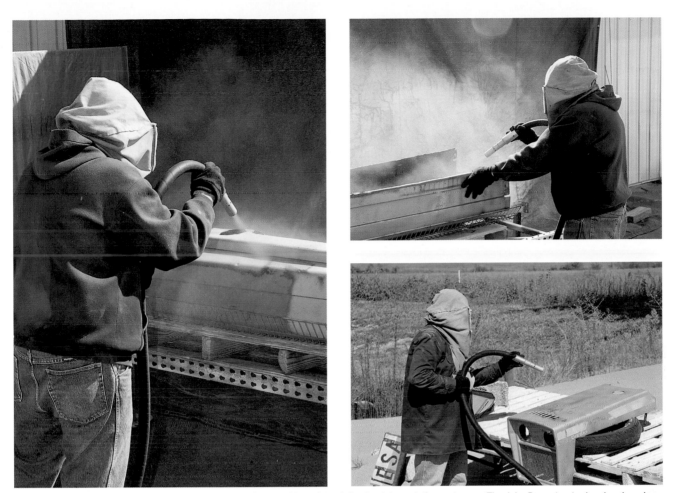

Deardorff routinely uses his media mixture to strip paint from a wide variety of sheetmetal panels for customers. The John Deere tractor hood and garden tractor hood shown here are just a few examples. However, he has also stripped classic automobile bodies and even a jet airplane.

CHEMICAL STRIPPING

Another paint removal method that is widely practiced by a number of restorers, particularly to remove paint from sheetmetal parts, is using a quality metal stripper. Unlike media blasting, using chemical strippers doesn't pose any risk of warping or pitting the sheet metal. Still, it can remove multiple layers of paint, primer, wax, and rust rather easily. Another advantage of chemical paint strippers is that they can often be as effective as media blasting, yet they won't warp or affect the metal in any way.

Just keep in mind that chemical strippers are generally toxic and require adequate ventilation. In addition, you should always wear eye protection and rubber gloves when using them.

Perhaps the best option for stripping sheet metal if you're doing the job yourself is using aircraft stripper. It may have been formulated at one time for aircraft sheet metal, but it's available at any paint and automotive supply store. For best results, it generally helps to scuff the old paint surface prior to any application. It doesn't matter whether you use coarse sandpaper or a rough pad, such as those marketed by Scotch-Brite. The idea is to scratch the surface enough to allow the paint stripper to penetrate deeper into the paint coating.

As mentioned earlier, some restorers like to use a combination of processes, such as using a paint stripper followed by media blasting, particularly on components like the engine, transmission, and frame. Jim Deardorff is one of those restorers. Furthermore, he says he has found a water-based stripper called DoradoStrip that he likes better than any of the chemical-based strippers. Even though it contains no toxic or hazardous air pollutants, he says it effectively lifts epoxies, urethanes, and powder coatings.

Deardorff typically applies the material to any surface he wants to strip, then lets it soak overnight before washing it off the next morning with a strong stream of water. Most of the paint, he insists, washes right off with the material.

While it's not as easy as using a sandblaster, using a wire brush on an electric grinder can take off years of accumulated rust, according to Estel Theis of Savannah, Missouri.

A number of parts, like the steering shaft, will require hand sanding, due to their shape. Any part that can bind or stick should be refinished to like-new condition.

PAINT STRIPPER APPLICATION

Before applying chemical strippers of any kind, it's important that you mask off any areas that you don't intend to strip, just as you would if you were going to media blast the area. In this case, it's best to apply

Your local automotive parts dealer should be able to direct you to a wide assortment of paint strippers for cleaning sheet metal down to bare metal. Many restorers say they have the best luck with aircraft paint remover (far right).

In addition to media blasting, Jim Deardorff also uses a chemical stripper at times. However, he prefers a product called DoradoStrip that claims to contain no toxic or hazardous air pollutants.

a double layer of masking tape or other material. Be careful, too, to make sure you cover any crevices that could allow the material to seep into an area that you don't intend to strip. Any chemical residue that isn't removed will prevent paint from adhering to the area later on.

As for application, it's best to read and follow the directions on the container. Unless you're using a product that comes in an aerosol can or instructs you to apply it with a hand sprayer, it generally works best to use a cheap bristle-type brush and apply the stripper in one direction only. Don't be too conservative, either. If you get it too thin, you'll just end up repeating the process.

Next, allow time for the stripper to work into the paint layer before scraping it off with a putty knife, steel wool, or a special pad. In most cases, this is at least fifteen minutes or until the paint has completely softened. If you start scraping the paint off too soon, you'll also remove the stripper before it has a chance to work deeper. Even then, it may be necessary to apply more stripper as undercoats are exposed.

Ford collectors who have been fortunate enough to acquire a 1939 Model 9N with an aluminum hood leave the aluminum parts unpainted and polish them to a bright shine. Only around 700 tractors were built before the aluminum hood was replaced with steel, so it's only natural for a Ford enthusiast to show it off.

This is a good example of an engine hood that has been stripped and prepared. All that is left to do here is to prime and paint.

Once you've stripped away all the loose paint and exposed the bare metal, it's important that you neutralize any stripper material that remains with plenty of clean water. If you haven't used them to this point, a fine steel wool or a fine-grade cleaning pad work well to remove any paint particles. These also will hold enough water to help dilute the stripper at the same time.

The final step, after all paint and stripper residue has been removed, is to dry the surface and wipe it down with a quality wax and grease remover. If the surface isn't going to be coated with a filler primer or another type of primer for immediate painting, you should also finish it off with a coat of epoxy primer to prevent any rust from forming on the bare surface.

If you can find someone to do it for you, another good way to strip paint from sheetmetal parts is to dip them in a caustic soda bath. A lye solution is added so that any grease that may be on a part is removed. You may need to check around with some of the automotive repair shops or tractor or auto restorers to find someone in your area that specializes in this type of service. Don't try to do it yourself, though, even if you find a lye-based paint remover recipe on the Internet. Lye can burn skin and clothing just as quickly and easily as acid. It just happens to be on the other end of the pH spectrum.

If you do take the parts to a professional paint stripper, it's still important that you rinse and dry each of the parts once you get them back and then coat them with an epoxy primer as soon as possible.

Chapter 16
Sheetmetal Repair and Parts Fabrication

Once you have all the paint off, the first thing you're going to notice on an older tractor are all the dents, dings, scratches, and rust spots that need to be filled in, pounded out, and otherwise hidden from view. You may even have to splice in one or two pieces of sheet metal, create a new bracket, or, in the worst-case scenario, fabricate a whole new sheetmetal section. This is particularly true if you're trying to restore a vintage tractor that hasn't been used for a half century.

If you're lucky, you'll be able to find or repair every part and piece on your vintage tractor that needs replacing. But few tractor restorers are that lucky. Sooner or later, they come across a component that is simply too elusive to be found.

The other scenario is the part or sheet metal piece that you simply don't feel like you can afford. That's when parts fabrication comes into play.

Some parts fabrication can be as simple as bending a piece of sheet metal on four sides to make a new battery box that has rusted away. Or it can be as advanced as cutting, bending, and shaping a new front grille.

PARTS REPLACEMENT OR FABRICATION?

If you've discovered a significant amount of sheetmetal damage on your tractor, you may want to consider the options before going much further. If you choose to keep the original piece, you're still going to have to remove the old paint and then make the appropriate repairs before it is usable. As a result, you may be thinking that if a new hood or fender is available, as mentioned in the previous section, you could be further ahead just by buying a new one.

Certainly, if a fender or hood has a few large dents in it, it can be repaired for less than it will cost to replace it—even if you have to hire someone to do it. However, if the piece is rusted out or torn, and you can replace it at a reasonable cost, you may want to consider a reproduction part.

Following are a few additional thoughts to consider when making that "repair or replace" decision:

- Is there a replacement component available for your tractor brand and model? You certainly won't find any for vintage tractors like a Twin-City or orphan tractors like a Silver King. But they are available for many of the most popular brands like Ford, John Deere, and Farmall.
- What is the value of the tractor? In essence, you can justify the cost of replacement parts on a tractor that is one of only fifty built a lot easier than you can on a Ford 8N.
- Where is the damage located? Near the edge or right in the center? Is it on a flat portion of the hood or fender or on a curved portion of the part?
- How bad is the damage? Are the edges torn and gouged or rusted through?
- How much time do you have available to make the repair? And do you have the experience: for instance, if welding is required to make the repair?
- How does the cost of a new fender or hood compare to that of taking the part to a professional for repair? Can the component be easily transported or relocated to an area where it can be repaired?

It's hard to tell here whether body putty is cracking under the paint or rust is working its way through from the backside. What appears to have been a nice paint job, though, is going to waste.

A number of materials on the market, including brands such as Liquid Steel and J-B Weld, can be used to repair metal parts that shouldn't be subjected to a lot of pressure.

- How accessible is the part and/or what will shipping cost? Some parts, like a pair of fenders for a John Deere B, can't be shipped via UPS and must be shipped by freight to an acceptable location with a loading dock.
- Can the component be repaired with a part? For example Restoration Supply and others stock hood patches for repairing the area around a John Deere A or B muffler. They also have grille inserts (a piece that was easily lost) for several Farmall H and M tractors.

It may be that you don't even have the necessary part to begin with, which means your only options are a salvage yard or reproductions. The engine side panels on a Massey-Harris Pacer or Oliver 70 are good examples. Reproductions will certainly be cheaper than originals—if you can even find originals.

Finally, keep in mind that even the replacement part may require some work to get it to fit properly. So seek out a supplier that will be honest with you about the fit and finish.

In the end, though, you're the one who has to make the decision. At the time of this book printing, a replacement hood for an Allis-Chalmers WD was priced at around $349 plus shipping, while a flat-top fender for a John Deere B was around $215. If the satisfaction of restoring the old piece is worth more than a few hundred dollars, and you have the skills to tackle the job, go for it.

How much time do you have available to make the repair? And do you have the experience—that is, if welding is required—to make the repair?

How does the cost of a new fender or hood, for example, compare to that of taking the part to a professional for patching?

All of these things need to be considered before you take on sheetmetal repair or place an order for the new hood. And there's nothing to say you can't compromise and have a professional weld in a patch, leaving you to do the body filler repairs and preparation. On the other hand, it's true that time is money. At the time of this book's publication, a replacement clamshell fender for a John Deere Model A, B, 50, 60, 70, 620, 630, 720, or 730 was listed at $129 plus postage. A flat-top fender was $215. Similarly, the fender panel for a Ford 9N, 2N, or 8N without the mounting bracket and no Ford script was listed for $79.

So the choice is really yours. If the satisfaction of restoring the old piece is worth more than $100 to $200, go for it.

PARTS FABRICATION BASICS

For the sake of a beginner, let's start with a flat or nearly flat piece that is cut and drilled to become a tractor

The engine side panels found on many Oliver and Cockshutt tractors were some of the first parts to disappear and are currently some of the hardest to locate.

sidesheet. There were a number of vintage tractors that came equipped with sidesheets, including the Allis-Chalmers D Series, some Massey-Harris models, and the Oliver Fleetline Series. Unfortunately, the sidesheets had a tendency to disappear. Most were simply taken off by the original owner and stashed in a shed or next to the barn and left to rust or be thrown out at a later date.

And it's easy to see why. After fighting with the engine shields day after day while performing routine service or maintenance, many farmers simply got tired of them and permanently pulled them off. A few others got tired of the enclosed engine compartment playing host to rodents that were looking for shelter or a place to build a nest. Again, the shields came off.

According to Chris Pratt, with *Yesterday's Tractors*, who provided the following outline, you'll need to start your project by making a pattern or template. This can best be done if you know someone with a similar tractor model from which you can borrow the original sidesheet. Then it becomes a simple matter of tracing the sidesheet onto your template material. If you can't locate an original, you'll have to resort to looking at product photos to determine the appropriate fit and then measuring each section and opening to create a makeshift template.

You'll need to make sure your template material is heavy enough to stand up to the project, yet flexible enough to withstand the twisting and handling it's going to take to get it right. A piece of cardboard from the side of a shipping carton or a large piece of poster board will generally suffice.

Now, you'll simply need to cut, check for fit, and cut again until the template properly matches the original.

Once you're satisfied with the pattern, trace it onto the sheetmetal using a marker that is bold enough to see clearly through the sparks that will be flying off the piece. If you can get it straight in your mind, it's also best to trace the pattern so you're cutting out the piece from the back side. That way, any grooves or scuffs you make by mistake won't show up in the finished product.

Most restorers suggest using 22-gauge sheetmetal for something like a sidesheet or hood. It's not as thick as the original material used on most tractors, but it will be easier to bend, and it will still be imperceptible from the original when completed and painted.

One of the best tools for cutting out sheetmetal is a paper pattern angle grinder with a 1/8-inch-wide cut-off wheel. Regardless of what tool you're using, though, remember to wear safety glasses. Equally important, make sure you're cautious about the way you hold the grinder. You don't ever want to be in a position where a kickback could cause an injury. As a final precaution, make sure you cut on the waste side of the line. You can always grind off more material if the piece doesn't fit perfectly, but you can't add it.

Depending upon your tractor model and pattern, there will probably be some areas where you have to cut out a section by hand. Examples include cutouts for a choke knob, steering shaft, and so on. In those cases, you'll need to go as far as you can with the angle grinder and finish out the contour with a drill and flat and round metal files.

Once you have the rough cutting and drilling done, you'll need to go over every surface edge with a good-quality file. This step eliminates the sharp edge left by the grinder and creates a professional-looking smoothness.

From a distance, this tractor looks like a quality restoration . . . until you get close enough to notice the dent in the fuel tank.

Obviously, you still have just a flat sheet of metal at this point, and many sidesheets or hood pieces have a few bends. The best way to address this challenge is with a hammer and a piece of pipe approximately 3 to 5 inches in diameter, depending upon the degree of the curve. The best way to ensure accuracy is to determine where the center of the bend should be on the sheet. Then, draw a line from one side of the piece to the other at the center of the curve. Work back and forth on the sidesheet on both sides of the line, slowly moving outward.

Be sure to fit the sidesheet to the tractor at regular intervals to make sure you aren't going too far or at the wrong angle. Once you have finished and have a piece that fits to your satisfaction, you'll need to use a hammer and dolly or heavy piece of steel to work out any marks left during the bending and shaping process. Slight imperfections, of course, can be covered later with a coat of filler primer prior to painting. The only step left is to finish off the piece with a file or sandpaper as required to leave a smooth surface and edges.

RUST REPAIR

Depending on the age of the tractor you're painting and how long it has been sitting around in the weather, rust is often a bigger problem with sheet metal than dents and dings. That's particularly true of an older tractor you intend to restore. Unless you're lucky enough to find one that has spent the last fifty years in a barn, chances are it was parked out in a tree row or pasture once the owner thought its life was over.

The first thing you need to do is determine the extent of the rust damage. Is it just surface rust, or does it go deeper? If the rust has gone all the way through the sheet metal, you'll need to consider two options. One is to replace the entire piece, as mentioned in the previous chapter. That's easy enough to do if you're looking at a hood or fender for a vintage John Deere B, a Farmall M, or a Ford 8N. But that isn't an option with some of the less-popular brands, or with a rare model like an orchard version. In those situations, you'll have to cut out and repair the hole with a patch as covered later in this chapter.

If the rust is only on the surface and there is solid metal behind it, you can often sand it out with 80- to 100-grit sandpaper, wipe the entire surface down with a wax and grease remover, and apply a coat of epoxy primer to protect against any additional rust.

If the rust goes a little deeper or includes pitting, another option is to carefully sandblast the surface as described in the previous chapter. That will still leave a

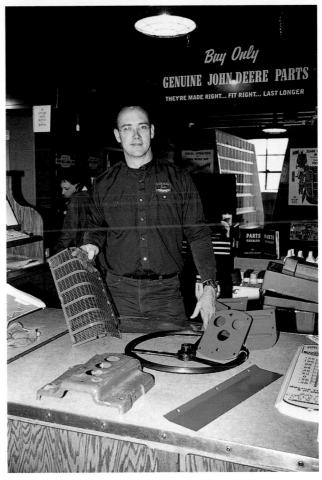

Even replacement dash panels and replacement nose pieces are available from a number of sources if your old piece is unusable.

lot of deep pits, though, which will need to be filled with one or more applications of filler primer or, perhaps, a light coat of body putty.

DENTS AND CREASES

While it's unfortunate, it's not unusual to find one or more dents and/or creases in a tractor's sheet metal. Being the work tool that it was or still is, dents just seem to happen, particularly if the tractor is equipped with a front-end loader. The fenders seem to be a vulnerable area on most tractors, too, as they often come in contact with everything from tree limbs and fence posts to towed implements on a tight turn.

If a dent or crease is more than 1/8 inch deep, it's best to smooth it out with a body repairman's hammer and dolly. Do not simply fill it in with body putty. Not only is the area likely to crack or sag if it is too deep, but the vibration that is inherent with tractor operation can

You can add as many coats of paint as you want, and you still won't hide the dents and wrinkles in the sheet metal on this tractor. In fact, a coat of paint just makes them show up even more. It would have been better to replace the panel or spend some time on bodywork before getting to this point.

One option to consider instead of getting new replacement parts is to search out original salvaged parts that need a little work. One place to find these is in the vendor section at many tractor shows.

John Deere owners were notorious for peeling back the hood around the exhaust to save time during a muffler replacement. That's because you had to remove the hood, steering shaft, and everything connected to get to the bolts. Cutting a hole around the bolts was a lot faster.

cause body putty to pop right out of a deep dent, leaving you with an ugly hole that will require more work and a new coat of paint.

If there aren't a lot of dents to take care of, you might be able to fix them with a ball-peen hammer and a mallet or large hammer to back up the piece. The thing you have to keep in mind is that the original metal stretched as the dent was created. So you may have to shrink it as it is straightened. One way to do that is to heat the spot with an oxy-acetylene torch before beating out the dent.

Another technique, particularly if you are trying to remove a sharp crease, is to drill or punch a series of small holes (approximately 1/16 inch in diameter) along the crease. This will allow the metal to shift as it goes back into place. The holes can be filled later with epoxy or filler putty. If you're drilling holes in the panel, this also gives you the opportunity to use a dent puller instead of

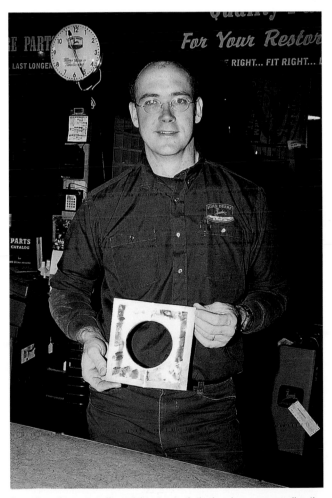

A number of sources offer patches to repair the hood area surrounding the exhaust on A or B model tractors.

a hammer and dolly (although you may need them to finish the job).

When straightening any type of dent or crease, it's important that you don't go too far and end up with an outward bulge. If that ends up being the case, you'll need to carefully hammer the high spot back into the contour. In essence, the repaired area needs to be slightly lower than the surrounding area so the body filler can be matched to the undamaged surface. But that isn't possible if the dent ends up being higher than the surrounding surface.

REPAIRING HOLES AND INSTALLING PATCHES

If the damage you're trying to repair is too severe, you may just want to replace the entire component, such as the hood, side panel, or fender. For newer tractors and any of the popular restoration models, these are readily available.

There may be some instances, however, that call for cutting out an old piece of metal and welding in a new piece. If you decide to do this, first remove all the paint from the area to be worked, if you haven't already done so. At least 2 inches of solid, bare metal should surround the area to be replaced. Next, make a clean cut around the damaged area so you have removed all the bad metal and have left a clean, solid edge.

Although tin snips might work in some situations, the best way to cut out the area is to use a die grinder with a cut-off wheel, a plasma cutter, or a reciprocating saw. It's important that you cut beyond the damage because when you take the pieces to a welder, or do the work yourself, any thin, pitted surfaces will self-destruct. You'll also want to remove the section in a shape that will be easy to reproduce. A square section with clean right angles tends to work best.

Now, find a scrap piece of sheet metal that is the same thickness or gauge as the original piece. The biggest mistake people make at this stage is to use a slightly thicker or thinner replacement piece. Next, you'll want to trace the hole you have created onto a piece of cardboard and make yourself a template. This will be particularly helpful when you go to cut out the new piece.

If necessary, bend the new piece to match the contour of the hood, grille, or fender where it is being installed. Finally, clamp or tape the new piece into position and tack weld it in place being careful not to set the welder at a temperature that is too high and would cause it to burn through the sheet metal.

To make it easier to hold the patch in place, you may want to follow the lead of some body shops and use a body hammer to form a depression for the patch material. Simply tap the hammer around the outside of the opening until the surrounding good metal has formed a depression that is about 1 inch wider on each side than the dimensions of the hole. It should also be just deep enough to allow the patch to rest flush with or just slightly below the surrounding metal. Naturally, the patch will need to be a little larger so it overlaps the good metal by ½ to ¾ of an inch in each direction. This method also gives you the option of using rivets or screws instead of welds—as long as they can be ground down far enough and covered with body filler when you complete the repair.

As you finish welding around the splice, you also need to be careful not to heat the area to the point where it warps or disfigures the sheet metal. It generally works best to skip around or alternate between the different sides of the patch to avoid building up too much heat in one spot. Another trick some bodywork specialists use is to grab the air hose from your compressor and blow cool air onto the welds as you move around the patch.

In the process, try to hide as much of the weld as possible. If you use a series of spot welds around the patch, you can fill in the seam with body putty a little later. Finally, to complete the patch, grind the welds down to remove any high spots, and fill the area with J-B Weld, body filler, or Bondo (see the Using Body Filler section, which follows). This will also fill any rust pits and gaps that have been left. Once the filler has hardened, you can sand it down to the point where the patch is flush with the clean sheet metal, using finer and finer sandpaper to finish the surface.

One likely spot for repair on early-model John Deere two-cylinder tractors is around the exhaust pipe where it exits through the hood. As mentioned earlier, a lot of original owners didn't go through the effort to remove the

A new grille screen makes a tremendous difference in the appearance of this restoration.

Because of its somewhat fragile nature, the corrugated screen used in many tractor grilles is often torn, dented, or gouged. Fortunately, replacement material is available.

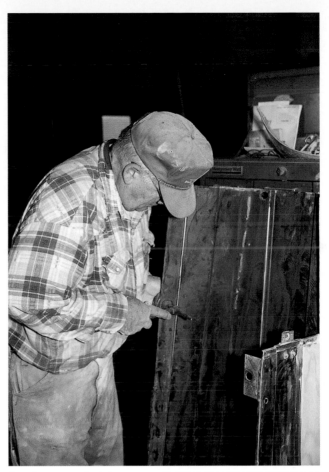

Small dents in sheet metal can often be removed with a ball-peen hammer and a mallet or a large hammer to back up the piece. On stubborn dents, however, it may be necessary to apply heat to help shrink the metal back into place.

If you have many dents to remove, you may want to invest in a bodyman's hammer and dolly.

hood, steering shaft, and grille just to replace a muffler. So they simply cut or peeled away enough of the hood to reach the bolts from the top.

The good news is that there is now a patch available to correct the problem on Model A and B tractors. Available through Moline Tractor and Plow Company, among other sources, the patch is already sized and contoured to fit the back side of the hood. Plus, it has a raised section that surrounds the exhaust pipe hole that is the exact thickness of the hood. As a result, all you have to do is cut a clean, square hole large enough to accept the raised lip and carefully weld the patch to the underside of the hood as previously explained. Then, simply fill the gap between the hood and the patch and sand it smooth.

If you're dealing with rather small holes in a sheetmetal component, you can often get by with putting a piece of fiberglass cloth on the back side of the cavity and filling it with Bondo or body filler. It may take several thin coats

before you get the hole filled to surface level. At that point, you can sand and treat it just as you would any other patch. For fiberglass patches, it's best to purchase a complete fiberglass repair kit, which includes nearly everything you'll need for the job, including the fiberglass cloth, liquid or jelly epoxy, release film, and hardener. The kit will also contain the appropriate instructions for installing a patch on sheetmetal damage.

USING BODY FILLER

Unless you're simply repainting a tractor that's already been restored, or you're not bothered by a few dents on a work tractor, chances are you're going to need to use some plastic body filler or Bondo.

The first thing that's necessary, if you haven't already done so as part of the rust removal or repair process, is to sand the area down to bare metal. The process of sanding away the paint should also reveal any other high or low

Once the hardener has been added, the material will begin to stiffen rather quickly, so don't mix more than you can spread in a few minutes. Using too much hardener will only speed the hardening process, so be careful about overdoing it.

Now, using a body filler spreader, work the filler into the dented or damaged area using long, smooth strokes, or use the spreader to apply a thin film over the rust-pitted section. Be sure you apply a reasonable amount of pressure during application to ensure good adhesion with the surface. In the meantime, always follow the directions on the particular brand you are using, as it may differ on application instructions. As soon as the filler starts to ball up under the spreader, it's generally time to stop and mix up a new batch. Don't worry about getting filler on the unsanded area or any remaining paint. You'll be sanding off the excess and feathering it out as soon as it cures.

Generally, you can start shaping the area as soon as the filler has dried to where you can still scratch it with your fingernail. In other words, it shouldn't be completely hardened. At this point, you can begin rough shaping the material with a Surform or cheese-grater file.

On the other hand, some plastic fillers recommend the material be completely hardened before you start working it or that it can be worked with an 80-grit sanding disc mounted on an electric drill. So be sure you read the instructions for the material you're using.

Don't worry if you end up with a low spot or a place where a bubble has formed. All you have to do is mix up a little more filler and apply another light layer. In fact, it's better to build up the filler in several layers on large or deep areas, rather than trying to apply one thick coat. There's less chance of forming bubbles or leaving voids this way, and you'll end up with a smoother patch. Just remember to decrease the angle of the applicator with each ensuing layer.

Here are a couple of other tips: If you're applying filler to a large flat area, start with a light strip of filler near one edge and then overlap the next few strips by about a third until you get to the opposite edge. This automatically places the heaviest amount of filler near the center of the repair. Also, if you're applying filler to a curved surface, use an applicator made from soft plastic or hard rubber so the filler can be shaped to the contour of the surface.

Once the entire area has hardened and you're satisfied with the patch contour, you can begin final shaping with coarse 80- to 100-grit sandpaper. Don't forget to wear an approved dust-filtering mask!

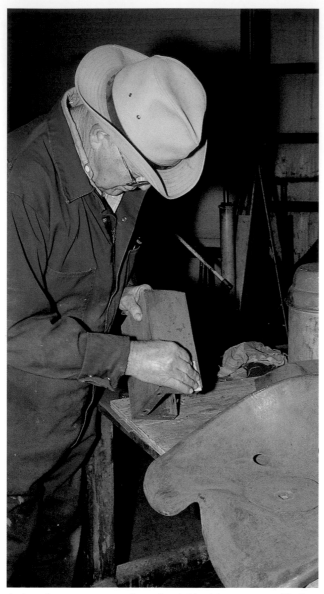

Just as when you were removing rust and old paint, you may need to do some hand sanding and use some elbow grease when doing bodywork on your tractor.

spots in the area. Now switch to a 100-grit sanding disc and feather any remaining paint out to at least an inch from the dented area. Finally, clean the repair area with wax/silicone remover to get it as clean as possible.

Now that you're ready for the plastic filler, mix the appropriate amount of filler with the hardener. If you don't have a mixing palate, you can easily substitute a clean piece of cardboard. Just be sure you get the two components mixed thoroughly. If there are streaks in the filler, you haven't folded and stirred it enough yet. It should all be one color when properly mixed.

With the paint removed from this hood piece, it's ready to be finished off with a little body filler for a glass-smooth surface.

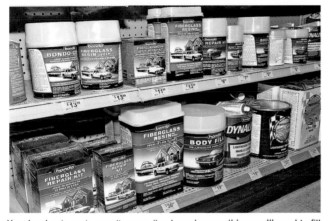

Your local auto parts supplier can direct you to everything you'll need to fill and cover minor imperfections. Just remember that body filler or Bondo should not be used to correct deep dents or creases.

When mixing body filler, it's important to get the right mix of material and hardener. Otherwise, the material may begin to harden before you have a chance to spread an even coat.

Whether you use a Surform file or course-grit sandpaper for the initial shaping, make sure you leave enough material to allow for finish sanding, which will allow you to sand out all the rough file marks and course sanding scratches.

Move the sander back and forth, up and down, and diagonally over the entire area, switching to finer grades of sandpaper until it blends in with the surrounding surface. After every two or three minutes of sanding, run your hand over the surface to determine the progress. Any irregularities will show up clearly when covered with paint, so it's best to find them now. Also, check the area where it blends into the surrounding sheet metal for any rough spots. No matter the pattern, try to blend as much multidirectional movement as possible into the job to prevent grooves and potential patterns. Regardless of where the filler is used, the key to a smooth, flat surface is a long sanding board or DA sander for finish work. While a short sanding block follows the contours, a long board tends to bridge the high spots, so they can be worked down to a level surface. Finish up with 180 grit or finer sandpaper until the filler material has been perfectly smoothed and feathered into the surrounding area.

Once any added body filler has hardened, it should be sanded to a smooth finish that is flush with the original sheetmetal surface, using finer and finer grit paper as you finish it off.

Depending on the brand, some body fillers allow you to start shaping the material with a cheese grater–type file before the material has hardened. Others recommend No. 30 grit sandpaper for initial shaping.

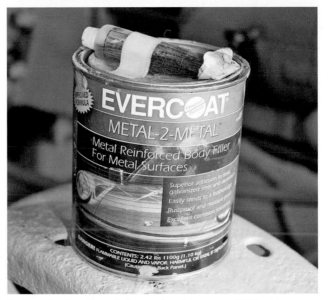

For the extra strength needed on some patches, you might want to consider something other than plastic body filler, such as this metal-reinforced filler.

Using long sanding boards, whether you're sanding by hand or with a power sander, will help ensure a smooth surface when finishing body filler or a coat of primer.

Estel Theis uses a straight-edge ruler to check for any remaining depressions while using body filler on a nose piece.

Ed Hoyt of St. Joseph, Missouri, smoothes out a spot on the fender of a Model D he recently restored.

Fortunately, the hood on this 520 didn't need much filler or bodywork to get it ready for painting.

There may be times when it is necessary to splice in a new piece of metal to replace a rusted-out area. The answer is to spot-weld a metal piece of comparable thickness in place and then cover the patch with body filler. The entire area can then be sanded to a thin layer that only covers imperfections.

A new gauge panel was among the other items fabricated by Anderson while he was rebuilding the Cletrac.

There may come a time when you actually have to fabricate a part or hire a metal worker to do it for you. After a fruitless search for a new grille for a vintage Cletrac crawler, Bill Anderson, a full-time tractor restorer from Superior, Nebraska, simply built one himself.

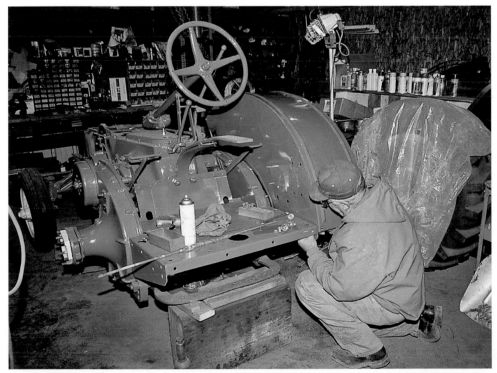

Don't be surprised if large sheetmetal parts like fenders and hoods don't fit perfectly when it comes time to reassemble the tractor—particularly if you had to apply heat to a part. It doesn't take much to shift a bolt hole ever so slightly.

Chapter 17
Painting Preparation

Even though you've spent the last few chapters—and who knows how many hours—stripping paint and making sheetmetal repairs, you're still not quite ready to start painting. The good news, though, is that you're getting close.

Unless you totally media blasted every inch of the tractor, chances are some areas are still covered with old paint. And applying any primer and new paint without scuffing up the old surface would be a mistake. Paint must have an absorbent base to adhere to. If you removed the old paint to bare metal, or if the paint that is left is tight with no chance of flaking off later, then using a fine grade of Scotch-Brite pads works well for scuffing the surface, particularly on hard paint surfaces. Just be sure the old paint feathers into the bare metal surfaces without any hard edges. A coat of filler primer will generally take care of any differences later.

The one advantage of painting a tractor, in comparison to an automobile, is that the surface is usually rougher to begin with, which gives the paint something to hold on to. That is especially true of the cast components, like the engine, frame, and transmission. It's the sheet metal that will be of greater concern.

CLEANING PARTS

Perhaps the most obvious advice for preparing the tractor for painting is to make sure it is clean. If you previously media blasted the tractor to remove paint, make sure you have gone over the entire unit with an air hose to remove any medium from cracks and joints. Similarly, if you used a chemical stripper, make sure every trace of the product has been removed and neutralized with clean water. Finally, make sure that you've removed the dust and residue from any body filler you've used and that you have wiped all sheetmetal surfaces with a tack cloth to remove dust and debris that may have settled. That applies, too, to any dust created by scuffing old paint. In fact, if at all possible, you should go over the whole tractor with soap and water, just to make sure you've got everything.

At this point, some automotive paint books will tell you to use a wax/silicone remover solvent on all surfaces that will be painted. Again, that's because paints need a rough, but clean surface for adhesion. However, most automotive painters are now using urethane, while most tractor painters are still using enamel. Not only is the latter more forgiving, but you're dealing with a lot of cast-iron

Once all surfaces have been stripped, cleaned, and smoothed or filled, it's time to make sure the tractor and the sheetmetal panels have been thoroughly cleaned of any stripping residue or media blasting material.

Jim Deardorff often uses a product called Chlor*Wash to clean surfaces a final time before they're painted to remove salt, dirt, and exhaust residue. He often uses the same product to wash restored tractors after they've been exposed to the elements.

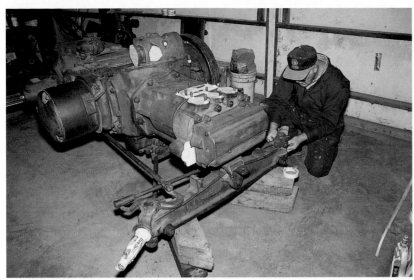

Make sure all openings have been covered and any parts you don't want painted have been masked. That includes wheel spindles, the distributor, gauges, etc.

One way to mask a large opening is to cut a piece of cardboard to cover the void and punch holes for any bolt holes.

and heavy-gauge sheet metal as opposed to glass-smooth engine hoods and fiberglass fender panels. Perhaps the best bet is to talk to your paint supplier to see if he or she recommends any additional cleaner.

Jim Deardorff, owner of Superior Coatings in Chillicothe, Missouri, says he has had good luck with a product he recently discovered called Picklex 20. Although he hasn't had many months to test it long-term, he notes that it can be applied to any metal surface as a combination metal surface cleaner, surface rust remover, surface preparation, and pre-treatment for finishing. The product also promises to provide long-term rust protection on surfaces that have been prepped, but are waiting on a sealer or primer coat, to prevent oxidation.

Deardorff says he has also used a product called Chlor*Wash to clean tractors prior to painting. Because it was initially developed for industrial use, Chlor*Wash is actually blended to remove road films, dirt, and chloride, as well as sulfate and nitrate salts. In essence, it has the cleaning ability of a soap but has the added feature of removing any salts.

MASKING

To protect components or parts from primer and paint, they need to be covered with masking paper and/or tape. Perhaps you've done this to some extent already, if you did any media blasting. Masking for media blasting and masking for paint, however, are really two different things.

As you learned earlier, the purpose of masking prior to media blasting is to protect vulnerable areas from the effects of sandblasting or media blasting and to keep sand

and material from getting into areas where it can cause damage. These areas include brake adjustment holes, water pump drain holes, and open bolt holes. That generally requires something more substantial than a single layer of paper or tape.

The purpose of paint masking is to prevent unwanted paint from covering an area. Fortunately, you shouldn't need to do a lot of masking on a tractor. Most of the parts that need to be protected from paint can simply be removed, including the glass fuel sediment bowl, the muffler, and tires. That also applies to emblems and nameplates. It is far easier to remove these types of parts than to try to mask them, and it will take less time in the long run, too.

The other advantage you'll have with most tractors is that most, if not all, of the tractor will be painted the same color. Even if the sheet metal happens to be a different color, it will have been removed so you can paint the frame and engine separately. That really just leaves items such as the headlight lenses; mating surfaces, which require a gasket; wheel spindles; and/or wheel hubs that will need to be masked.

The one exception will be those tractor models that have a two-tone hood or grille. Examples include Oliver tractors on which the grille is painted red with a yellow center stripe; the Ford Powermaster line, which has a red band down the center of the gray hood; and John Deere's 30 Series two-cylinder models like the 530 and 630, which have a green hood with a yellow stripe down the side. In each of these cases, you'll need to prime the entire piece, but mask off the individual areas for painting.

One of the most important things about masking is to make sure you have quality tape and that it is relatively fresh. If tape gets too old and brittle, it can be extremely hard to work with and even harder to remove. That's one advantage of the new blue plastic painter's tape that came out a few years ago. It provides more time to finish the job and remove the tape than the average roll of masking tape. The bottom line is that an automotive paint store is probably a better source for materials than the local discount store.

Speaking of materials, the same logic goes for masking paper. Granted, you may be tempted to use newspaper, and that may be fine for masking some parts. But it's not your best option when masking something that really needs to be protected. Newspaper tends to tear much more easily than masking paper designed for the job. Paint can also seep through if the newspaper becomes too saturated, particularly if the paint has been thinned quite a bit to work in your spray gun. Lastly, newspaper doesn't lie as flat on most surfaces as masking paper does. That leaves pockets that can pick up dust and dirt that has been kicked up while you're making other preparations. The next thing you know, that dust and dirt have been transferred and are now embedded in the paint surface.

If you're masking off an area of the hood that is to be a different color, you may want to start with a narrow roll of tape that is only 1/8- to 1/4-inch wide. This is particularly important if you have to deal with any curves, as it's much easier to follow the contours with the narrow width. Then you can come back with a wider piece of tape and your paper to completely cover the unpainted portion.

Also, if you're painting a two-tone tractor, like a Farmall 350 or 450, that has white panels on the red hood or a John Deere 530 or 630 that has the yellow panel on the side of a predominantly green hood, most restorers suggest masking the hood and painting the smaller areas first. Then go back and carefully mask off the entire white or yellow panel while you paint the remainder of the hood. This is a little easier on most two-tone Ford tractor hoods because the colors, in most cases, are separated by a seam or panel edge.

When laying down masking tape, it's generally best to use the longest strips possible. Every seam you make leaves the potential for a leak. On the other hand, you don't want to start weaving in an attempt to lay one strip over too much distance. If you prefer to use shorter strips that overlap and you've done a good job of sticking them down, then do it your own way. If you're working on a vertical surface, though, and you're putting on more than one strip, start from the bottom and go up, so the upper strips overlap the lower ones.

No matter what your technique is, lay the tape down evenly without stretching it. Then cut it off cleanly with a trim knife, razor blade, or X-Acto knife, rather than tearing it. Tearing it just leaves more ragged edges that can allow paint to seep under the tape.

Finally, if you're painting a tractor with a cab, you'll need to mask around the edge molding first. The best way to do this is to run a 1- or 11/2-inch-wide strip of masking tape over the molding around the window. Then come back with masking paper to cover the glass. Attach the masking paper to the first strip of tape with more tape, making sure you've covered all the seams between the two.

Masking Tires

It's always easiest to remove the tires before painting the wheels. If you're painting a restoration tractor, you've probably done this anyway so you can check the condition of the wheel rim for rust. Or you may have needed to replace one or more tires that were badly rotted or weather checked. If that was the case, you can simply sandblast the wheels and prepare them for painting as you would any other part; otherwise, you'll need to mask the rubber.

With most tractor brands and models, the wheels are a different color than the rest of the tractor or the frame. That's not the case with a Model 9N or 2N Ford, as the entire tractor is painted the same color. But it's true on most everything else.

Consequently, you'll need to cover any wheels and/or tires that haven't been removed until you've painted the rest of the frame, engine, and other components that have a different color. One way to do this is by covering smaller

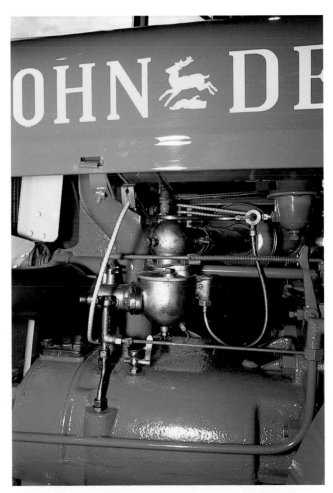

You certainly don't want to paint something as unique as the brass carburetor or vintage magneto on some early tractor models. Either mask them carefully, or remove them altogether and carefully mask the engine openings.

One way to mask an area is simply to cover the entire surface and then cut away the excess with a sharp knife.

If necessary, clean the surface you'll be masking to make sure the tape doesn't come loose or lift at an edge while you're applying paint.

You'll find masking tape available in a number of different sizes from your paint supplier.

Masking paper that has been specifically designed for automotive painting is best for masking off large areas, such as the two-toned hood on some tractor models.

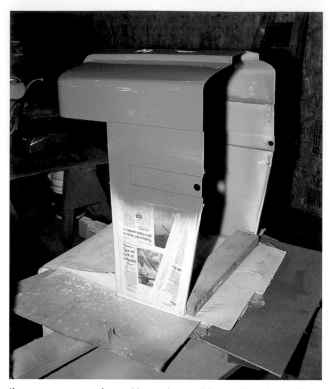

If you use newspaper for masking, make sure it is smooth and doesn't contain pockets that can gather and hold dust. Also, make sure you use enough layers to keep paint from seeping through to the surface below.

wheels with plastic trash bags. In the same manner, you can use larger sheets of plastic or plastic drop cloths to cover the rear tires and wheels. Use tape where necessary to hold them in place, and be careful about letting dust accumulate in any folds.

Once you finish the main part of the tractor, you'll need to mask off the rubber tires with tape and masking paper and paint them separately. You'll also need to protect the rest of the tractor from overspray if the wheels haven't been removed. Considering that you'll need to mask and paint both sides of each wheel, you can see why it's in your best interest to put the tractor on stands and remove the wheels at the start of the job. The same goes for the tires.

Granted, not everyone has the means to haul a set of tractor tires to the local tire shop, but most farm cooperatives have a mobile tire service that supports farmers with field repairs. So it may just be worth your time and effort to have them make two stops at your shop, too: once to remove the tires from the wheels and once more to put them back on when the paint has cured.

If any part of the tractor has to remain outdoors, it is a good idea to protect it with a coat of primer as soon as it has been cleaned and prepped.

Unless you're painting a newer tractor or a classic model like the Minneapolis-Moline UDLX, which featured a cab as early as 1938, you probably won't need to worry about masking off any glass surfaces. If you do, however, simply use wide masking tape and masking paper to cover both the rubber molding and the glass.

Clothes might not make the man nor does paint make the tractor—but it sure helps! A good paint job begins with exemplary preparation. Don't cut corners here, as it'll show later on when it's too late. This 1919 Case Model 10/18 Crossmotor was done right. Owner: John W. Davis. *Ralph W. Sanders*

Chapter 18
The Primer Coat

Once the sheet metal has been stripped, smoothed, and filled as necessary and the body and frame have been cleaned and prepared, it's time to apply a quality coat of primer. Some restorers recommend applying a coat of etch primer immediately after the tractor frame and/or sheet metal have been cleaned, even if they won't be painted for a while. According to Gary Ledford, a paint technician from St. Joseph, Missouri, bare metal can begin to rust in as little as four hours. Consequently, a coat of etch primer on bare metal not only helps prevent rust, but may make it easier to clean away any grease or oil before you add additional primer coats or the paint coat.

The primer stage also gives you the opportunity to take care of a lot of the imperfections that may remain after most of the bodywork has been completed. By putting on two or three coats of filler primer, you can easily fill a lot of pits and crevices.

CHOOSING THE RIGHT PRIMER TYPE

A number of different types of primers can be used to prepare, fill, or seal the surface prior to the final coat of paint. Each has its own unique role and application. For example, while epoxy and urethane primers protect components from new rust, some form a harder finish than others. However, you need to ensure that the primer you select is not only compatible with any paint that remains on the tractor or engine, but also with the paint you have selected to finish the project.

Ledford explains that the type of primer you start with depends to some extent on the type of finish you're covering—old paint, bare metal, or cast iron. If an alkyd enamel is being applied over lacquer, which is often the case with classic tractors if they haven't been totally stripped or media blasted, a sealer must be used. A sealer should also be used with enamel over enamel. Basically, the bottom line is that if you're in doubt about the old paint or primer, use a sealer.

Epoxy Primers

If you're shooting primer over bare metal or cast iron that could be exposed to the weather before you get it covered with additional primer, Ledford generally recommends using epoxy or self-etch-type primer. This is particularly the case with parts of the frame or cast wheels that have been sandblasted and are in no need of further work or sanding.

Epoxy is generally the easiest to use because, in many cases, depending on the brand, it combines the qualities of a metal etch, a primer surfacer, and a primer sealer in one product. A self-etching primer, on the other hand, is basically a phosphoric-acid-type etch. Self-etching primers have to have another primer over the top of them, Ledford adds. It can't be an epoxy primer, but it can be a urethane primer. Ledford cautions, however, that you need to check with your paint supplier to learn the characteristics of each product, as these principles don't apply to all brands.

You'll find several different kinds of primers on the market, including filler primers and those that are self-etching, as well as epoxy and urethane primers. Your paint supplier can help you select the best type for your needs and application.

Filler primers have been described by some as "little more than liquid body filler," since they're formulated to fill and smooth surface imperfections.

You normally cannot paint directly onto a self-etching primer because the paint won't adhere. That's why painters generally recommend that tractor restorers go over bare finishes with an epoxy primer, since it will give you a more durable finish, and it will etch aluminum and metal in one shot.

Although epoxy primer is primarily used for corrosion protection, it can be used in two other ways. It can be used as a primer-sealer, where you spray it on, wait 15 to 20 minutes, and start top coating with your color. Or it can be used as a primer-surfacer to cover minor flaws in the surface. In this case, you will want to put down two to three coats, giving it 15 to 20 minutes to dry between coats. Then, wait at least six hours before sanding the surface.

Finally, epoxy primer can be sprayed over the top of old lacquer paint—which was often used on older tractors—without a problem. It is a good idea, however, to seal the original lacquer just to be sure the two surfaces remain compatible. It is not recommended that you ever put lacquer on top of enamel.

Dave Henderson, a tractor repair and restoration specialist from Colo, Iowa, applies a coat of primer to a vintage Farmall tractor.

"We have one epoxy primer in our inventory that can go right over a partially painted surface or bare metal," Ledford says. "Then, you can either paint over it when it dries or wait a few days to apply a top coat. The best part is it gives you a seven-day window to finish the job before it becomes necessary to resand it."

Urethane Primers

Although urethane primers are very popular with restorers due to their hard finish, they do not include any kind of chemical agent to prevent rusting. In fact, if you put a urethane filler primer over bare metal, it actually soaks up the moisture and the metal will begin to rust beneath the paint. Therefore, you either need to ensure that the surface is completely free of rust before you apply a urethane primer, or you need to lay down a coat of epoxy primer or an etching primer and put the urethane over it. Otherwise, you may find rust popping through the surface four or five months down the road.

Since urethane is only a primer-surfacer, you may need to apply a sealer of some kind before you paint, depending on the brand. Some let you paint right over the top as long as you haven't sanded through the primer layer. If not, a coat of epoxy primer over the top will serve the purpose. Plus, a coat of epoxy will serve to bridge any scratches in the urethane that have been left after sanding and leave a smooth surface for the top-coat color.

The only thing you shouldn't do with urethane is put it under a top color coat of lacquer; however, since lacquer seems to be on its way out, the use of lacquer as a top coat isn't even covered in this book.

Lacquer Primers

Just like lacquer paint, lacquer primers are pretty much outdated. Although lacquer primers air dry fairly quickly, they tend to shrink for days and weeks after they have been applied. As a result, the primer can shrink for up to a month under any coat of paint that has been applied too early.

"If you use lacquer primer, it's best to let it set for at least a week minimum before you even do anything with it," paint technician Gary Ledford says. "And that's under perfect drying conditions . . . say 70 degrees or above; otherwise, you can start to see sanding scratches show up where it pulled away under the paint."

If you do use a lacquer primer, Ledford recommends putting a urethane-type primer over it before moving on to a top coat.

In most cases, the primer is applied in the same manner as paint. Consequently, it's important to follow the same procedures you'll find in Chapter 20.

Filler Primers

For complete coverage of any imperfections, you might want to follow the lead of several tractor restorers and use a filler primer, heavy-bodied primer, or high-build primer on top of the etch primer or epoxy primer. No matter what you call it, a filler primer is basically formulated to fill in any pits in the surface from sanding or rust even quicker than an epoxy primer alone. As one restorer put it, filler primer is little more than a liquid body filler.

Although some tractor enthusiasts use fine-grit sandpaper, such as a No. 240 grit, to smooth the surface between coats of primer, others say they simply apply one coat of primer over the next, once it's had time to dry. On the last sanding before painting, though, you'll want to use an even finer sandpaper sheet, like No. 400 grit, if you're using enamel, and up to No. 600 grit for urethane. At the very least, you will have to sand the surface before applying a sealer and the top coat. Because it has the texture to fill pits and imperfections in the sheet metal, an unsanded primer coat would be too rough to paint over without further preparation.

It's important to note, too, that most urethane primers will need a sealer coat before the top coat of color is applied, particularly if there is a chance you've sanded through in spots. In general, you can apply one coat of primer every seven to ten minutes, or when the first coat is dry to the touch. After the last coat, wait about three hours before sanding.

Jeff McManus, a John Deere enthusiast and former manager of the Moline Tractor and Plow Company, has

Estel Theis shoots a coat of primer on the hood of a John Deere two-cylinder tractor. Note that primers tend to come in a variety of colors, depending on the type and manufacturer.

Since the primer on this John Deere radiator is a dull yellow, it will make it easier to judge adequate paint coverage when it is ultimately painted green.

been known to apply up to fifteen coats of filler primer on a sheetmetal part that has had a lot of work done to it, just to get a glass-smooth surface. Between every three coats, he uses long sanding boards to smooth the finish. This helps prevent high and low spots from being formed by the sander itself.

Jeff Gravert, a Cockshutt enthusiast and professional restorer from Clay Center, Nebraska, says he has put as many as twenty coats of primer on a tractor, sanding between each coat. Regardless of how many coats he applies, though, he usually ends the sanding job with 600-grit sandpaper.

Another trick used by some body specialists is to switch between different colors of compatible primers so they can better identify hills and valleys in the finish. Be sure to finish with finer and finer grades of sandpaper, ultimately ending up with wet sanding paper.

Urethane primers are usually 1 to 3 millimeters thick per pass, Ledford explains, noting that one of his brands averages 2.5 millimeters per pass. So if you go around the tractor three times, you've got 7.5 millimeters of primer on there; whereas most new cars today have about 4.5

millimeters total, including all primers and paints. In the end, you'll have a much thicker paint coat.

Sealing Primers

The final step before applying a coat of paint should involve applying a coat of sealing primer, or sealer, as it's more commonly called. This closes the surface and prepares it to accept a coat of paint. The sealer does this in two ways. First, it helps minimize sand scratch swelling, which can make scratches more visible under the top coat. This is particularly important if you used a filler primer. If the sand marks aren't sealed, the paint solvent can cause the sand scratches to swell; plus, as solvents evaporate, paint solids fill the voids in the surface, leaving a microscopic series of hills and valleys, which results in a dull finish. In contrast, a coat of sealer provides a uniform base that, in turn, leads to uniform paint distribution and solvent evaporation.

Second, the sealer also acts as a barrier to protect the undercoat primers from any reaction with the top coat. Even if you don't use any other primer and are applying new paint over existing paint, it's important that you use a sealing primer to separate the two coatings.

As has been mentioned more than once here, enamel and urethane paints are totally incompatible with any lacquer-based paint or primer. If there's any doubt about what kind of primer to use at any stage of the painting process, it's best to discuss it with your paint supplier or refer to the applications guides and/or information sheets that are available for the products you plan to use. Regardless of what type of primer you use—and you'll probably need to use more than one type—you'll also need to mix it with thinner or reducer for it to be sprayable through a paint gun. Of course, your paint dealer can help with this decision, as well.

Before you apply any primer or sealer, though, use a tack cloth a second time to get the surface extra clean. You don't want to seal in any dirt or sanding dust.

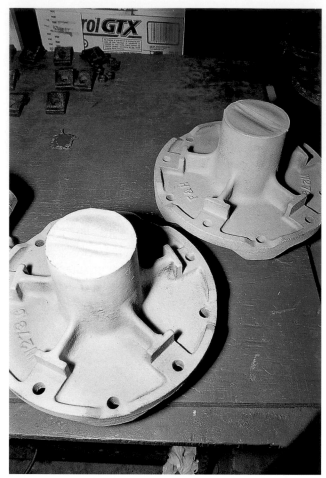

When possible, go ahead and shoot a coat of primer on cast parts, like these wheel spindles, as soon as they have been stripped and prepped to prevent the formation of rust. They can wait a while for paint.

The same holds true for the tractor frame, which is generally constructed of cast iron.

Everything that will receive a coat of paint needs some kind of primer to seal the surface, including the fuel tank.

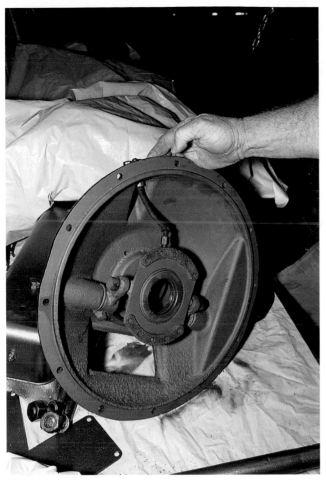

Covering tractor parts that have already been primed with a sheet of plastic will help prevent an accumulation of dust until it's time to paint.

Chapter 19
Paint Color Selection

If there was ever a topic of discussion and debate among tractor restoration enthusiasts, it's paint color. Sure, it's easy to say that an Oliver tractor is green and an Allis-Chalmers tractor is orange, but the real debate comes when you question which shade of green or orange. With little exception, most of the manufacturers changed the color tint two or three times over the history of the brand.

There's an equal amount of debate, too, about the color of the trim, wheels, etc. Some companies made a change between models or between model years. Other companies switched from one color or shade to another with less planning . . . like when they ran out of paint in one color. This undoubtedly occurred even more often during the war years when supplies were tight.

For these reasons, don't assume you can go to the implement store or a farm supply and get the correct paint color. Granted, the farm and ranch supply outlet may have cans of paint labeled International Harvester Red or Allis-Chalmers Orange, but they may or may not be an exact match to the paint color originally used on your tractor.

Similarly, Oliver went through several changes in the shade of the color used over the years. According to Lyle Dumont—an Oliver collector from Sigorney, Iowa, and a partner in the Oliver Decals business with his wife, Helen—Oliver used as many as four different shades of green from 1930 through 1975, when the company became part of White.

Canned paint can also vary in color from one can to the next. Because of this, these paints are generally best left to farmers who want to touch up their work tractors. If you're going for a true restoration, it's best to purchase an enamel product formulated by the manufacturer or go with automotive paint and have it custom mixed to the true color.

The bottom line, as most people will tell you, is that you should paint your tractor the shade and color that makes you happy.

ALLIS-CHALMERS

Beginning with the first tractor the company produced in 1914, Allis-Chalmers painted all of its early tractors with a shade of green that is today best replicated by DuPont No. 2619D. The company switched to its infamous Persian Orange color in 1929—supposedly after Harry Merritt, manager of the tractor division at the time, saw a field of brilliant orange poppies while on a trip to California. Of course, that's just one story concerning the origin of the paint color.

Allis-Chalmers changed the original Persian Orange to a more brilliant shade in 1960 and called it Persian Orange No 2. The tractor line was also highlighted with cream-colored wheels, grilles, steering wheels, and nameplates. So it's important to know the model year of your tractor if you want to keep the paint color authentic. At practically every tractor show, true Allis-Chalmers enthusiasts will find a tractor that carries the wrong shade of Persian Orange for the model year.

CASE

Tractors were nothing new to Case in the early 1900s, when farm tractors were really coming of age. The company had already become the largest producer of steam engines between 1870 and 1925. Naturally, it continued using most of the same colors, which meant its first tractors were dark green followed by gray.

Although Allis-Chalmers tractors have been orange since 1929, the color tint of the Persian Orange changed three times before the company was sold in 1985.

Case tractors changed from gray to Flambeau Red, which actually looks closer to orange, in 1939. Later, the sheet metal changed to Desert Sunset while the cast components remained Flambeau Red.

The colorful change from gray to Flambeau Red came in 1939, which was around the same time that other tractor manufacturers opted for brighter colors. That was also the same year Case introduced new styling on models like the D and the R; however, the color changed again in 1957 when Case introduced the Desert Sunset paint scheme. While the cast iron remained Flambeau Red, the lighter color dominated the sheet metal, including the hood and fenders.

COCKSHUTT

Founded as a company in 1877, Cockshutt got its start in the tractor business in 1924 by marketing Hart-Parr

tractors with red and cream paint and the Cockshutt name on the radiator shell.

Following World War II, Cockshutt finally had the resources to come out with its own tractor, the Model 30, in 1946. Naturally, it continued the red-and-yellow paint scheme as a Cockshutt model. The same tractor was also sold in the United States as the Co-Op E3 by the National Farm Machinery Cooperative, based in Ohio, and as the Farmcrest tractor through the American Gambles Stores chain. During their reign, the Co-op tractors supposedly carried at least two different shades of orange, with the latest represented by Martin-Senour No. 90T-22014.

In the meantime, Cockshutt continued with the red and yellow paint scheme until the early 1950s, when the Deluxe models were introduced. At that time, the color of the hood, grille, and fuel tank was changed to a cream color, while the rest of the tractor remained red. Finally, in 1958, Cockshutt debuted the new 500 Series with a new squared-off grille and an all-yellow paint scheme called Harvest Gold.

A few years later, in 1961, the "red belly" paint scheme came into play, which featured a Vermillion Red transmission, engine, and frame to contrast the Harvest Gold sheet metal.

FARMALL/INTERNATIONAL HARVESTER

Like most other tractor brands, IH started painting its first tractors with a drab color—Tractor Gray, as the company called it—that seemed to match the times. In November 1936, International Harvester made the change to Farmall Red for its 1937 models.

Imports from Canada, Cockshutt tractors carried some version of red and cream paint until the 1950s when the Deluxe models were introduced with red and yellow paint. In 1958, Cockshutt switched to a Harvest Gold paint scheme.

Although the red color remained the same over the years, Farmall and McCormick tractors did go through a number of changes in trim colors, which included cream, blue, and black. Wheels, meanwhile, were either red or galvanized; most restorers reproduce the galvanized look with silver paint.

As you'll discover in the chapter on decals, International Harvester also complicated the paint issue with a program in the 1950s in which customers could have the local dealer repaint their tractors. In many of these cases, employees at the dealership weren't as careful about masking off certain parts as the factory workers had been. For example, on Letter Series tractors, such as the M, C, and H, engineering specifications called for leaving electronic components unpainted. This included the magneto, spark plugs, coil wires, and, in most cases, the distributor cover. It's not uncommon, however, to see many of these parts painted red today—especially the distributor cap and some wires.

If you really want to do your research on the correct paint scheme, you might want to go to the Wisconsin Historical Society website (www.wisconsinhistory.org) and search through its library of documents from IH. All of the IH paint committee decisions from 1924 through 1960 are listed on the site.

If, for instance, you have a 1931 F-20, you'll discover in a paint committee memo dated June 5, 1930, that the drawbar on Farmall tractors was to be painted Harvest Red instead of Tractor Gray as it originally had been. The decision was made at the request of the works manager, who stated that "because of the physical layout of the Farmall equipment," some money could be saved by painting the drawbar the same color as the wheels. The trunnion castings and braces were to remain gray, as in the past; however, if you look around at many tractor shows, most Farmall tractors continue to have a gray drawbar, regardless of the year.

Another memo, dated September 24, 1946, states that all tractor weights are to be painted the same color as the tractor. No notation is made as to what color they were previously.

International Harvester tractors are easily recognized today by their bright Harvest Red paint coat. In fact, about the only thing in their paint scheme that has changed since 1937 has been the trim color.

Until the company introduced its 1937 models in 1936, most Farmall and International Harvester tractors were painted Tractor Gray.

The best resources for determining the original colors of the various components are vintage photographs found in tractor ads or literature, since other restorers have occasionally been wrong.

FERGUSON

After dissolving his partnership with Henry Ford, Harry Ferguson continued to build and market his own brand of tractors from 1948 until 1953, when Massey-Harris acquired the Ferguson company and renamed the company Massey-Harris-Ferguson. To keep the company afloat after Ford split on the agreement, Ferguson imported tractors from Europe as the TE-20. Then, in 1951, Ferguson introduced the TO-20, which was produced specifically for the American market. Other tractors that followed included the TO-30 and TO-35.

In an effort to build on the reputation that had been established by the Ford-Ferguson 9N and 2N models, the Ferguson tractors continued to use an all-gray paint scheme for a few years. In fact, one of the company's early ads proclaimed, "Fortunate is the Dealer who offers the all-gray tractor with the Chevron Nameplate."

Although the gray color looks very similar to the solid gray on Ford 9N and 2N models, it does have a different paint code number, which is referred to as Ferguson Gray. However, in 1954, Ferguson switched to a Ferguson Light Gray paint on the TO-35 with yellow-green metallic on the TO-35 castings and F-40 grille screen panels.

The company changed paint color again in 1956 when Old MF Red or Tractor Red was used on the sheet metal on the TO-35s and the F-40 grille screen panels. A Flint Gray Metallic, meanwhile, was used on the castings of TO-35 and F-40 models, giving rise to the red and gray paint scheme that followed with Massey Ferguson.

FORD

It doesn't take much planning to paint a Ford 9N tractor, which made its debut in 1939, or a Model 2N, which followed in 1942. It just takes the right shade of gray paint, since the entire tractor, including the wheels and frame, are all the same color on both models. Although the Ford Motor Company generally gets most of the credit for the 9N and the 2N, the first two N Series models were actually the result of a partnership between Henry Ford and Harry Ferguson.

Unfortunately, that partnership dissolved in 1946, and by 1947, it was clear that each of them was going in his own direction—especially when Ford introduced the 8N with its distinctive red castings and wheels. The rest of the 8N was painted a lighter gray than the previous 2N and 9N models. Even after Ford introduced several larger tractors, including the NAA, 600, and 861 Powermaster, the company continued to use a mix of red and gray paint.

All Ford tractors were painted solid gray until 1948, when Ford split from Ferguson and introduced the 8N with its red and gray paint scheme.

Whether it's because the previous owners wanted their tractor to look like an 8N, you'll find more 9N and 2N tractors that are painted red and gray than those painted only gray.

While a number of manufacturers offered industrial tractors, they were almost always painted a different color than the companies' agricultural tractors.

This Ford 8N, beautifully restored by Chris Mercer with some help from his father, Dallas, shows the true colors for a Model 8N. *Chris Mercer*

The only difference was that a few models, like the 601, used more red than gray.

The paint scheme changed completely, though, in 1958, when Ford introduced a new line of tractors that included the Model 5000. At that point, Ford introduced the famous blue color that was recognized until the company was purchased by New Holland.

Although there are a number of sources that carry both the dark gray and the lighter gray introduced on the 8N, the biggest debate today centers around which shade of gray is correct. Many claim, for example, that several brands or paint codes specified for the 8N are too white, while other paint codes have too much of a tan or beige tint.

Later-model Ford tractors carried various color schemes of the red and gray until the colors were changed to blue and gray in 1964.

JOHN DEERE

John Deere tractors are unique in the vintage tractor world in that they have always been green and yellow, unless of course you're restoring an industrial model. If you're going for a true restoration, you have a couple of choices. One is to go to an automotive paint supplier and have the paint custom mixed to the true color. The other is to go to the John Deere dealership for your supplies. Keep in mind, though, that John Deere changed the shade of green around the time it introduced its New Generation tractors, which included the 3010, 4010, etc., in 1960. If you shop for paint at the dealership, you'll find it has two Deere shades: Agricultural Green and Classic Green. The latter is primarily used on two-cylinder models.

According to technical representatives for the Two-Cylinder Club, nearly 80 percent of the tractors at John Deere expos have John Deere–brand paint. On the other hand, Dan Peterson, with Rusty Acres Restoration, says he prefers a regular acrylic enamel, specifically a product produced by Martin-Senour.

As one of the most recognized tractor brands today, John Deere tractors have been green and yellow since the day the company introduced the Waterloo Boy in 1918.

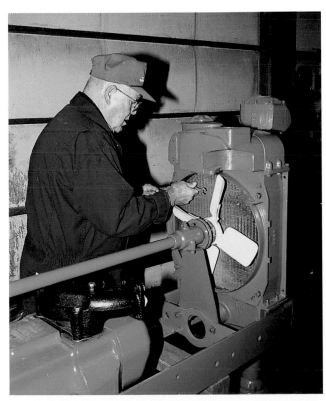

If you're striving for an authentic look, you need to know which parts of the tractor were painted different colors. Some painters, for example, might assume the fan on a John Deere two-cylinder tractor would be painted the same color as the engine. Instead, it's painted yellow, undoubtedly to make it more visible when the engine is running.

Although the difference is subtle, vintage John Deere tractors were painted with what is today called Classic Green paint, while newer tractors carry an Agricultural Green paint coat.

MASSEY-HARRIS/MASSEY-FERGUSON

Although the first Massey-Harris Challenger tractors were painted gray, most of us know Massey as the brand that sported Radiant Red paint with Straw Yellow wheels. In fact, that trend actually started with the Challenger, following its restyling around 1938. It continued until 1955, which was shortly after the merger of Harry Ferguson's tractor company with Massey-Harris.

Under Massey-Harris-Ferguson, new sheet metal and a new red and gray paint scheme were introduced on the MF-35. Eventually, the "Harris" portion of the name was dropped. As a division of AGCO Corporation, Massey Ferguson continues to build tractors today with the familiar red and gray paint scheme.

MINNEAPOLIS-MOLINE

According to Minneapolis-Moline enthusiasts, M-M used three recognized shades of Prairie Gold paint on the tractors the company manufactured from 1936 to 1963. Prior to that, the brand was known as Twin City and carried a shade of gray.

In general, it is believed that M-M used the original Prairie Gold for only two years—from 1936 to perhaps as late as 1938. At that time, the company switched to Prairie Gold No. 2, which was used from

Minneapolis-Moline first introduced its Prairie Gold paint color in 1936, shortly after acquiring the Twin City tractor line.

This lineup of Minneapolis-Moline tractors shows the transition from Prairie Gold to Prairie Gold No. 2 to Energy Yellow. Note how the trim color also changed over the years.

1938 (some say 1939) until 1955 (and until 1959 on the GB models). The biggest question when it comes to paint shade concerns the 1938 ZT, GT, and UT, which some say used the original Prairie Gold and others believe were painted with Prairie Gold No. 2.

In 1956, Minneapolis-Moline made another paint change to Power Yellow, sometimes referred to as Late Prairie Gold. Although the tint is very close to Prairie Gold No. 2, it does have a little more of an orange tint (hence the designation by some as Orange Prairie Gold). This color was primarily used on all Powerline models built from 1956 to 1961 and on the early 335, 445, Four

It was in 1938 that Massey-Harris switched from gray paint to the Radiant Red and Straw Yellow paint scheme that has since become associated with Massey tractors.

State, Four Star Super, M5, M-504, GVI, and G-704 models built through 1962 and 1963.

Finally, in 1962 or 1963, M-M switched to an Energy Yellow paint, which is sometimes referred to as an industrial yellow. Models painted this color include the G-705 and G-706.

Like most brands, the trim colors were another story. In general, the Prairie Gold tractors all carried Cherry Red trim and wheels. However, things began to take a twist in 1959, when the entire Jet Star tractor was painted Metallic Brown with wheels trimmed in Power Yellow. The rest of the tractors were painted Power Yellow with a Metallic Brown frame. In addition, the hood on the M5, M-504, GVI, and G-704 tractors had a dark maroon-red accent stripe and the wheels were painted Power Yellow. If the tractor was equipped with power adjustable wheels, though, the rims were silver.

According to most sources, M-M also used two different brown colors during the later years. The early Four Star, Four Star Super, M5, M-504, GVI, and G-704 used the same metallic brown color used on the Jet Star. Then around 1963, supposedly at the same time M-M switched to Energy Yellow, the change was made to Dyna Brown. Basically, this means that Metallic Brown goes with Power Yellow and Dyna Brown goes with Energy Yellow.

That doesn't mean that rule is set in stone, however. Most likely, the company used up existing supplies before making the switch on a few models. As a final change, M-M dropped the Dyna Brown in favor of white in 1967 and continued that trend until 1970. As a result, the paint scheme consisted of a yellow and white two-tone hood with a black trim band, and the fenders and cast metal were Energy Yellow.

In the 1970s, some wheels were white with silver rims—most likely from the Oliver influence. That's because M-M was purchased by White Motor Company in 1963 as a sister brand to Oliver Farm Equipment Corporation, which was purchased in 1960, and Cockshutt Farm Equipment Corporation, which was acquired in 1962. That, of course, led to a whole series of crossover models that were simply painted different colors.

As a result, any models produced after 1970 often shared colors with White, Oliver, and/or Cockshutt, which means that, yes, there were even a few red and white Minneapolis-Moline tractors. But that's a subject perhaps best left to a brand-specific publication. Besides, the 1970s are really getting beyond the scope of vintage tractors in most books.

OLIVER

Oliver tractors came about as the result of a merger of five related companies in 1929 under the umbrella of Oliver Farm Equipment Corporation. One of those, of course, was the Hart-Parr Company, which built the first farm tractor in 1903. With this head start, Oliver Hart-Parr introduced its Model 18/28 in 1930, setting the stage for green tractors with red wheels.

Like a few other brands, though, Oliver went through several changes in the shade of the color used over the years. According to Lyle Dumont—an Oliver collector from Sigorney, Iowa, and a partner in the Oliver Decals business with his wife, Helen—Oliver used as many as four different shades of green from 1930 through 1975, when the company became part of White. Unfortunately, he says, there aren't any records that specify exact colors on specific models, which has forced him and other collectors to locate old paint codes and compare current paint numbers to pieces taken off the tractors.

Another problem, he says, is you can talk to ten different people and get close to ten different answers for paint color. The Martin-Senour numbers listed on the chart at the end of this chapter are the closest that Dumont has been able to come by matching actual sheetmetal panels with the paint chips.

Dumont says Oliver started with a dark green, which is essentially the same color used on Hart-Parr tractors. When the company came out with the four- and six-cylinder engines around 1935 to 1936, however, it switched to a lighter green. The color went to an even lighter shade around 1939, when Oliver came out with

Like several other companies, Oliver went through a series of color shades over the years, even though the main color always remained green.

For a while, Oliver continued to use the dark green color on its tractors that was previously used on the Hart-Parr brand (foreground) the company acquired.

Oliver's Steamline series used a new tint of green, highlighted by yellow and red details. These make for some of the most beautiful tractors ever, as with this 1945 Oliver Model 60 Row Crop. Owner: Ferrel Moots. *Ralph W. Sanders*

One of the last color schemes used on Oliver tractors was a light shade of green with Clover White trim.

the styled models that included the 60 and 70. The shade was lightened again when the company introduced the Fleetline Series. The final change came when Oliver introduced the Super Series.

According to some, there was one more change with the 55 Series, but Dumont says he has never seen much difference in the color after the Super Series.

In the meantime, trim colors consisted of yellow with red highlights followed by Clover White on later models. Dumont cautions, however, that even though there is a touch of green in the Clover White formulation, some colors go too heavy on the green, which looks unnatural.

AVAILABLE COLORS

As mentioned earlier, tractor paint is available from a wide range of sources, including the local hardware or farm supply store. As most collectors will tell you, though, those aren't the best sources for a quality paint job. The better option, they say, is to purchase your supplies from an automotive paint supplier. Most of them have paint codes for the major tractor brands; however, what they call Allis-Chalmers Orange could be Persian Orange No. 1 or it could be No. 2.

Valspar, for example, has a line of enamel called Restoration Series Tractor and Implement Finish, which is available in eight "classic colors." The colors include JD Green, Ford Gray, MF Red, AC Orange, JD Yellow, Ford Red, IH Red, and Ford Blue. Unfortunately, like the implement paint label at the farm supply store, the brochure doesn't specify a shade. Perhaps the dealer has more information, but the paint chip on the Ford Gray,

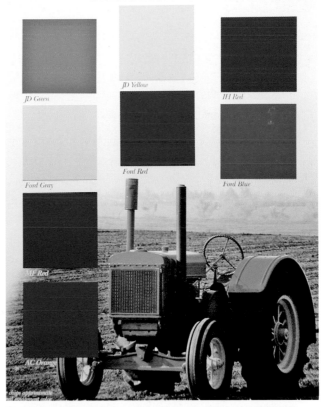

RESTORATION SERIES™
TRACTOR & IMPLEMENT FINISH
is available in these Classic Colors:

JD Green
JD Yellow
IH Red
Ford Gray
Ford Red
Ford Blue
MF Red
AC Orange

One of the most inexpensive options for tractor painting is implement enamel paint, which is generally available through farm supply stores and parts suppliers.

for example, looks more like the 8N gray than the 2N or 9N shade.

If you want to get a more specific or exact shade, you have a couple of options. One is to start with the paint codes listed in this chapter. These have been compiled from a number of sources, including paint color books, paint code charts posted on the Internet, and discussion boards on various tractor websites. Still, there is no guarantee of accuracy here. It's worth noting, however, that in many cases, more than one source agreed on a color. At least three different sources, for example, agreed that PPG's No. 60080 is a very close match to Allis-Chalmer's Persian Orange No. 1.

You'll also note that paint codes are supplied for five different suppliers. Dupont and PPG seem to be the predominant sources for most tractor restorers, as indicated by the number of available codes from those two suppliers. But others prefer Martin-Senour (NAPA), TISCO, and Sherwin-Williams. Those numbers are supplied in cases where they were available.

Keep in mind that most paint suppliers can cross-reference their number to that of another company. So if you at least have one number as a starting point, you can usually find what you're looking for. That doesn't mean you will have an exact match, though. According to several tractor restorers, one company's paint color may not match another company's color, even though they use the same number to cross-reference the shade.

With the advanced technology available today, tractor restorers have yet another option for selecting paint color. That is to have your paint supplier use a computer-based machine called a "color eye" or color spectrometer to determine the color. Not every paint outlet will have one, of course. But if you can find a professional paint store that does, it's simply a matter of finding a piece of sheet metal that hasn't faded over the years and having the technician take a color-reading scan. This information is then downloaded to a computer, which interprets the color and displays the appropriate paint formula. This is especially valuable when painting an orphan tractor or early model for which paint codes aren't available. Although the paint matching process can't always be 100 percent accurate, it does tend to be very accurate on single-stage paints.

If you're striving for authenticity, you may want to avoid implement enamel paints that are simply labeled Ford Gray or Allis-Chalmers Orange because several companies changed the color tint over the years.

Some places to check for original paint color are on the underside of the fuel tank or hood or on the backside of a mounting bracket. You may want to use some polishing compound on the area to remove oxidation, but if the area has been protected from exposure, it should be pretty close to original. Even without the use of a color spectrometer, an unfaded paint sample will give you something to compare paint chips to when shopping for the color coat.

As a final hint on tractor painting, it may be helpful to check out some of the websites maintained by individual tractor enthusiasts and a number of tractor clubs. The paint color data on some websites goes so far as to tell you which parts of the engine are painted and what the correct color should be. One of the most common questions, for instance, is whether the exhaust manifold should be painted and, if so, what color. Often, the radiator fan on various brands and models was painted different colors over the years. Sometimes it was black or painted to match the engine, and sometimes it was painted a color that made it more visible for safety reasons.

Of course, all this only matters if you're interested in complete accuracy in an attempt to restore a tractor to its original appearance. If you're painting a work tractor or a pulling tractor, it probably doesn't make any difference to anyone.

Virtually any color you could ever need can be mixed with the toners stocked by automotive paint stores and many body shops. Custom paint mixing is done by weight (note the scales on the far left) as the base and different amounts of toner are weighed out one at a time.

PAINT COLOR CODES

Here is a listing of the most commonly sought-out paint colors and various paint suppliers' shade codes for them.

	DUPONT	TISCO	PPG	MARTIN-SENOUR	SHERWIN-WILLIAMS
Allis-Chalmers					
Persian Orange 1	655	TP280	60080	99L3723	
Persian Orange 2			60396		
A-C Orange	29047		60691	90T-3723	
Yellow	421		81330		
Cream		TP270	8638		
Green	2619D	TP380			
Case					
Gray	24938		32678		
Green	262				
Black	93-005		9000		
Flambeau Red	016DH	TP140	70138	99L3724	
Desert Sunset		TP580	81357		
Power Red	G8156 UAD	TP890			
Caterpillar					
Cat Yellow	H7947 D	TP170	80021		
Highway Yellow	421		80979		
Cletrac					
Orange	017 D		60045	90T-3728	
Green	GS380				
Cockshutt					
Red			78210	99-23797-0	JK8522-G
Yellow			88234		JK6475
Harvest Gold			83761		JK8523
Co-Op					
Late Orange				90T-22014	
Ferguson					
Gray (1946–54)	652		32676	10039	1337
Light Gray (1954–56)	N9650		33965	3740	4030
Yellow-Green	B9533		47383	2245	11558
Tractor Red (1956-60)	7505	70738	4763	7191	
Flint Gray Metallic	L7949		34690	3746	4650
Bamboo Beige	L8071		25035	22986	32145
Ford					
Modern Dark Blue	29509		12908		
Ford Gray	29665		31657		
Empire Blue	27863D	TP360			
Industrial Yellow		TP760			
Light Gray		TP330		99L3732	
Medium Gray		TP240			
Red	RS465	TP310	70075	99L4338	
Hart-Parr					
1918–19 Green				99L8753	
1928–29 Green				99L8747	
1929–37 Green				99L11513	

	DUPONT	TISCO	PPG	MARTIN-SENOUR	SHERWIN-WILLIAM
International Harvester					
IH Gray	98620				
IH Green	93-84155				
IH Red	7410 D	TP1101	71310		
IH White	24440	TP900			
Blue	24160		10067		
Cub Cadet Yellow	79535 D		81518		
Cub Cadet White	57350 A		8665		
John Deere					
Green	262 D	TP210	46180		
Yellow	263 D	TP190	80186		
Industrial Yellow	43007 D	TP530	82295		
Massey-Ferguson					
Red	77932 D	TP300	72598		
Tractor Red			70837		
Gray	652	TP230			
Metallic Flint Gray	LM447	TP320	31644		
Silver Mist Gray	83825 D	TP750	31991		
Industrial Yellow		TP540	81518		
Massey-Harris					
Red	27958 D		70364	99-4354	
Straw Yellow	3274		80533	99-4341	
Bronze	B8191				
Minneapolis-Moline					
Prairie Gold	006 D		60098		
Prairie Gold 2	020DH		60039	99L3749	
Industrial Yellow	K9590AK				
M-M Red			71528	90G540	
M-M Cherry Red			70385	99G540	
Metallic Brown	C8194AH				
Dyna Brown			22394		
Dyna Brown 2			23049		
Oliver					
Dark Green	0149 or 030	TP220	99L8758		
Lighter Green				99L11513	
Styled Tractor Green			99L8748		
Fleetline Green	1317			99L8746	
Fleetline/Super Green	GS911		99L3751		
Yellow	44087			99L11611	
Red (wheels)	M9218			99L3752	
Clover White	4775		DAR46536		
Silver King					
Silver	5476A				
Twin City					
Gray			31953		
White					
Blue	G8164			12773	
Orange				2235	
Red				72231	

Chapter 20
Primer and Paint Application

If you're doing a paint job as part of a restoration, you probably can't wait to get the tractor assembled and get started painting. But try to restrain yourself just a little longer. You'll achieve the best results and have the easiest time painting your tractor if it is still disassembled. That means you should look at priming and painting individual sections of sheet metal, as well as the frame and engine, separately.

By leaving as many parts off the tractor as possible, you also have the opportunity to paint both sides of a piece in one session. Components like the seat, grille, battery box, and instrument panel can be hung on wire hooks, for example, and coated on all surfaces, without having to let one side dry first.

Also know that the safety precautions and application techniques that apply to painting also apply to the primer coat (which you should complete first). So now that you know about the different types of primers and paint, here's a look at how to apply them.

PRACTICE MAKES PERFECT
If you haven't done much painting in the past, the first step should be to find an old tractor fender or a sheet of plywood and practice your application technique. Read through the following procedures on adjusting and using the paint gun and then simply practice.

Also, use a can of inexpensive paint to get a feel for holding the gun on vertical and horizontal surfaces. Then adjust the paint volume and pattern adjustment knobs and see what kind of difference it makes. Use the spray gun air cap to adjust the spray pattern orientation from horizontal to vertical or vice versa. Learn how to overlap each pass with the gun to obtain a happy medium between thin spots and runs caused by too much paint. Once you've become proficient on your practice panel, you can be assured you'll do a better job on the actual application.

Using the hood from a Farmall tractor as a demonstration panel, Jim Seward, a tractor restorer from Wellman, Iowa, shows the transition (right to left) from original finish through bare metal with some filler, etch primer, epoxy primer, sealer, base-coat paint, and clear coat.

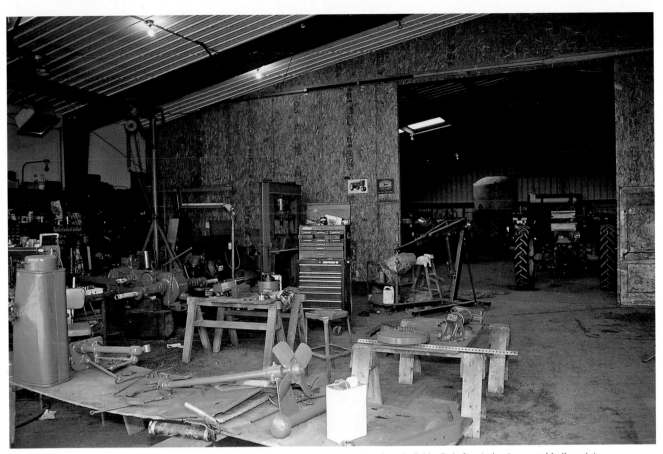

Painting a tractor is also much easier if you have room to spread out the parts and paint them individually before trying to assemble them into a finished project.

PAINT MIXING

Whether you're using implement enamel from the farm equipment dealership or you had paint professionally mixed by the NAPA dealer or automotive paint store, you should have a container of paint that is ready to go as soon as you open the can. The paint won't be your only ingredient, though. You'll also need to mix in the reducer or thinner to dilute it to a sprayable liquid and improve the spray pattern. You'll need to follow the specifications provided by the paint label or your paint supplier, but you can generally figure on something close to a one-to-one ratio of paint or primer to thinner or reducer.

Your paint supplier will tell you that thinners and reducers do basically the same thing and that they're usually referred to as thinners when used with lacquers and reducers when used with enamels, including urethane products. While they may do the same thing, they're certainly not the same product. You may remember using paint thinner to clean brushes or fix mistakes with glue or paint. Paint reducers, on the other hand, are

formulated specifically for acrylic enamels and urethanes and don't offer crossover applications. Reducers also come in different speeds to match the size of the job and the temperature. Again, your paint supplier can help you determine the correct "speed" of reducer for your needs.

Whatever you do, don't use gasoline in place of a reducer or thinner, even though some people have done so. It's not safe, and any money you save won't be worth the risk to the quality of the end product, not to mention risking your own safety.

In addition, you'll need to add a specific amount of hardener to the products, assuming your preference and if the label calls for it. In addition to helping the paint dry faster, an acrylic hardener will increase the gloss and provide a more durable finish. Adding a hardener has the negative effect, though, of reducing the pot life of the mixed paint. In the case of enamel, the pot life goes from about twenty four hours without hardener to about four hours once the hardener has been added. If you have any questions about the ingredients or the amounts that need to be mixed, talk to your paint supplier.

FIRE SAFETY FIRST

As you're setting up shop and getting ready to paint, remember that paint, thinners, and solvents are highly flammable, particularly when atomized by an air-powered spray gun. So be sure the area is free of any open sources of ignition, and keep a fire extinguisher nearby. Some additional safety precautions provided by PPG include:

- Make sure paints, solvents, and other flammable liquids are safely stored in a secure area.

- The quantity of flammable liquids stored in the spraying area should not exceed what is required for one day's use.

- Paint and solvent products should be kept away from all sources of ignition, including heat, sparks, flames, motors, burners, heaters, pilot lights, and welding.

- Paint- or solvent-soaked rags should be replaced frequently.

- Be sure the filtration system is clean at all times.

- Check frequently to ensure that the exhaust system is operating efficiently.

- Be aware that the high pressure of airless spraying can inject coatings into the skin, which can cause serious injury requiring immediate medical treatment.

- Never smoke or allow smoking in the painting area.

Hanging small parts on coat hangers or pieces of wire allows you to paint all sides of the part in one pass. It also allows you to get parts up on a level where you can keep the gun on a horizontal plane.

One of the easiest ways to measure and mix the paint is to use a clear mixing cup that has calibrations printed on the outside. Simply pour in the paint or primer, followed by the thinner or reducer until the liquid reaches the appropriate calibration mark for each. Do the same with the hardener. You can then use a stir stick to mix the components in the mixing cup before pouring it into the paint gun canister or gravity cup.

Paint manufacturers and their vendors also offer calibrated paint mixing sticks that work in a similar manner to the mixing cups. In this case, you can pour the paint into any straight-sided container and use the calibrated stick to measure out the appropriate amount of paint. Then add the thinner or reducer until the level on the stick hits the next appropriate mark. Add any necessary hardener in the same manner and use the stirring stick to mix the liquids together.

Once all the components have been measured and blended by either method, pour the mixture through a paint filter placed over the opening of the paint gun cup or canister. This is your last chance to prevent any impurities or clumps from entering spray gun passages and causing a clog or misspray.

Make sure the canister is securely fastened to the paint gun or the lid on a gravity-feed unit has been screwed on straight or secured, and you're ready to start painting.

ADJUSTING THE SPRAY PATTERN

Before you start shooting paint on the tractor, it's important that you adjust both the spray mixture and the spray pattern. One, of course, can affect the other. In general, several thin coats of paint are better than one or two thick ones. On the other hand, if you get the paint too thin, it can have a dusty appearance that reduces gloss and shine.

Assuming you've created a paint/reducer mixture that sprays smoothly and evenly, adjust the nozzle to spray an oval that is approximately 3 inches by 6 inches at about 1 foot distance. Most guns have two control knobs on the back—one for the fan spray and the other for the volume of spray that exits the nozzle. The air pressure, meanwhile, should be adjusted at the compressor or your air filter unit. Naturally, different products and different ratios of paint and thinner will spray differently. The best way to adjust the spray is to simply spray a small amount of paint onto a test panel or sheet of cardboard.

One of the easiest ways to set up a test area is to tape sheets of masking paper to an old sheet of plywood and set it nearby. Once the paint has dried, you can just tear

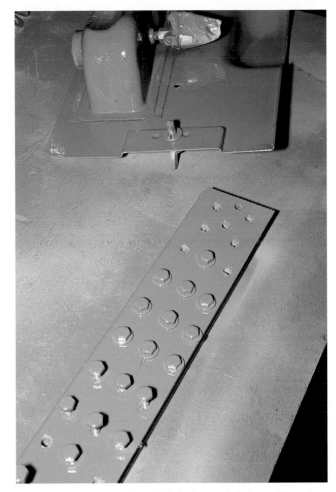

One trick that saves a lot of hand painting is to push fasteners into a piece of cardboard or to insert them into holes drilled in a board. This lets you spray paint all the bolt heads of a like color in one pass.

Because they have the tractors custom painted off the premises, the staff members at N-Complete built a set of carts to haul the remanufactured chassis between the facility and the nearby paint shop. This also allows the painter to move around and under the frame without obstruction.

Before you start painting on the tractor, test the spray pattern on a scrap of metal or a sheet of masking paper. You want a uniform oval pattern at a distance of 8 to 12 inches.

When painting a tractor, it's important that you use a thinner or reducer to obtain the correct consistency. Several thin coats are better than one or two thick ones. Adding a hardener, to improve drying time and strengthen the paint coat, is also a good idea.

off that sheet and tape on a new one. This will also let you quickly retest the pattern each time you refill the gun or if you suspect it may not be spraying an even pattern.

PAINT APPLICATION

If there are two keys to paint application and paint gun maneuvering, they are smoothly moving the gun in a back-and-forth motion and holding the gun perpendicular to the surface as much as possible at a distance of 8 to 12 inches. Both are important to produce a smooth, even coat.

If the gun is tilted too much in relation to the surface, the spray won't be uniform, which can lead to other problems. If you can picture the spray pattern hitting the surface at an angle, you can imagine the impact. The paint on one side of the circle or oval you're spraying will go on thicker because the nozzle is closer to the surface, while the other side of the oval will be thinner because the nozzle is farther away. The same thing happens if you swing the gun in an arc as you move it back and forth. As you curve your arm at the end of the arc, you're moving the gun and especially the outer edge of the spray pattern farther from the surface.

This creates the potential for the thinner paint to dry faster than the thicker paint. Unfortunately, if you apply the second coat, based on the drying time for the thin spots or the average, there may still be thick spots where the solvent is still evaporating, which can lead to various problems including solvent pop. The other problem is that the paint you've sprayed at the far end of an arc may be too dry by the time it hits the surface, resulting in poor adhesion or a thin coat of paint.

How and when you pull and release the trigger on the paint gun is also important. You don't want to have it simply pointing at the panel when you pull the trigger. It should be aimed off to the side and then smoothly twisted into the panel as the paint starts to spray. Keep it moving at a steady, even pace until you get to the end of the panel where you can twist it away from the panel. If you've had experience with an aerosol paint can, you'll do fine. You'll just need to learn from experience that if you go too slow, you may leave runs in the paint and if you move too fast, you may fog the paint rather than putting down a full coat. Practice on an old panel, not the tractor hood.

Since the paint will generally be thinner on the outer edge of the pattern, try to overlap the previous pattern by one-third to two-thirds of the pattern width. When painting large areas, spray around the edges first and finish up by filling in the center.

Jim Deardorff says he also likes to go around any openings, such as those for the radiator cap or fuel fill, before moving to the main portion of engine hood. Speaking of tractor hoods, one of the best ways to paint a hood is to set it over the top of a single sawhorse. This will allow you to hit all the edges and even come up underneath the edges, whereas if you place it across two sawhorses, there will always be edges touching one or both supports.

One more tip: Always hold the hose in your free hand or drape it over your shoulder while you're moving around the tractor or sheetmetal components. You don't want the hose dragging across the wet surface. At the

Most reducers come in three different speeds, which is based on temperature range of the work area and the size of the job—slow, medium, and fast. Since reducers and thinners act as carriers that evaporate as the paint cures, the speed is basically the evaporation speed. Consequently, you'll note that each speed has a temperature range. In general, fast reducers are designed for cooler temperatures and slow reducers are for use in higher temperatures. Using a fast reducer in 90-degree weather can cause the paint to dry too fast for the job, and using a cool temperature reducer in an extremely warm shop can cause paint to blush, fade, or cause other problems.

Most paint obtained from a professional paint dealer has a tech sheet that tells you everything you need to know concerning flash times, drying time, protective equipment required, pot life, required pressure, and more.

very least, it will smear the paint coat and it may even introduce dirt into the wet surface.

FLASH TIMES AND RECOATS

Yes, your tractor paint job will require more than one coat. That is particularly true if you're using enamel. Most restorers and paint suppliers recommend at least two to three coats of paint; some even use up to five or six on sheet metal for extra durability and shine. One

tractor restorer, who specializes in museum-quality restorations, applies at least seven coats of enamel on sheet metal, putting one coat on right after the other. After he finishes the last coat, he lets it cure for three or four days, then wet sands all sheet metal with 1,200-grit sandpaper, staying clear of any edges. Finally, he applies the decals and sprays clear coat over both the paint and the decals to produce a gleaming shine. Any cast parts, however, receive only paint to avoid a glossy, unnatural appearance.

Even if you use a polyurethane base coat and a clear coat, you should put at least two coats of paint on your tractor. The key is to make sure the timing between paint coats is sufficient, particularly if you're using an enamel without a hardener. That's another reason most restorers and paint specialists recommend the use of a hardener. It causes the coat to dry from the inside out and allows recoats without a lift problem. The next coat can be applied as soon as the first coat is dry to the touch.

The time required for the solvents to evaporate and the paint to cure enough for the next coat is referred to in professional circles as flash time. Basically, you can't apply additional coats until the solvents from the first coat, as well as each successive coat, have had time to evaporate. If you haven't allowed sufficient flash time, you may be trapping solvent vapors under the new coat and that can lead to blistering, cracking, lifting, sagging, or any of a number of other problems.

Carefully measure out the correct amount of paint, reducer, and hardener for each canister or spray cup refill. If you don't know the exact amount needed, measure each ingredient into a calibrated measuring cup and then transfer it into the gun canister. Remember, never pour any mixed paint back into the can.

On the other hand, since the coats rely on a chemical bond for adhesion, you don't want to wait too long between coats either. Most paint coatings, or your paint supplier, will provide some kind of guidance, so follow those recommendations. Realize, though, that additional coats may require longer flash times than the initial coat. Some painters say they have learned to test the surface with their thumb on a hidden area. If the paint doesn't show their thumbprint, it's ready to accept the next coat.

As a final note, don't set or lay anything on the paint coat once you've finished, even if it looks totally dry. The solvents will continue to evaporate for some time, and the paint is continuing to cure underneath. Setting a can on the surface before it has cured may just leave you with a nice little indented circle in your beautiful paint coat. Gary Ledford says he knows of a painter who put a mat

on the surface and left it there without thinking, only to see the full outline when it was later removed.

FINISHING THE JOB

Once you've finished painting the tractor, you may or may not be really finished, depending on the type of paint you used and your own preferences. First of all, you'll need to remove any masking tape and paper after the paint has completely cured. Keep in mind that the layers of paint have no doubt bridged the lip between the paint and the tape, so you need to carefully lift the tape in such a way that it doesn't tear the paint coat. To do this, pull the tape away from the painted area and back on itself rather than straight up or toward the paint. The idea is to create a sharp angle where the tape contacts the surface. If there is any concern about

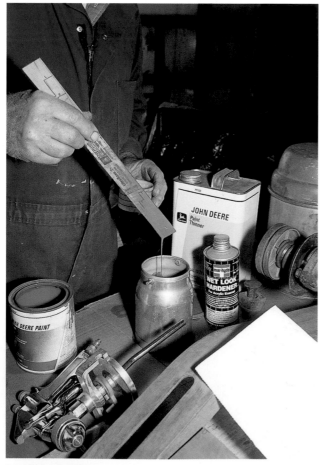

Even if you thoroughly stirred the paint in the can and it appears to be free of clumps, you should pour it through a paint strainer. Foreign material can easily clog the tiny passages in the gun and negatively affect the paint job.

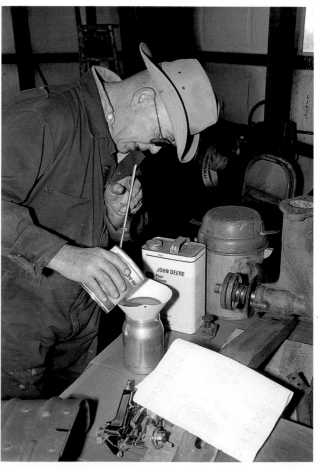

Most spray guns have two knobs located on the back of the gun housing for adjusting the paint material and airflow. The amount of material is usually controlled by the knob that is in line with the air nozzle, while airflow is controlled with the other knob. Always consult your manual for exact adjustment procedures.

whether it is going to pull away cleanly, use a sharp razor blade to cut the paint film next to the tape.

As mentioned earlier, some painters like to wet sand the final coat of paint to attain the ultimate smoothness before polishing the surface or applying a clear coat. Others use very fine sand-paper to simply remove the nibs that interfere with a smooth surface. Not all paint coatings will accept wet sanding, so check with your paint supplier ahead of time or at least before doing any wet sanding on the finish. If you do plan to do any wet sanding, use very fine paper with 1,500- to 2,000-grit on a hand-sanding block. Then use just enough light pressure to remove nibs or dust and dirt in the finish.

To be honest, most tractor painters are satisfied with the finished appearance that comes with several coats of enamel that contains a hardener to strengthen the paint and add luster.

Another option, assuming it is permissible with the paint you are using, is to "rub out" any minute imperfections with rubbing compound or polishing compound. Suffice to say polishing compounds include polishing grit to remove blemishes and oxidation of old paint. In this case, the idea is to remove any imperfections and polish the surface to a deeper shine. If you do use a polish, make sure the finish has completely cured and that all the solvents have evaporated. This is one time you can use an electric polisher or buffer, as long as you're using a machine polishing compound.

Finally, if you plan to apply a coat of wax after the polish, it's best to wait at least 90 to 120 days for that step. In the meantime, you're ready to move on to applying the decals and putting your tractor back together.

Smoothly move the gun from side to side as you paint the tractor, overlapping each previous spray by about half. This is particularly important on sheet metal. On the first paint coat, it's often best to spray a light "tack" coat, especially with thin paints that can run.

Be sure to direct paint spray into all the cracks and crevices around the engine and frame. But be careful. It's easy to hold the gun in one spot too long, causing a run. While applying primer and paint, it's also important that you move any control or adjustment levers to ensure that the area behind them gets painted.

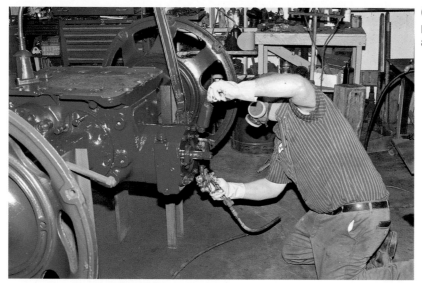

One or more sawhorses make a good support for painting larger tractor components like fenders, allowing you to cover the top surfaces evenly.

Tractor wheels can best be painted with the tires removed. Estel Theis usually places them between two secured sawhorses, which allows him to paint both the inside and outside surfaces.

Having been painted in a contrasting color to the frame, the wheels and fenders for a Ford 8N tractor are set off to the side to await the tires and final assembly.

It helps if you have room to spread out parts after they have been painted so they're easier to find when reassembling the tractor.

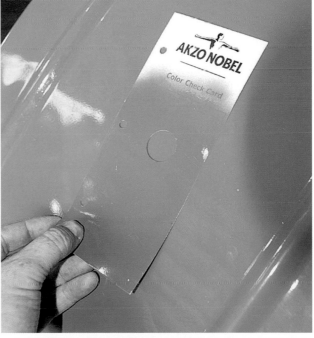

Spray out cards, which are available from most paint suppliers, are handy to have when painting a solid panel. Prior to painting the tractor, spray the black and white grid with enough coats to attain full coverage. This will tell you how many coats it should take to sufficiently cover the tractor. Also, the hole in the middle of the card allows you to make a color-matching check before spraying a panel that needs to match the rest of the tractor.

Once you finish painting, be sure to thoroughly clean the gun as instructed in the owner's manual, using thinner to clean the canister, as well as the internal components. Never use a piece of wire to try to clean clogged passages.

Once the paint has thoroughly cured, you can begin to carefully remove any masking tape and masking paper.

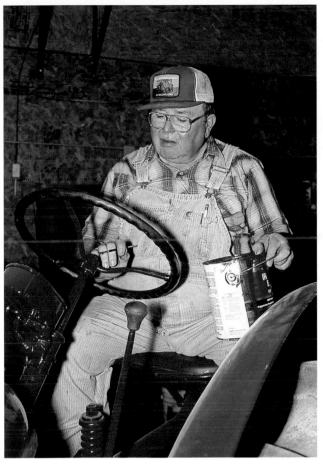

No matter how good of a job you did painting the tractor, there are often spots, such as nuts and bolts, that have been tightened during reassembly that require touch-up.

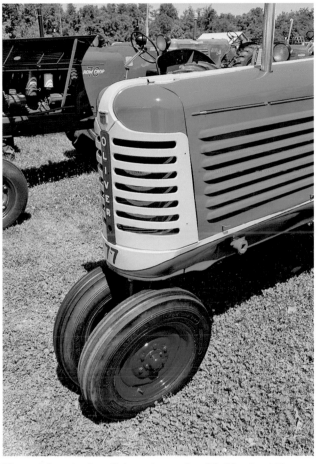

When painting a tractor with two colors, such as this Oliver hood, it's vital that you carefully mask off each colored area. Most restorers also recommend that you paint the smallest color area first, which in this case is the yellow. Fortunately, sections of the grille on some models can be removed and painted separately.

Jeff McManus, who has restored more than seventy tractors for himself and Deere and Company, likes to use a "cast gray" pigment on manifolds and rear axles.

Some restorers like to finish off the sheet metal with clear coat, while others prefer the look of hand-buffed enamel.

Taking your time to do the job right can yield a tractor that is better looking than the day it left the factory decades ago, as with this gorgeous 1937 Fordson All-Around. Owner: Earl Resner. *Ralph W. Sanders*

Hopefully, you've made it to this point, having completed the paint job, without any problems. In case you did run into some, though—or you encounter any later—the most common problems that plague a painter are listed in the following outline (which is strictly alphabetical and not in any order of most common occurrence).

Although there are several references to base-coat/clear-coat finishes and metallic finishes, which won't be applicable to most painters, they have been left in, since some readers may choose to use these types of finishes. This is particularly the case with those who restore show tractors and/or customized tractor pulling tractors.

These tips come courtesy of the Martin-Senour Paint Company.

AIR ENTRAPMENT

Small craterlike openings in or on the paint film. Some cases of air entrapment may have an appearance very similar to solvent pop or dust contamination; however, air entrapment normally occurs when the film is still wet and can be removed with compounding procedures. On the other hand, solvent pop will appear after the film is "skinned over" and, when sanded, will have pinholes. Dust contamination will appear while the film is drying, but still "tacky." These craters, under close examination, will have a speck of dirt in the center of the crater.

Cause
Trapped or buried air pockets in the wet paint film that rise to the surface and "burst," causing small craters. Lack of atomization is the cause of air entrapment and may be due to one or more of the following:
- Spray gun travel too slow.
- Spray gun distance too close.
- Air pressure too low.
- Improper spray gun setup.

Repair
- Sand with 1,200 or finer grit sandpaper, then compound and polish to restore gloss.
- Or sand smooth and refinish.

Prevention
- Maintain correct spray gun speed.
- Maintain correct spray gun distance.
- Use the recommended air pressure.
- Use the correct air cap/nozzle/needle recommended for clear coats.

BLEEDING OR DISCOLORATION

A red or yellow discoloration in the top-coat color.

Cause
Solvent in the new top coat dissolves soluble dyes or pigments in the original finish, allowing them to seep into and discolor the new top coat.

Repair
- Allow color to cure. Isolate with two-component undercoat(s) and refinish.
- Or remove original paint film and refinish.

Prevention
Isolate suspected bleeding finish by applying a two-component surfacer and/or sealer. Allow to cure following product recommendations; then apply desired top coat.

BLISTERING, PIMPLES, BUBBLES, OR BUMPS

Swelled areas appearing as pimples or bubbles in the top-coat film, often months after application.

Cause
- Moisture trapped beneath the paint film due to improper dry time after wet sanding; contaminated air lines; or spraying in extreme high humidity conditions.
- Using a poor grade and/or too fast of an evaporating thinner/reducer for spray conditions.
- Trapped solvents from applying wet heavy coats with insufficient flash time between coats.
- Improper dry time of undercoats before top coating.
- Painting over grease, oil, or rust.

Repair
- Remove affected area and refinish.
- Extreme cases must be stripped to bare substrate before refinishing.

Prevention
- If wet sanding is preferred, allow sufficient time for moisture to evaporate. Avoid wet sanding lacquer-type primer surfacer when possible. Drain moisture from compressor and air lines regularly. Allow additional flash time between coats and/or add retarder when spraying in humid conditions, or spray at times of low humidity when possible.
- Select proper thinner/reducer for spray conditions.
- Apply materials according to product recommendations, allowing sufficient flash time between coats.

- Allow undercoats to thoroughly dry/cure before top coating.
- Clean and prep substrate using recommended products and procedures.

BLUSHING OR MILKINESS

A milky gray cloud appears on the surface of the paint film immediately or shortly after application.

Cause

When spraying during humid conditions, air from the spray gun and solvent evaporation lowers the substrate temperature below the dew point, causing moisture in the air to condense in or on the paint film. The condition is aggravated when unbalanced thinner/reducer is used or the thinner/reducer is too fast drying.

Repair

- Should blushing occur during application, you should apply heat to the affected area or add retarder and apply additional coats.
- If the finish has dried, minor blushing may be corrected by compounding or polishing; however, severe blushing will require sanding and refinishing.

Prevention

- Always use good-quality solvent and thin/reduce material according to label directions.
- Select proper thinner/reducer for spray conditions.
- Add the recommended amount of retarder when spraying in humid conditions.
- Apply heat after application to evaporate moisture.

CHALKING, FADING, OXIDATION, OR WEATHERING

A chalky white appearance on the surface of the paint film.

Cause

Pigment is no longer held and protected by resin, resulting in a powderlike surface and lack of gloss due to:
- Natural weathering of the paint film.
- Improper application of paint material.
- Using generic thinner/reducer and/or hardener in the paint material.
- Excessive use of mist/fog coats when applying single-stage finishes.

Repair

- Use compound to remove oxidation and polish to restore gloss.
- Or sand the area to remove "weathered" paint film and refinish.

Prevention

- Weekly washing and occasional polishing or waxing will remove oxidation from the finish.
- Thoroughly stir, shake, or agitate all paint materials.
- Use the recommended thinner/reducer, hardener, and measure accurately.
- When spraying single-stage metallic finishes, apply mist/fog coats panel by panel while finish is still wet.

CHEMICAL STAINING, ETCHING, SPOTTING, ACID RAIN, OR DISCOLORATION

Irregular-shaped pitting, etching, or discoloration on the paint film.

Cause

A chemical change occurs when harmful environmental contaminants, such as acid rain, tree sap, bird droppings, or road tar remain on the surface for an extended period of time.

Repair

- Wash the component or panel with soap and hot water; then rinse and dry.
- Clean with appropriate surface cleaner.
- Wash with baking soda solution and rinse thoroughly. (Use one tablespoon baking soda per one quart water.)
- Compound damaged surface and polish to restore gloss.
- If polishing does not remove the damage, wet sand with 1,500- to 2,000-grit sandpaper. Then compound and polish to restore gloss.
- If refinishing is necessary, sand to remove damaged area with appropriate grit sandpaper, wash with a baking soda solution, then refinish. In severe cases, the finish must be removed to bare metal.

Prevention

- Remove harmful water-soluble contaminants by regularly washing with detergent and clear water.
- Polish or wax periodically.
- Refinish with an acrylic urethane base-coat/clear-coat system to provide the maximum protection.

- When sanding and buffing a base-coat/clear-coat finish, a minimum film thickness of the clear coat (2 mils) is required to maintain adequate ultraviolet protection. If correcting the damage will result in removing more than 0.5 mils, refinishing is recommended.

CHIPPING, NICKS, STONE PECKS, CHIPS, OR BRUISES

Small areas of damage to the paint film, leaving a nick, notch, or void in the finish.

Cause

Loss of adhesion of the paint film to the substrate caused by an impact from stones or other hard objects.

Repair

Sand and featheredge damaged areas to remove chips; then refinish.

Prevention

- Use premium two-component undercoat and top-coat system.
- Use a flex agent in undercoat and/or top-coat system in areas that are prone to chipping.

COLOR MISMATCH, OFF SHADE, OR OFF COLOR

The original finish and repair exhibit a noticeable difference in color when viewed under the same lighting conditions.

Cause

- Original finish has drifted from manufacturer's standard.
- Old finish weathered and oxidized.
- Color over- or underreduced.
- Improper spray procedures.
- Color not properly stirred or shaken.
- Improper spray gun setup.
- Inaccurate mixing of the color formula.
- "Panel" painting instead of blending.
- Evaluating color under a light source other than color-corrected lighting or natural light.
- Adjusting a color before it has been sprayed, or adjusting a base coat before applying clear coat.

Repair

- If color is close enough to blend: prepare adjacent panel(s) for blending, then blend color into adjacent panels.
- If color must be tinted: tint the color for a blendable match; prepare adjacent panel(s) for blending, then respray the repair, blending into the adjacent panel(s).

Prevention

- Check alternate color selector for variances. Choose the alternate that provides a blendable match.
- All color must be viewed under equal gloss; compound or polish the area to be matched.
- Thin/reduce according to label directions.
- Follow label directions for proper application of color coat.
- Stir or shake materials thoroughly to be sure all pigments and metallics are mixed properly and the solution is in suspension.
- Refer to product label or data sheet for spray gun, fluid nozzle, and air cap recommendations.
- Recheck color code, formula number, or formula weights before mixing colors.
- Spray a test panel prior to application to determine if blending or tinting is necessary.
- Always use natural daylight or color-corrected lights to make color-matching decisions.
- All color must be sprayed out for an accurate evaluation. Base coats must have clear coat applied. Check color from all angles—face (90 degrees) and side tone (20 to 60 degrees).

CRACKING, CHECKING, CRAZING, SPLITTING, ALLIGATORING, OR CROWSFEET

Cracks or lines of various lengths and widths in the top-coat finish, often resembling the cracking of dried mud.

Cause

- Excessive film thickness of the undercoat and/or top coat.
- Refinishing over a previously crazed/cracked surface.
- Insufficient flash time between coats and/or force drying undercoats using air from the spray gun.
- Mixing incorrectly or using too much hardener.
- Not thoroughly stirring or agitating paint ingredients.
- Breakdown of finish due to prolonged exposure to sunlight, moisture, and extreme temperature changes.
- Using generic reducers and/or hardeners.

Repair

Remove all cracked paint film and refinish.

Prevention

- Apply all materials following label direction.
- Completely remove crazed/cracked finishes before refinishing.
- Do not force-dry undercoats by fanning with spray gun air.
- Mix ingredients thoroughly using the recommended additives. Add each component in proper sequence following the recommended mixing ratio.
- Stir or agitate materials thoroughly before use to ensure all ingredients are in solution.
- Use premium two-component undercoat and top-coat system to provide maximum gloss and durability.
- Use the recommended thinner/reducer and hardener, and then measure accurately.

DUST CONTAMINATION OR DIRT IN FINISH

Foreign particles embedded in paint film. Fine dust particles that fall on a tacky surface can be encapsulated by the finish, creating an appearance almost identical to solvent pop. This "solvent pop" appearance usually occurs on vehicles that are removed from the booth in a tacky condition and placed in another location to dry. Fine dust contamination can be removed by sanding and polishing; however, if the condition is solvent pop, the finish will contain pinholes or small craters after sanding.

Cause

- Inadequate cleaning of the surface to be painted.
- Dirty spraying environment.
- Inadequate air filtration or unfiltered air entering the booth.
- Dirty or unsuitable work clothes that contain dust, lint, or fibers.
- Particles from deteriorated air supply lines.
- Poor-grade masking paper.
- Dirty spray gun.
- Removing the vehicle from the spray booth before the finish is "dust-free."

Repair

- Sand with 1,200-or finer grit sandpaper. Then compound and polish to restore gloss.
- Or sand smooth and refinish.

Prevention

- Thoroughly blow off all parts to be painted and clean all surrounding areas. Wipe the surface to be painted, along with any masking paper, with the tack rag.
- Maintain a clean working area.
- Wear a lint-free paint suit during the spray application.
- Use quality masking materials. "Wicks" found on newspaper can break away and blow into the wet paint.
- Repair or replace defective air compressor lines and/or hoses.
- Properly clean and maintain spray equipment.
- Tractor or components should be kept in a clean environment until finish is "dust-free."

EDGE MAPPING, EDGE RINGING, OR FEATHEREDGE LIFTING

Raised or lifted edges in the wet or dry paint film that outline sand-throughs or featheredges.

Cause

Solvent from the new top coat penetrates a solvent-sensitive substrate, causing a lifting or wrinkling that outlines the featheredge.

Repair

- Sand smooth or remove the affected area. Final sand with 400 or finer grit sandpaper.
- Isolate affected area with a two-component primer surfacer and refinish.
- Or apply waterborne primer surfacer, sand smooth, and refinish.
- Or apply acrylic lacquer primer surfacer thinned with nonpenetrating thinner, sand smooth, and refinish.

Prevention

- Check questionable finishes by rubbing a small, inconspicuous area with a shop towel saturated with lacquer thinner. Finishes susceptible to lifting will soften, wrinkle, or shrivel as lacquer thinner is applied.
- Use acrylic urethane primer surfacer, waterborne primer surfacer, or an acrylic lacquer primer surfacer thinned with nonpenetrating thinner over sensitive substrates.
- Use 400-or finer grit sandpaper when featheredging.
- Avoid sanding through insoluble top-coat color or clear coat, exposing solvent-sensitive or solvent-soluble finishes.

FISHEYES, SILICONE CONTAMINATION, OR CRATERING

Small, circular, craterlike openings that appear during or shortly after the spray application.

Cause
- Spraying over surfaces contaminated with oil, wax, silicone, or grease.
- Use of thinner/reducer in place of a solvent cleaner.
- Spraying over previously repaired areas containing "fisheye eliminator" additive.

Repair
- Remove wet paint film with solvent, clean, and refinish.
- Add the recommended fisheye eliminator and respray the affected area.
- If fisheyes appear in a base coat, allow the color to flash; then spray a mist coat over affected area. Do not use fisheye eliminator in undercoats or base-coat color.
- If the paint has dried, sand to a smooth finish below the fisheye cratering and refinish.

Prevention
- Thoroughly clean the surface to be painted with detergent and hot water, followed by the recommended solvent cleaner. Wipe dry with clean rags.
- Use fisheye eliminator that is specifically recommended for the top coat.
- Install an air-filtering system that removes and prevents oil and moisture contamination.
- Maintain air supply by draining, cleaning, and changing filter(s) on a routine basis.

LIFTING, WRINKLING, RAISING, ALLIGATORING, SHRIVELING, OR SWELLING

The existing paint film shrivels, wrinkles, or swells during new finish application or drying.

Cause
Solvents in a newly applied product attack the previous finish, causing wrinkling, raising, or puckering of the paint film due to:
- Recoating enamels or urethanes that are not fully cured.
- Exceeding maximum flash or recoat times during application.
- Recoating a base-coat/clear-coat finish, where existing clear coat has insufficient film build.

Repair
Remove lifted areas and refinish.

Prevention
Check questionable finishes by rubbing a small, inconspicuous area with a shop towel saturated with lacquer thinner. Finishes susceptible to lifting will soften, swell, or shrivel as lacquer thinner is applied. If any of these reactions occur, the following recommendations should be considered.
- Do not exceed a product's maximum recoat time during or after application.
- Allow enamels or urethanes to thoroughly cure before recoating or attempting a repair.
- Avoid applying undercoats or top coats excessively wet.
- Avoid the use of lacquer products over an air-dried enamel finish.
- When insoluble material (enamel/urethane) has been applied over a soluble material (lacquer):
  - Avoid sanding through and exposing areas of the soluble material.
  - Apply two-component primer surfacer and/or sealer as a barrier between the new and the old finish. When applying two-component undercoats over soluble finishes, the complete panel must be coated.
- Use waterborne undercoats to repair extremely sensitive finishes.

LOSS OF GLOSS, HAZING, DULLING, DIEBACK, MATTING, OR WEATHERING

A dulling of the gloss as the film dries or ages.

Cause
- Top coat applied in heavy, wet coats.
- Inadequate flash time between coats.
- Insufficient film thickness of top-coat color or clear coat.
- Insufficient drying/curling of undercoats before applying top coats.
- Using a poor grade and/or too fast evaporating thinner/reducer for spray conditions.
- Improper cleaning of the substrate.
- Insufficient air movement during and after application.
- Spraying over a deteriorated or solvent-sensitive substrate finish without proper priming or sealing procedures.
- Natural weathering of the finish.

Repair
- Allow finish to cure thoroughly, compound, or polish to restore gloss.
- Or sand and refinish.

Prevention

- Apply the top coat according to product label directions, using the recommended gun setup and air pressure.
- Allow all coatings sufficient flash between coats.
- Apply sufficient number of coats to achieve recommended proper film thickness.
- Allow undercoats to thoroughly dry/cure before top coating.
- Select recommended thinner/reducer based on temperature, humidity, air movement, and size of repair.
- Clean substrate thoroughly before and after sanding.
- For air dry situations: (1) allow exhaust fan to run forty minutes or longer after spraying; (2) open booth doors after finish is dust-free; and (3) maintain a shop temperature of 60 degrees Fahrenheit or above, especially when drying overnight.
- For maximum holdout, use a premium two-component undercoat system.
- Properly wash and care for the finish on a regular basis.
- Using a premium top-coat color or clear-coat system will provide maximum gloss and durability.

MOTTLING, STREAKING, TIGER OR ZEBRA STRIPES, FLOATING, OR FLOODING

A streaked, spotty, or striped appearance in a metallic color.

Cause

An uneven distribution of metallic flake caused by:

- Using a spray gun that gives an unbalanced spray pattern.
- Improper application technique, such as tilting the spray gun during application, causing the spray pattern to become heavy at the top or bottom.
- Holding the gun too close to the surface (flooding).
- Uneven spray pattern overlap.
- Omitting/improper use of mist coats.
- Too much thinner/reducer. Color overthinned/reduced.
- Applying clear coat to a base coat that has not thoroughly flashed/dried.
- Improper application of base coat (e.g., failure to apply or an improper use of a low-pressure mist coat or wet base-coat application).

Repair

- To uniform single-stage metallic finishes, apply a higher-pressure mist coat, panel by panel, while previous coat is still wet.
- Or allow base-coat color to flash; then apply a low-pressure mist coat.
- Finishes that have dried must be sanded and refinished.

Prevention

- Use recommended spray gun, including fluid tip and air cap, for the material being sprayed. Always adjust the gun for best atomization and balanced spray pattern before paint application.
- Use the correct ratio of thinner/reducer.
- Allow base coat proper flash/dry time before clear coating.
- Follow base coat application procedures.

ORANGE PEEL, POOR FLOW, OR TEXTURE

Paint film having an uneven texture that resembles the skin of an orange.

Cause

- Underreduction and/or air pressure too low.
- Thinner/reducer evaporates too fast for spray conditions.
- Excessive film thickness or piling on of heavy wet coats.
- Improper spray gun setup.
- Improper painting technique.

Repair

- Compound or polish to reduce surface texture.
- Or sand smooth with 1,200-or finer grit sandpaper, compound, and polish to restore gloss.
- Or sand smooth and refinish.

Prevention

- Use proper reduction ratio and spray at recommended air pressure.
- Select recommended thinner/reducer based on temperature, humidity, air movement, and size of repair.
- Avoid heavy coats and excessive film thickness.
- Use recommended spray gun, fluid tip, and air cap for the material being sprayed. Always adjust the gun for best atomization and balanced spray pattern before paint application.
- During paint application, hold the gun perpendicular and parallel to the surface. Adjust speed of pass, pattern overlap, and distance from the panel to achieve the desired appearance.

PEELING, FLAKING, OR DELAMINATION

A loss of adhesion or separation of the paint film from the substrate.

Cause

- Improper preparation of the substrate (sanding and cleaning).
- Omitting or applying an incompatible undercoat to a specific substrate (e.g., aluminum, galvanized, plastics).
- Insufficient flash/dry time or exceeding the product's maximum recoat time.
- Insufficient film thickness of undercoat or top coat.
- For clear-coat finishes: (1) insufficient film thickness of clear coat; (2) solvent cleaning base coat before clear coating; (3) sanding base coat before applying additional base coat or clear coat; (4) base coat applied too dry; (5) clear coat applied too dry; (6) baking base coat before applying clear coat; (7) using fisheye eliminator in base coat; (8) incompatible clear coat; (9) use of incompatible "adhesion promoter"; (10) excessive base coat film thickness; (11) overreduction, underreduction, or incompatible reducer used in base coat.

Repair

- Remove the finish in the affected area, featheredge, and refinish.
- Or strip to bare substrate and refinish.

Prevention

- Clean and prepare all substrates according to product recommendations.
- Use the recommended undercoat (primer) for the substrate being finished. Plastic parts may require use of a special primer and flex additive for maximum performance.
- Recoat all products within their recommended minimum and maximum recoat time.
- Apply a sufficient number of coats to obtain the recommended film thickness.
- Follow base coat/clear coat application procedures using only recommended/compatible products.
- "Adhesion promoter" should only be used when specifically recommended.

PINHOLING IN BODY FILLER, BUBBLES, OR AIR POCKETS

Small holes or bubbles located in or on top of putties or body fillers.

Cause

Air or gas bubbles become trapped inside putty or filler during mixing or product application. These bubbles are exposed during the sanding process, creating small holes or craters in the surface. Air or gas is trapped when:

- Filler and hardener are mixed together using a "whipping" motion (fast circular motion).
- Too much hardener is added.

- Heavy, thick coats have been applied, producing excessive heat and causing gas bubbles to form inside the product as it cures.

Repair

Apply a thin layer of polyester glazing putty (properly catalyzed and mixed), sand smooth, and continue the repair process.

Prevention

- Mix putty/filler components by folding together and pressing down to eliminate air pockets.
- Apply putty/filler in thin coats. Do not exceed manufacturer's recommended total film thickness.
- Follow manufacturer's recommendation of correct ratio of putty/filler to hardener.

RUNS, SAGS, HANGERS, CURTAINS, OR SIGNATURES

Coatings that fail to adhere uniformly, causing beads, droplets, or slippage of the total film.

Cause

- Overreduction and/or too slow evaporating thinner/reducer.
- Applying paint materials without proper flash time between coats.
- Applying excessively wet coats due to:
- Holding the gun too close to the surface.
- Slow gun speed.
- Double coating.
- Air pressure too low during spray application.
- Improper spray gun setup or an unbalanced spray pattern.
- Material and/or substrate temperature too cold.

Repair

- Remove the wet paint film with solvent, clean, and refinish.
- Or, after finish is completely dry, remove excess paint by block sanding with 1,200 or finer grit sandpaper, compound, and polish to restore gloss.
- Or block-sand smooth and refinish.

Prevention

- Mix according to product directions. Select recommended solvent for spray conditions based on temperature, humidity, air movement, and size of repair.
- Spray medium wet coats and allow sufficient flash time between coats.

- Adjust the spray gun for the best atomization and balanced spray pattern before paint application. Hold the spray gun perpendicular and parallel to the panel.
Adjust speed of pass, pattern overlap, and distance from the panel until the desired results are achieved.
- Set air pressure at the gun according to product recommendations.
- Use recommended spray gun, including fluid tip and air cap combination.
- Allow the paint material and substrate to reach room temperature before application.

SANDING MARKS, STREAKED FINISH, OR SAND SCRATCHES

Dark and/or streaked marks that resemble sand scratches in the paint film.

Cause
Scratching or distorting metallic/mica flakes close to the surface of the paint film due to:
- Sanding single-stage or base-coat metallic finishes prior to clear coating.
- Sanding single-stage metallic finishes prior to buffing.

Repair
Allow finish to dry, then sand and refinish.

Prevention
- Avoid sanding base-coat finishes before clear coating. If sanding is necessary, apply additional color following label direction.
- When sanding single-stage finishes, confine the sanding to minor imperfections (nib sanding rather than entire panels). For best results, use 1,200-or finer grit sandpaper.

SAND SCRATCHES, SWELLING, SINKING, OR SHRINKAGE

Visible lines or marks in the paint film that follow the direction of the sanding process.

Cause
- Sanding the substrate with too-coarse-grit sandpaper.
- Insufficient dry/cure of undercoats before sanding and top coating.
- Refinishing over soft, soluble substrates (e.g., lacquers, uncured OEM).
- Using poor grade and/or too fast evaporating thinners/reducers for spray conditions causing:

- Primer surfacer to "bridge" over sand scratches.
- Top coat to "skin over," trapping solvent, which swells sensitive substrates.
- Using a solvent cleaner that is too strong for the substrate or using thinner/reducer as a surface cleaner after sanding.

Repair
- Allow finish to dry/cure, sand smooth, compound, or polish to restore gloss.
- Or sand and refinish.

Prevention
- Sand with recommended grit sandpaper.
- Allow undercoats to thoroughly dry/cure before sanding and top coating.
- Rub a small area of the old finish with a shop towel saturated with lacquer thinner. If the old finish is soluble or undercured, apply appropriate sealer.
- Select recommended thinner/reducer based on temperature, humidity, air movement, and size of repair.
- Avoid "bridging" existing scratches by applying primer surfacer in thin, wet coats, allowing adequate flash time between each coat.
- Use solvent cleaner designated for either lacquer (soluble) or cured enamel/urethane (insoluble) substrates.

SEEDINESS, GRITTY, DIRTY, GRAINY, OR SPECKLED

Solid particles of various shapes and sizes embedded evenly throughout the paint film.

Cause
- Material not properly stirred or agitated.
- Failure to strain material.
- Using material exceeding its shelf life.
- Using generic reducers and/or hardeners.
- Using materials beyond their specified pot life.
- Using contaminated thinner/reducer or hardener.
- Using contaminated waterborne products.

Repair
- Remove the wet paint film with solvent, clean, and refinish.
- Or sand smooth and refinish.

Prevention
- Stir or shake materials thoroughly to be sure all pigment/resin is in solution.
- Strain all undercoats and top coats.

- Do not use material that cannot be stirred or strained. Caution: Repeated straining will not completely remove seediness.
- Use the recommended thinner/reducer and hardener, and then measure accurately.
- Mix only enough material as can be used within specified pot life.
- Use material as soon as possible; close and tighten container lids immediately after use.
- Do not allow thinner/reducer to come into contact with waterborne products.

SHRINKAGE, BULLSEYES, RINGING, OR EDGE MAPPING

The repaired area, featheredge, or sand scratches become visible within hours, days, or weeks after the repair is completed.

Cause
- Top coating before undercoats have thoroughly dried/cured.
- Undercoats applied excessively wet with inadequate flash time between coats.
- Undercoats underreduced.
- Using a poor grade and/or too fast evaporating thinner/reducer for spray conditions.
- Finishing over body filler that has not thoroughly cured.
- Using too strong of a solvent cleaner or using thinner/reducer as a surface cleaner.

Repair
- Allow the affected area to thoroughly dry/cure; then sand and refinish.
- If additional filling is necessary, apply a primer surfacer, sand smooth, and refinish.

Prevention
- Allow undercoats to thoroughly dry/cure before sanding and/or top coating.
- Thin or reduce undercoats according to product label directions. Apply in thin wet coats, allowing adequate flash time between coats to avoid "bridging" scratches.
- Select recommended thinner/reducer based on temperature, humidity, air movement, and size of repair.
- Follow body filler manufacturer's recommended cure time.
- Use solvent cleaner designated for either lacquer soluble or cured enamel/urethane insoluble substrate.

SOFT FILM OR SLOW DRY

The paint film is soft to the touch and will fingerprint or waterspot within hours/days after application.

Cause
- Applying undercoat and/or top coat excessively wet.
- Insufficient dry time between coats.
- Improper shop ventilation or heating.
- Adding too much or too little hardener to the paint material.
- Using an incorrect thinner/reducer for spray conditions.
- Omission of drier in enamel/urethane top coats.

Repair
- Allow additional dry time, maintaining a shop temperature of 70 degrees Fahrenheit or above.
- Or force dry following temperature and time recommendations.
- Or remove soft paint film and refinish.

Prevention
- Use recommended spray gun, fluid tip, and air cap for the material being sprayed. Always adjust the gun for best atomization and balance spray pattern before paint application.
- Allow sufficient flash time between coats.
- Maintain shop temperature at 70 degrees Fahrenheit or above for proper dry/cure.
- Use the recommended hardener and measure accurately.
- Select appropriate thinner/reducer based on temperature, humidity, air movement, and size of repair. Allow additional flash time when spraying in high temperature/high humidity or low temperature/high humidity conditions.
- Add the correct amount of drier that is specifically listed in the color formulation.

SOLVENT POPPING, BOILING, OR BLOWING

Small bubbles, pinholes, or craterlike openings in or on the paint film. Fine dust particles that fall on a tacky surface can be encapsulated by the wet film, creating an appearance almost identical to solvent pop. This "solvent pop" appearance usually occurs on panels or components that are removed from the paint area in a somewhat tacky condition and placed in another location to dry. Fine dust contamination can be removed by sanding and polishing; however, if the condition is solvent pop, the finish will contain pinholes or small craters after being sanded.

Cause

Liquid solvent (thinners/reducers) becomes "trapped" in the paint film when the surface layer skins over too quickly, preventing its evaporation into the atmosphere. Solvents that vaporize within the paint film leave bubbles, pinholes, or craters as they push through and "pop" the surface. Solvents can be trapped due to:

- Thinner/reducer evaporating too fast for spraying conditions.
- Inadequate flash time between coats.
- Excessive film thickness or "piling on" of heavy/wet coats.
- Too much air movement causing surface to "skin over" before solvents evaporate.
- Excessive purge/flash time before force drying.

Repair

- Allow finish to thoroughly dry/cure, sand smooth, and refinish. Inspect surface carefully to ensure all craters have been removed.
- Severe popping will require removal of the affected film. Prime, seal, and recoat as necessary.

Prevention

- Select recommended thinner/reducer based on temperature, humidity, air movement, and size of repair.
- Allow for proper flash time between coats.
- Avoid "piling on" or double wet coats.
- Restrict air movement over the surface being painted.
- Avoid extended purge/flash time before force drying.

STAINING, PLASTIC BLEED-THROUGH, OR DISCOLORATION

A yellow-brown discoloration appears in the top coat over areas repaired with polyester body filler or glazing putty.

Cause

- Using too much or too little hardener in the putty/filler.
- Insufficient mixing of putty/filler components.
- Applying a surfacer, sealer, and/or top coat before putty/filler has thoroughly cured.
- Applying undercoats and/or top coats excessively wet.
- Clear coating a white or light color without using a stain-free body filler.

Repair

- Allow top coat to thoroughly cure.
- Sand affected area, isolate with two-component undercoats, and refinish.

Prevention

- Use correct amount of body filler hardener.
- Mix components thoroughly.
- Allow putty/filler to cure thoroughly before top coating.
- Apply undercoats and/or top coats in medium-wet to wet coats, always allowing proper flash time between coats.
- Use nonstaining body filler, especially when clear coating light colors.
- Isolate suspected staining filler by applying a two-component surfacer and sealer.
- Allow to cure, following product recommendations; then apply desired top coat.
- Two-component acrylic urethane primer surfacer and acrylic urethane sealer may be used to top a majority of body filler staining problems. Both are required and must be allowed to fully cure for maximum stain resistance. For 100 percent assurance against body filler staining, use a nonstaining body filler, following manufacturer's recommendations.

TAPE TRACKING

An imprinted line or texture in the dried paint film following the use of masking tape.

Cause

- The finish is not dry before taping, causing solvent entrapment between finish and tape.
- Using a nonautomotive tape for multicolor finishes. Solvents from additional color soak through the tape and into the previous color.

Repair

- Compound and polish to remove texture.
- Or sand with 1,500- to 2,000-grit sandpaper, compound, and polish to restore gloss.
- Or sand and refinish.

Prevention

- Allow the finish to thoroughly dry before masking.
- Use only high-quality automotive masking tape.
- Determine if it is safe to tape on freshly painted surfaces by applying a small piece of tape to the surface for 10 to 15 minutes; then remove and check for imprinting.
- Untack the tape before applying by pulling the adhesive side of the tape over your pant leg or between your fingers.
- Remove the tape as quickly as possible after applying additional color(s).

TRANSPARENCY, POOR HIDING, POOR COVERAGE, OR TRANSLUCENT

The original finish or undercoat is visible through the top coat. Spray monitors (hiding power labels, opacity charts) provide a contrasting feature by which to observe the hiding power or transparency of top-coat color during spray application. When black and white can no longer be seen through the color, complete coverage is achieved.

Cause

- The color is not thoroughly stirred/agitated.
- The color is overthinned/reduced.
- Substrate not uniform in color.
- Wrong color undercoat used.
- Insufficient number of color coats applied.

Repair

- Apply additional coats of color until hiding is achieved.
- Or sand and apply similar colored undercoat/ground coat and refinish.

Prevention

- Stir or shake paint material thoroughly, making sure all pigment is in solution/suspension.
- Thin/reduce according to product label directions.
- Use a sealer or ground coat to provide a uniform color before top coating.
- Use an undercoat that is similar in color to the top coat.
- Spray until hiding is achieved.

WATER SPOTTING OR WATER MARKING

Circles with raised edges or whitish spots resembling the various shapes of water droplets appear on the surface of the paint film.

Cause

- Allowing water to come into contact with a finish that is not thoroughly dried/cured.
- Washing finish in direct sunlight.

Repair

- Wipe with a damp cloth, then polish.
- Or compound and polish.
- Or sand smooth with 1,500- to 2,000-grit sandpaper, compound, and polish to restore gloss.
- Or sand and refinish.

Prevention

- Do not allow water to come into contact with newly painted finish.
- If a new finish does get wet, dry immediately with a soft cloth.
- Wash new finishes in the shade and wipe dry.

WRINKLING, CRINKLING, PUCKERING, OR SHRIVELING

The surface of the paint contains irregular grooves or ridges resembling the skin of a prune.

Cause

- Excessive film thickness or "piling on" of heavy wet coats.
- Placing a newly painted finish in the hot sun too soon after spraying.
- Using lacquer thinner to reduce synthetic enamel.
- Spraying in extreme hot, humid weather conditions.
- Using underreduced and/or too fast evaporating thinner/reducer for spray conditions.
- Air pressure is too low during spray application.
- Force drying air-dry enamels without the recommended additives.

Repair

- If defects are minor, sand the top surface smooth, allow to cure, and refinish.
- If defects are severe, remove the affected area and refinish.

Prevention

- Avoid excessive film thickness and heavy coats. Always allow for sufficient flash times.
- Keep newly painted finish away from direct sunlight until finish has dried/cured.
- Use reducer that is specifically recommended for the top coat.
- Use the recommended reducer, additive, and/or retarder when spraying in hot, humid weather.
- Select recommend thinner/reducer based on temperature, humidity, air movement, and size of repair.
- Use the proper reduction ratio and spray at recommended air pressure.
- Select the recommended additives to suit drying conditions. Follow force-dry temperatures and time recommendations.

Chapter 21
Decals, Name Plates, and Serial Number Plates

When it comes to decals, the good news is they have never been easier to apply or easier to find. In the past, it was nearly impossible to locate decals for anything but the most popular antique tractor models. You might have been able to purchase a John Deere decal at the local dealership, and many aftermarket vendors were starting to release copies for brands like Allis-Chalmers, International Harvester, and Minneapolis-Moline. But if you were trying to restore an old Cletrac or Hart-Parr, you were out of luck.

Fortunately, the interest in antique tractor restoration—coupled with advances in computer-graphics technology—has changed all that. It started when a few collectors commissioned a printer to produce a set of decals that they couldn't locate. Soon, those people found there was a demand and began selling them to others.

That was certainly the case for Lyle Wacker, an antique tractor enthusiast from Osborn, Nebraska. He hired a printer to make up his first Allis-Chalmers decal more than twenty-five years ago. Today, he mails A-C and Case decals all over the world.

However, tractor collectors can also thank the young minds who have designed today's computers. Using modern scanning technology, decal companies are now

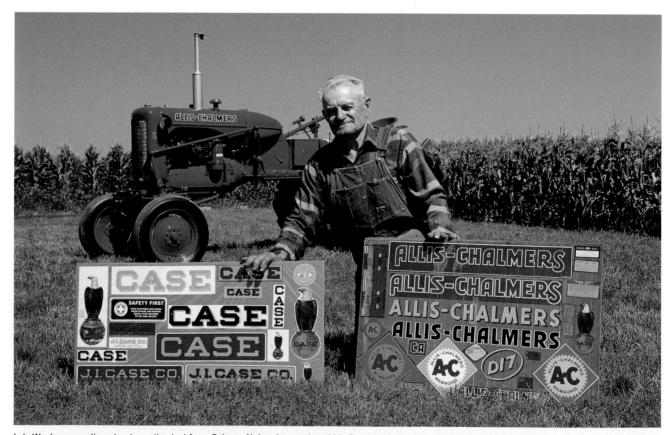

Lyle Wacker, an antique tractor enthusiast from Osborn, Nebraska, produced his first tractor decal more than twenty-five years ago. Today, he is just one of many vendors offering reproduction decals for vintage tractors.

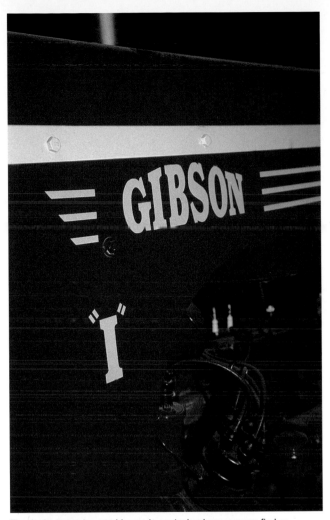

Thanks to computer graphics and new technology, you can find or reproduce decals for even the most unusual orphan tractors.

able to produce decals from drawings, literature, operating manuals, or even pencil rubbings. Chances are you won't have to go to those lengths, considering that decal sets are already available for just about any tractor you may choose to tackle. In the event you find an old Farmaster you just have to restore, though, there are a number of firms that offer custom services.

The other thing that has changed in the industry is the type of decals available. At one time, almost all of the decals on the market were the old water-transfer type, similar to the ones we used to apply on plastic airplane models. After soaking them in water, the backing paper is slipped off and the decal is applied and left to dry.

While decals of that type are still available—and used by those who prefer a nostalgic appearance or are going for an authentic restoration—the majority of the decals sold and used today are made by applying ink through a

silk-screen stencil onto Mylar plastic. With this type of decal, you simply remove the backing paper, which protects the adhesive, carefully press the decal into position, and remove the front layer of paper that protects the letter surface, much like you would apply a bumper sticker.

Also gaining popularity are vinyl-cut decals. Like the Mylar decals, the decal is sandwiched between two layers of protective paper. However, each letter or number is individually cut out of vinyl. Hence, the paper on the back protects the adhesive, while the paper on the front holds each of the letters in place as they're being applied. Unfortunately, vinyl-cut decals are often a one-shot deal, without any chance for adjustment, since the letters are all separated from each other.

RESEARCHING DECAL AUTHENTICITY AND PLACEMENT

Before you get started with any type of decal, let's make sure you are armed with the right knowledge. This is particularly important. You may think you know where all the decals go, but even experienced restorers get fooled at times. Decal configurations occasionally changed from one year to another, even within the same model. And not all models were equal, either.

Eugene Mohr, who creates decals for Minneapolis-Moline tractors, relates that there is a difference, for example, between the decals used on a propane-fueled M-M model and those used on a gas model, even though the model may be the same. So, do the research before you start. Look up old sales brochures or owners manuals, examine old photographs, and talk to club members from collector organizations.

Some people are misled, too, when they buy a package of decals that includes logos and lettering for more than one tractor model. If there are extra decals in the package, they feel they need to use them. So remember, if the decal pack is applicable to other models besides the one you're working on, you need to find out which decals are right for your tractor, and use only the ones you need.

Tools and Supplies

You should collect the appropriate supplies before you start. This should include a roll of paper towels; a clean, soft cotton towel; a roll of masking tape or drafting tape; and a rubber or plastic squeegee (you can find these in most craft, automotive, and wallpaper supply stores). A sponge may be helpful, as well. Plus, you might want to have a pair of tweezers handy for holding the edges of smaller decals. If you're using wet-application decals, you'll also need a water tray large enough to immerse the decals being applied.

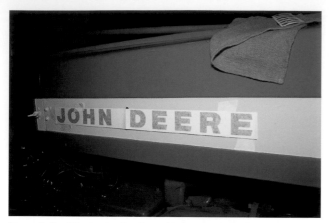

The majority of the tractor decals used today are made of vinyl-cut numbers or letters, or a silk-screened piece of Mylar. In both cases, the decal is sandwiched between two layers of protective paper.

SURFACE PREPARATION

Next, make sure the surface is ready. The surface needs to be thoroughly dried and cured, which means you should wait at least a week after the tractor has been painted. If a hardener was used in the paint, you may need to wait even longer to make sure the paint isn't going to give off gas bubbles that form under the decal. The paint surface must be smooth and absolutely clean, as well. If there are any pits or surface imperfections, the decal may not adhere properly. Make sure your hands are clean, too.

You need to make sure the room temperature is within a comfortable range, too. This isn't just for your comfort: Decals don't do well when the temperature or metal is too cold. The shop should be between around 60 and 90 degrees Fahrenheit to ensure that the decals adhere correctly.

The decals on this Farmall AV add the finishing touch to a fine restoration. *Hans Halberstadt*

The first step in decal application is positioning the decal in the proper location and marking the edges with pieces of tape or a fine pencil line.

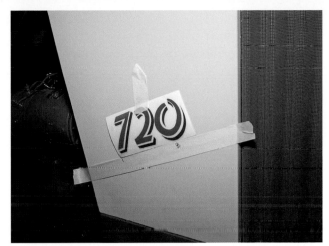

Unless you've taken measurements before you stripped off the old paint and decals, or used an accurately restored model as a reference, it can be difficult to position decals in the correct location, especially if they don't run parallel to a seam or the edge of the hood.

An extra pair of hands can come in handy when applying decals—especially when you need to reach for something and you've got a wet or sticky decal in your hands.

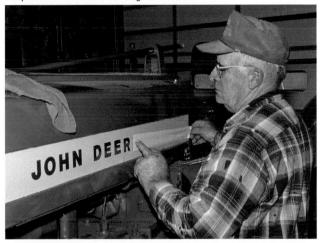

Once the decal has been pressed in place, carefully peel off the protective backing paper.

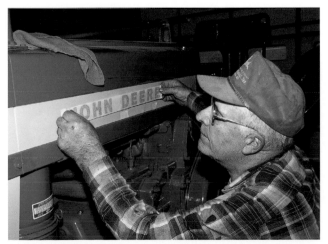

Once the protective paper has been removed, carefully apply the decal to the clean surface, lining it up with your reference marks.

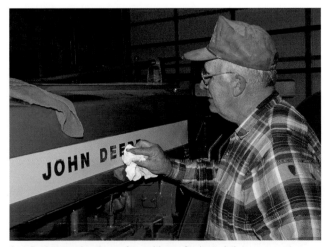

As a final step, wipe the surface with a soft, clean cloth to press out any air bubbles and dry the surface.

DECAL APPLICATION

Now that everything is ready, the first step in applying the decal is to hold it in the proper location and mark the edges with a piece of tape. You should be able to see the actual decal outline, even if it does have a protective film on each side. A few pieces of tape to mark the bottom edge and a piece of tape on one or both ends will give you a reference point.

At this point, it's simply a matter of peeling off the backing and applying the numbers or lettering to the tractor. Still, there are a few tips that will make the job easier. If you're using Mylar decals, you might do what many veteran restorers do and make sure your hands and tools are clean and wet. This will help keep the decal from sticking to surfaces it's not supposed to.

Lyle Wacker says he likes to carry a spray bottle filled with water, or water with a drop of soap or Windex in it, to lightly spray the back of the Mylar decals before placing them on the metal. You can also mist the surface of the metal, as well. This allows you to shift the decal slightly, when necessary. Once it is in the exact location you want it, use the squeegee to press the decal into place and remove any water and air bubbles from beneath it. Start in the center and work outward. Then, use a soft cloth to dry the surface and remove any adhesive left on the surface.

As a final tip for those who want the look of individual letters but can't find vinyl-cut decals for their model, you can do what some restorers do and cut out the individual letters or numbers on a Mylar decal with a razor knife or X-Acto knife. However, if you choose to go this route, which, in effect, will remove the film between the letters, you'll need to first place a strip of masking tape above or below the decal to note the position where each letter needs to go. Then you can cut the letters out and apply them one at a time.

Although some restorers like to finish off the decals with a shot of clear coat, others say they never put paint or clear coat over any kind of decal. For one thing, you have to know that the decal can take it and that the protectant won't cause it to lift off the surface. Water-transfer decals, for one, can't take it.

In addition, some decals have a tendency to yellow when covered with clear coat, even if the surface is better protected. Finally, body shop owner B. J. Rosmolen says he never puts clear coat over any kind of decal or appliqué, including pin stripes on an automobile, simply because it's a lot easier to replace a decal in the future than it is to restore the paint finish.

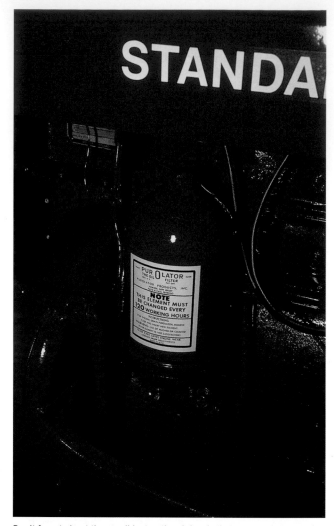

Don't forget about the small instructional decals that were a vital part of the original model. However, it's important to know which ones were used and where, since decal kits often apply to several tractor models and include extra decals. The new decals on this McCormick W-9, owned by Walter Bieri of Savannah, Missouri, sets off the whole tractor.

EMBLEMS AND NAME PLATES

On most early tractors, a decal was the extent of any adornment or identification. However, just as automakers started adding chrome and special emblems, so did some tractor manufacturers. Instead of a decal, some companies affixed a stylish metal or plastic name plate to the hood. Others, like International Harvester, added stainless steel or raised numbers to distinguish the model.

Unfortunately, it's one more thing that you, as a restorer, have to be concerned about. In many cases, it's easier to find a reproduction than to restore the original—and it will look a lot better in the end, too.

Care and research—and a steady hand—in decal placement and painting trim work are rewarded in a beautiful restoration, as with this Oliver 70 Orchard model. *Hans Halberstadt*

The best paint and decal job in the world will lack something if the emblem that adorns the grille on many tractors is not restored or replaced.

This is certainly true of the John Deere emblem found in the grille of many late-model two-cylinder tractors. It's also true of the plastic grille inserts used on the Case 400 and Ford Jubilee tractors; both can be replaced with new reproductions, assuming you can find a supplier.

In the case of letters, you might be able to straighten out the old ones and polish them up or repaint them, depending upon the type. But, again, there are suppliers who can sell you a reproduction.

Finally, you may be able to get around the problem with modern technology. A case in point is the name plate attached to the hood on Cockshutt 60 Series tractors. According to Cockshutt enthusiast Jeff Gravert, some decal suppliers make a decal to replace the lettering that was originally painted on the raised name plate. As a result, restoration consists of cleaning and repainting the plate and applying the decal. "It's a little tricky to get the decal in place, but you can't tell it from the original when you're done," he says.

SERIAL NUMBER PLATES

For most vintage tractor restorers, restoration of the serial number plate is not only the last step in the project, but a source of pride. Having a tractor with a low serial number is kind of like acquiring a limited-edition painting with a low number. Consequently, tractor collectors don't take this step lightly.

If you're working with an older-model tractor, you may be lucky enough to have a brass serial number plate. If so, a good polishing with brass cleaner will suffice.

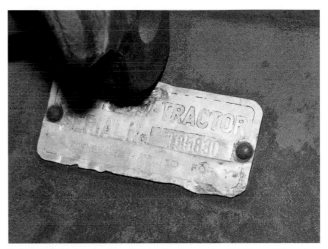

To finish off your restoration, be sure to clean and polish the serial number plate. Some restorers like to paint aluminum plates with black paint and then lightly sand the paint off the raised lettering.

Most of the serial number plates on later-model tractors, though, were made of aluminum. Still, you can make it stand out in a couple of ways. If the numbers are stamped into the plate, you may just want to clean and polish the plate with steel wool or a quality cleaner.

If the serial number is raised, however, you may want to follow the lead of Dennis Funk, a John Deere enthusiast from Hillsboro, Kansas. Funk likes to paint the serial number plate with black paint. Then, once it has dried, he lightly sands the raised areas with fine-grit sandpaper so the letters and numbers stand out in stark contrast to the black background.

Chapter 22
Taking the Next Step

Now that you have completed the restoration project, it's time to show off your pride and joy. Hopefully, the whole restoration process has been an enjoyable endeavor, despite the frustrations you've no doubt encountered. But it doesn't have to end there.

As the interest in antique tractor restoration has grown, so have the number of tractor clubs, shows, and events specifically designed for antique tractor owners. Granted, there are a number of antique tractor enthusiasts who are content to restore a tractor and drive it in the local parade every few years. Others look at tractor restoration as a way to build their collection. If you get to know many tractor enthusiasts at all, you'll find that, for many of them, collecting antique tractors is not much different than collecting coins, stamps, or models—just a little

more expensive. Some like to collect only two-cylinder John Deere tractors, while others prefer to specialize in Olivers or Minneapolis-Moline models. Still others like to look for unique orphan models.

Whatever route you take, though, you'll find that once you get involved in a club, tractor show, or antique tractor event, you'll build friendships that last for years.

ANTIQUE TRACTOR SHOWS

Each year, tractor enthusiasts put together literally hundreds of antique tractor shows throughout the United States, Canada, and Europe. While some of them are sponsored by clubs and cater to a certain brand of tractor, others welcome all tractor brands and are open to both steam- and gasoline-powered models. In

The goal of many restorers is simply to add to their collection, which often encompasses one favorite brand. This assembly of Minneapolis-Moline tractors, which totals more than forty models, belongs to Gaylen, Eugene, and Martin Mohr. It was started by their late father, Roger Mohr.

There's nothing quite as fulfilling as that first drive on a tractor you've spent several months restoring. If you don't believe it, just ask Ed Hoyt of St. Joseph, Missouri, who spent nearly a year restoring this John Deere Model D.

most cases, you don't even have to take a fully restored model. Go to any one of the shows, and you're sure to see at least one or two tractors sitting in the lineup that run just fine, but haven't seen a new coat of paint since they left the factory.

What you will also see are groups of men and women sitting under the closest shade tree, sharing stories and catching up on each other's lives since the last time they all got together. To your benefit, many of them also have tips to share about how they solved a particular problem or located a certain part. At any rate, you'll find that you're not alone in the challenges you face as show participants share their war stories.

If you're still in the process of restoring a vintage tractor, a tractor show will often give you the opportunity to closely inspect a like model and ask questions of its owner. Assuming that person has restored his tractor to original condition, there's nothing like physically examining the real thing to know what yours is supposed to look like.

If those aren't reasons enough to participate in a tractor show, consider that many shows also feature a swap meet or flea market where you can purchase parts for various models of antique tractors. Some of the shows also feature field demonstrations, tractor parades, and tractor games in which you can participate.

FARM EQUIPMENT DEMONSTRATIONS

As the interest in antique tractors has grown, so has the interest in antique farm implements and field demonstrations—and it's easy to see why. When you've got a vintage farm tractor that purrs like a kitten, it's hard to be content just driving it in parades or showing it off to friends. There's always the urge to put it to work in a nostalgic setting.

Hence, many antique tractor shows now feature field demonstrations as part of the agenda. While many started off with plowing demonstrations, the list of activities has grown to include such activities as threshing, baling, shelling corn, cutting silage, and so on. Some, of course,

The reward for all of your hard work will be a beautiful restoration, such as with this Ford 8N with its Funk Brothers six-cylinder overhead-valve-engine conversion. This glorious tractor is owned by Johnny Grist of Maple Hill, Kansas. *Chester Peterson Jr.*

will be stationary demonstrations that use the tractor's belt pulley to power the machine. Others are in the field, where antique tractors can be seen pulling implements that are appropriately matched for the time period and power requirements.

As an example, one Allis-Chalmers show, annually held in Minnesota, started off with wheat-harvesting demonstrations that featured vintage A-C tractors and several old pull-type combines. Next, the straw was raked into windrows and baled with an old A-C tractor and RotoBaler. That step was followed by tractors, wagons, and a couple of early mechanized bale loaders. Finally, the wheat stubble was attacked by a fleet of Allis-Chalmers tractors pulling plows matched to the era. All the while, the crowds watching numbered in the hundreds.

Whether you're watching or participating, however, it's important to remember one thing: Farm implements built in the early part of this century were not equipped with the safety features, nor the shields and guards, found on today's equipment. Carelessness could cost a finger, arm, or a life at the blink of an eye. So keep your distance from working machines. And if you're operating the equipment yourself, or helping a friend, never attempt

to make adjustments or clear out a crop slug without first shutting off the tractor. Remember, too, that tractors of the past were never designed for passengers. A tractor fender is not a seat.

TRACTOR GAMES

Gather a bunch of antique tractor enthusiasts together and they're bound to come up with other ways to show off their tractors than just a parade of equipment or a series of field demonstrations. Today, it's not unusual to see tractor shows that list such unusual activities as antique tractor square dances, slow races, and backing contests. All are designed to extend the fun associated with owning and restoring antique tractors.

A slow race, for example, not only tests your tractor-operating skills, but your mechanical skills, as well. The goal of the "race" is to see who can drive a certain distance in the slowest time without stopping or killing the engine. That means you have to decide which gear to start in, how far you dare throttle the engine back, and how often to apply the brakes. Naturally, the smoother the engine runs at low speeds, the better you'll be able to challenge the competition.

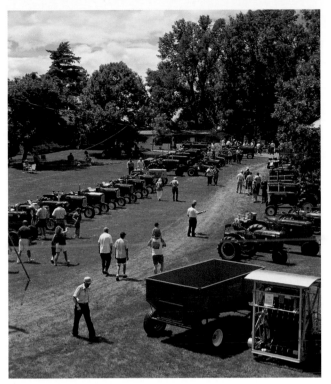

Each year, the Upper Midwest Allis-Chalmers Collectors Club brings together literally hundreds of vintage Allis-Chalmers tractors. And it is just one of several dozen tractor clubs in North America. Tractor shows such as this are an ideal place to meet other collectors and show off your accomplishments.

If maneuvering a tractor is your forte, you can find plenty of tractor games to test your skills in that area, too. The barrel race, for instance, calls for participants to push a barrel, which has been padded to protect tractor finishes, through an obstacle course. Naturally, drivers with narrow-front tractors tend to hold the advantage.

On the other hand, maybe you'd rather try backing. A couple of contest variations include backing a hay wagon up to a pretend loading dock or through an obstacle course. The winner in either case is the person with the fastest time. Another backing skill game requires participants to see who can back up and stop with the hitch positioned closest to an egg without breaking it. Obviously, this game is designed to test your skills at hitching up an implement and your ability to line up the hitch pin holes. Occasionally, just to level the playing field, the game organizers require all participants to use the same tractor.

Another popular game calls for antique tractor owners to balance their tractors on a low platform that functions much like a wide teeter totter. Each participant drives onto the platform until his or her tractor is centered over the fulcrum. The goal, then, is to try to balance the tractor in the middle by carefully inching it forward or backward. The ideal is to have both ends of the platform an equal distance from the ground.

As the interest in antique tractors has grown, so has the interest in antique farm implements. As a result, many antique tractor shows now include field demonstrations of baling, harvesting, raking, and so on.

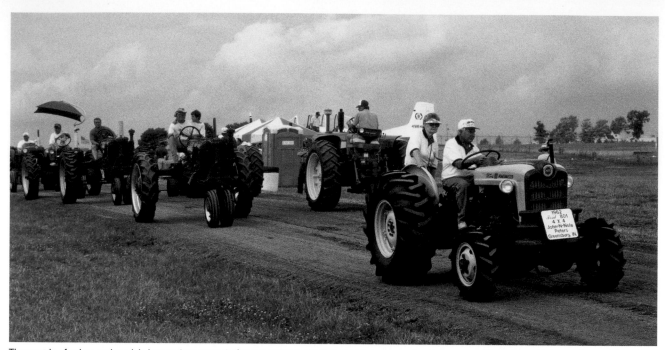

The parade of colors and models is a customary part of many tractors show. It can be a source of embarrassment if you haven't done a thorough job of restoration and your tractor dies and has to be pulled off the course. Most importantly, though, be careful about carrying passengers on tractors that were designed for only one occupant.

There are other games being played by tractor clubs all over the country. The latest, ever growing in popularity, is tractor square dancing. Needless to say, it takes a lot of room, because it is done a lot like real square dancing. A caller announces the moves to the tune of music, and the tractors drive in a circle and follow the calls.

ANTIQUE TRACTOR PULLS

There are a several reasons antique tractor pulling has become popular with tractor enthusiasts. The first is cost. Compared to modern-day pulling tractors, which are often equipped with multiple turbochargers and high-priced tires, an antique pulling tractor looks pretty much like the original. The only difference is the extra weight racks and the wheelie bars found on some tractors.

Consequently, an antique tractor enthusiast can participate in the sport for a fraction of the cost. On top of that, since the tractors in some classes are not significantly modified, they can still be used for work around the farm or acreage. Even if you weren't talking about pulling with a $3,000 tractor, instead of a $50,000 model, most antique tractor pullers simply prefer the slow pace of antique pulls to the glitz, smoke, and noise of modern tractor pulls.

In general, most antique tractor pulls are divided into four or five classes, depending upon the governing

body. It used to be that pulling tractors were classified as "antique," if they were built in 1938 or before, while tractors produced from 1939 to 1954 were designated as classics. The dividing year had more to do with tractor history than anything else. Prior to 1939, things like the radiator, fuel tank, and steering rod were pretty much left exposed, while later-model tractors were more streamlined and typically had more power.

Today, the National Antique Tractor Pullers Association (NATPA) and United States Antique Pullers (USAP), which generate the rules followed by most sanctioned pulls, have taken both history and tractor size into consideration. They realized, too, that there were getting to be fewer and fewer tractors built prior to 1939 participating in pulls. Hence, the NATPA now has five classes, or divisions, while the USAP recognizes four.

Division I in the NATPA, for example, is designed for beginning pullers and show tractors and is used to promote stock pulling. Only tractors built in 1957 or earlier, or production models that started in 1957, are eligible. In addition, almost everything must be stock and tractors can only pull in low gear with a 2.75 mph speed limit.

Divisions II is for near stock tractors that are 1957 or older models. Again, only low gear is permitted, even though some tire modifications are allowed and the speed limit has been increased to 3 mph. By the time you get into Divisions III and IV, drivers are permitted to use any gear, and any kind of cut is allowed on tires. Division III still has a speed limit, though, while IV does not.

Finally, Division V is for tractors that are 1959 or older. But by this stage of the game, any gear and any speed is allowed. So is turning up the engine to 130% over manufacturer's data. All divisions except Division I also require wheelie bars.

Meanwhile, tractors competing in USAP events generally have four classes to choose from: Super Farm Stock, Modified Stock, Pro Stock, and Super Pro Stock. Even though there are speed limits in each class, all four classes are limited to tractors that are 1958 or older models.

Keep in mind, though, that there are literally dozens of tractor pulling organizations around the country and many of them operate under their own rules and regulations. It's best to check the rules at any pull before

you go to the trouble of loading up the tractor and driving any distance.

Just as with modern tractor pulls, antique tractors in each class pull a mechanical sled, on which the weight increases as the sled is pulled down the track. However, there are basically two ways antique tractor pulls are run. One is by weight class and the other is by percentage pull. Weight classes for antique tractors generally start at 3,500 pounds and classes increase in 500-pound increments— usually up to 7,500 to 8,500 pounds. Determining the winner of each class is just as simple as it is in big pulls— the tractor pulling the sled the farthest wins.

Percentage pulls, on the other hand, require a little bit of math. In this case, you generally want the tractor to be as light as you can get it, or at least at the lighter end of the class. Consequently, any frills added for cosmetic reasons are often left off. Tractors are then weighed to determine their exact weight and participants attempt to

Tractor restoration can be a family affair, as evidenced by Tom Wingert of Sioux City, Iowa, who often receives help from his grandsons when getting ready for a parade.

pull as much weight as possible. In the end, if two tractors pull the same amount of weight the same distance, but one weighs 3,500 pounds and the other weighs 4,000 pounds, the lighter tractor would be declared the winner.

The one thing most antique pulls do have in common, though, is the ultimate goal. And surprisingly, it's not the trophy or prize money. What most participants are really after is the pride that comes with winning and the ability to settle the age-old argument—if only for a day—of whether a Farmall is better than a John Deere or whether an Oliver can beat an Allis-Chalmers.

Beauty may be in the eye of the beholder, but as the restorer of a machine like this 1939 Case RC, you will see lots of it. *Hans Halberstadt*

First published in 2013 by Voyageur Press, an imprint of MBI Publishing Company, 400 First Avenue North, Suite 400, Minneapolis, MN 55401 USA

Voyageur Press titles are also available at discounts in bulk quantity for industrial or sales-promotional use. For details write to Special Sales Manager at MBI Publishing Company, 300 First Avenue North, Suite 400, Minneapolis, MN 55401 USA.

To find out more about our books, visit us online at www.voyageurpress.com.

ISBN-13: 978-0-7603-4454-5

Library of Congress Cataloging-in-Publication Data

Gaines, Tharran E., 1950-
    How to restore your farm tractor / Tharran E Gaines.
        pages cm
    ISBN 978-0-7603-4454-5 (pbk.)
    1. Farm tractors--Conservation and restoration--Amateurs' manuals. I. Title.
    TL233.25.G353 2013
    629.28'752--dc23
                            2012050037

Editor: Michael Dregni
Design Manager: Cindy Samargia Laun
Layout by: John Sticha
Cover designed by: John Barnett

On the front cover: International Harvester Farmall Model 400. *Ralph W. Sanders*
On the title page: A beautifully restored International Harvester Farmall Model AV. *Hans Halberstadt*

Printed in China

10 9 8 7 6 5 4 3 2 1

Appendix

Parts and Information Sources

General Parts

Abilene Machine Parts
Box 129
Abilene, KS 67410
800-332-0239
913-655-9455

A-C Tractor Salvage
8480 225th Avenue
Maquoketa, IA 52060
319-652-2949

Ag Tractor Supply
Box 276
Stuart, IA 50250
800-944-2898
515-523-2363

All Parts International, Inc.
(API)
3215 West Main Avenue
Fargo, ND 58103
701-235-7503
www.stpc.com

Bob Martin Antique Tractor
Parts
5 Ogle Industrial Drive
Vevay, IN 47043
812-427-2622
www.venus.net~martin

Carter & Gruenewald Co., Inc.
4414 Highway 92
P.O. Box 40
Brooklyn, WI 53521
608-455-2411

Central Michigan Tractor &
Parts
2713 N. U.S. 27
St. Johns, MI 48879
800-248-9263

Central Plains Tractor Parts
712 North Main Avenue
Sioux Falls, SD 57102
800-234-1968
605-334-0021

Colfax Tractor Parts
Rt. 1, Box 119
Colfax, IA 50054
800-284-3001

CT Farm & Country
Box 3330
Des Moines, IA 50316
General parts: 800-247-7508
Used parts: 800-247-0128

Dick Moore Repair & Salvage
1540 Joe Quick Road
New Market, AL 35761
205-828-3884

Discount Tractor Supply
Box 265
Franklin Grove, IL 61031
800-433-5805

Dennis Polk Equipment
72435 SR 15
New Paris, IN 46553
800-795-3501
www.dennispolk.com

Draper Tractor Parts, Inc.
Rt. 1, Box 41
Garvield, WA 99130
509-397-2666

Fresno Tractor Parts
3444 West Whitesbridge Road
Fresno, CA 93706
209-233-2174

Iowa Falls Tractor Parts
Rt. 3, Box 330A
Iowa Falls, IA 50126
800-232-3276

J. P. Tractor Salvage
1347 Madison 426
Fredericktown, MO 63645
573-783-7055

Klumpp Salvage
Highway 165 S.
Kinder, LA 70648
800-444-8038
318-738-2554

Pete's Tractor Salvage, Inc.
2163 15th Avenue N.E.
Anamoose, ND 58710
800-541-7383
701-465-3274

PDQ Parts
Box 71007
Des Moines, IA 50322
800-274-7334
515-254-0014

Restoration Supply Co.
Dept. AP96 Mendon Street
Hopedale, MA 01747
508-634-6915

Silver Tractor Parts
Highway 40 East
Henager, AL 35978
800-828-1656
205-657-5191

South-Central Tractor Parts
Rt. 1, Box 1
Leland, MS 38756
800-247-1237

Southeast Tractor Parts
Rt. 2, Box 565
Jefferson, SC 29718
888-658-7171

Steiner Tractor Parts, Inc.
G-10096 S. Saginaw Road
Holly, MI 48442
810-695-1919
www.steinertractor.com

Surplus Tractor Parts Corp.
Box 2125
Fargo, ND 58107
800-859-2045
701-235-7503

The Tractor Barn
West Highway 60
Brookline, MO 65619
800-383-3678
417-881-3668

Thorne Farm Equipment
Box 358
Chesnee, SC 29323
803-461-7719

TTP, Inc.
3114 East U.S. Highway 30
Warsaw, IN 46580
800-825-7711

Van Noort Tractor Salvage
1003 10th Avenue
Rock Valley, IA 51247
800-831-4814

Watertown Tractor Parts
2510 9th Avenue S.W.
Watertown, SD 57201
800-843-4413

Wengers of Myerstown
814 South College Street
Myerstown, PA 17067
800-451-5240
717-866-2135
www.wengers.com

Worthington Tractor Salvage
Rt. 4, Box 14
Worthington, MN 56187
800-533-5304

Yesterday's Tractors
P.O. Box 160
Chicacum, WA 98325
www.ytmag.com

Specialized Parts

The Brillman Company
Box 333
Tatamy, PA 18085
610-252-9828
www.brillman.com
John Deere parts

Dave Geyer
1251 Rohret Road S.W.
Oxford, IA 52322
319-628-4257
JD two-Cylinder tractor hoods

Dengler Tractor
6687 Shurz Road
Middletown, OH
513-423-4000
513-423-0706
Deere two-cylinder parts

Dennis Carpenter
Ford Tractor Reproductions
P.O. Box 26398
Charlotte, NC 2821-6398
704-786-8139

Detwiler Sales
S3266 Highway 13 S.
Spenser, WI 54479
715-659-4252
Fax: 715-659-3885
*Specializing in Deere
two-cylinder*

250

John R. Lair
413 L.Q. P Avenue
Canby, MN 56220
507-223-5902
John Deere fenders

Little Red Tractor Co.
124 Marion Street
Howells, NE 68641
402-986-1352

Lynch Farms
1624 Alexandria Road
Eaton, OH 45320
937-456-6686
Oliver, including louvered engine side panels

N-Complete
10594 E. 700 N.
Wilkinson, IN 46186
Orders: 877-342-2086
Technical assistance: 765-785-2314
General: 765-785-2309
www.n-complete.com
Ford N Series parts

Shepard's 2 Cylinder Parts, Service & Repair
John Shepard
E633-1150 Avenue
Downing, WI 54734
715-265-4988

2-Cylinder Diesel Shop
Roger and Dana Marlin
Rt. 2, Box 241
Conway, MO 65632
417-589-2634

Zimmerman Oliver-Cletrac
1450 Diamond Station Road
Ephrata, PA 17522
717-738-2573

Carburetors and Governors
Burrey Carburetor Service
18028 Monroeville Road
Monroeville, IN 46773
800-287-7390
219-623-2104
Specializing in Deere two-cylinders

Denny's Carb Shop
8620 N. Casstown-Fletcher Road
Fletcher, OH 45326
937-368-2304

Link's Carburetor Repair
8708 Floyd Highway N.
P.O. Box 139
Copper Hill, VA 24079
540-929-4519
540-929-4719

McDonald Carb & Ignition
1001 Commerce Road
Jefferson, GA 30549
706-367-9952 (night)
706-367-8851 (7 a.m.–8 p.m. EST)

Motec Engineering
7342 W. State Road 28
Tipton, IN 46072

Robert's Carburetor Repair
404 E. 5th Street
P.O. Box 624, Dept. GM
Spencer, IA 51301
712-262-5311

Tredwell Carburetor Co.
HC 87 Box 24
Tredwell, NY 13846
607-829-8321
www.carbsandkits.com

Diesel Injection Pumps and Nozzles
Central Fuel Injection Service Co.
2403 Murray Road
Esterville, IA 51334
712-362-4200
www.centralfuelinjection.com

Roy Ritter
15664 County Road 309
Savannah, MO 64485
816-662-4765
Specializing in Deere two-cylinder pumps

Magnetos
Ed Strain
6555 44th Street N., #2006
Pinellas Park, FL 33781
800-266-1623
727-521-1597

Gag Electro Service
Glen Schueler
HCR 2, Box 88
Friona, TX 79035
806-295-3682
Larry G. Foster
905 McPherson Road
Burlington, NC 27215
877-556-5421
336-584-7563

Lightning Magneto
Rt. 1, County Road 54
Ottertail, MN 56571
218-367-2819

Magneeders
8215 County Road 118
Carthage, MO 64836
417-358-7863

Mark's Magneto Service
395 South Burnham Highway
Lisbon, CT 06351
860-887-1094

Gauges
Antique Gauges, Inc.
12287 Old Skipton Road
Cordova, MD 21625
410-822-4963

Wiring Harnesses
Agri-Services
13899 North Road
Alden, NY 14004
716-937-6618

Seals and Gaskets
A-1 Leather Cup and Gasket
2103 Brennan Circle
Fort Worth, TX 48180
817-626-9664

Lubbock Gasket & Supply
402 19th Street, Dept. AP
Lubbock, TX 79401
800-527-2064
806-763-2801

Olson's Gaskets
3059 Opdal Road E.
Port Orchard, WA 98366
360-871-1207
www.olsonsgaskets.com

Radiators
Omaha Avenue Radiator Service
100 E. Omaha Avenue
Norfolk, NE 68701
402-371-5953

Sieren's Reproduction Radiator Shutters
Tim Sieren
1320 Highway 92
Keota, IA 52248
319-698-4042

Wheels and Rims
Nielsen Spoke Wheel Repair
Herb Nielsen
3921 230th Street
Esterville, IA 51334
712-867-4796

TNT Poly Division
Taube Toll Corp.
1524 Chester Boulevard
Richmond, IN 47374
765-962-7415
Polyurethane replacement lugs for steel wheels

Wilson Farms
20552 Old Mansfield Road
Fredricktown, OH 43019
740-694-5071

Tires
M. E. Miller Tire Co.
17386 State Highway 2
Wauseon, OH 43567
419-335-7010
www.millertire.com

Tucker's Tire
844 S. Main Street
Dyersburg, TN 38024
800-443-0802

Replacement Seats
Speer Cushion Co.
431 S Interocean
Holyoke, CO 80734

Mufflers
Jim Van DeWynckel
RR 4
Merlin, Ontario
Canada N0P 1W0

Oren Schmidt
2059 V Avenue
Homestead, IA 52236
319-662-4388

Steering Wheel Repair
Tom Lein
24185 Denmark Avenue
Farmington, MN 55024
651-463-2141

Minn-Kota Repair
RR 1, Box 243
Ortonville, MN 56278
320-839-3940
320-289-2473

Tractor Steering Wheel
    Recovering and Repair
1400 121st Street W.
Rosemount, MN 55068
612-455-1802

Decals
Dan Shima
409 Sheridan Drive
Eldridge, IA 52748
319-285-9407

Jack Maple
Rt. 1, Box 154
Rushville, IN 46173
317-932-2027
Decals for a wide variety of
applications and models

Jorde's Decals
Travis & Shirley Jorde
935 Ninth Avenue N.E.
Rochester, MN 55906
507-288-5483
www.millcomm.com/-jorde/
    index.htm
Decals for John Deere

K & K Antique Tractors
5995 N. 100 W.
West Shelbyville, IN 46176
317-398-9883
www.kkantiquetractors.com

Kenneth Funfsinn
Rt. 2
Mendota, IL 61342

Lyle Dumont
20545 255th Street
Sigourney, IA 52591
515-622-2592
Decals for Oliver, Hart-Parr, and
Massey-Harris

Lyle Wacker
RR 2, Box 87
Osmond, NE 68765
402-582-4874
Decals for Oliver, Hart-Parr,
Case, and Massey-Harris

R-M Distributors
3693 M Avenue
Vail, IA 51465
712-677-2491
Decals for Minneapolis-Moline

Restoration Equipment
CJ Spray, Inc.
370 Airport Road
South St. Paul, MN 55075
800-328-4827
Spray systems

E & K Ag Products
HCR 3, Box 905
Gainesville, MO 65655
417-679-3530
Sleeve puller

TP Tools and Equipment
Dept. AP, 7075 Rt. 446,
P.O. Box 649
Canfield, OH 44406
800-321-9260
Info Line: 330-533-3384
www.tiptools.com
Parts washers, grinders, presses,
sandblasting equipment, etc.

Tractor Manuals
Clarence L. Goodburn
    Literature Sales
101 W. Main
Madelia, MN 56062
507-642-3281

Intertec Publishing
P.O. Box 12901
Overland Park, KS 66282
800-262-1954
www.intertecbooks.com

Jensales Inc.
P.O. Box 277
Clarks Grove, MN 56016
800-443-0625
507-826-3666
www.jensales.com

King's Books
P.O. Box 86
Radnor, OH 43066
Yesterday's Tractors
P.O. Box 160
Chicacum, WA 98325
www.ytmag.com

General Magazines
Antique Power
P.O. Box 500
Missouri City, TX 77459

The Belt Pulley
20114 IL Rt. 16
Nokomis, IL 62075

Engineers and Engines
2240 Oak Leaf Street
P.O. Box 2757
Joliet, IL 60434–2757

The Hook Magazine
P.O. Box 16
Marshfield, MO 65706
417-468-7000
Tractor pulling, including
antique and classic tractors

Polk's Magazine
72435 SR 15
New Paris, IN 46553

Steam and Gas Show Directory
Iron Man Album
Gas Engine
41 North Charlotte Street
P.O. Box 328
Lancaster, PA 17608–0328

Clubs and Brand Newsletters/
Magazines
Advance-Rumely
Rumley Collectors News
12109 Mennonite Church
    Road
Tremont, IL 61568
309-925-3925

The Rumley Newsletter
P.O. Box 12
Moline, IL 61265
309-764-7653

Allis-Chalmers
The Allis Connection
161 Hillcrest Court
Central City, IA 52214
319-438-6234

Old Allis News
10925 Love Road
Bellevue, MI 49021
616-763-9770

Upper Midwest A-C Club
22241 200th Street
Hutchinson, MN 55350

B. F. Avery
B. F. Avery Collectors Newsletter
RR 1, Box 68, 1373 E-100 N.
Paxton, IL 60957
217-379-9946

J. I. Case
Case Heritage Foundation
The Heritage Eagle Magazine
P.O. Box 8429
Fort Wayne, IN 46898-8429
Telephone: 213-639-6634

Old Abe's News
J. I. Case Collectors Association
400 Carriage Drive
Plain City, OH 43064

Caterpillar
Antique Caterpillar Machinery
    Owners Club and
    Newsletter
10816 Monitor-McKee Road
    N.E.
Woodburn, OR 87071
503-634-2474

Cockshutt
The Golden Arrow Magazine
N7209 St. Hwy. 67
Maybille, WI 53050
414-387-4578

International Cockshutt Club
Cockshutt Quarterly Magazine
12331 OR 316
Big Prarie, OH 44611
216-567-3951

Custom
Custom Club International
    Association and Newsletter
3516 Hamburg Road
Eldorado, OH 45321
513-273-5692

David Bradley
David Bradley Newsletter
Terry Strasser
Rt. 1, Box 280
Hedgesville, WV 25427
304-274-1725

Ferguson
The Ferguson Club and Journal
Sutton House
Sutton, Tenbury Wells
Worcestershire WR15 8RJ
Great Britain

Fordson and Ford
Ford/Fordson Collectors
    Association
F/FCA Newsletter
645 Loveland-Miamiville Road
Loveland, OH 45140

Ford 9N-2N-8N-NAA
Newsletter
P.O. Box 275
East Corinth, VT 05040-0275
www.n-news.com

Garden Tractor Collectors
Clubs
Vintage Garden Tractor Club
    of America
1804 Hall Street
Red Granite, WI 54970

Little G Lawn & Garden
    Tractor Collector's Club
13306 Black Hills Road
Dyersville, IA 52040

Gibson
Gibson Tractor Club
ADEHI News
4200 Winwood Court
Floyds Knob, IN 47119-9225
312-923-5822

**International Harvester/
    Farmall**
IH Collectors Association
310 Busse Highway, Suite 250
Park Ridge, IL 60068–3251

Red Power Magazine
Box 277
Battle Creek, IA 51006
712-365-4873 (evenings)

John Deere
Green Magazine
Dept. SG
2652 Davey Road
Bee, NE 68314
402-643-6269
www.cnweb.com/green

Two Cylinder Club/
    Publications
P.O. Box 10
Grundy Center, IA 50638-0010
www.two cylinder.com

**Massey-Harris and Massey
    Ferguson**
Massey Collectors Association
13607 Missouri Bottom Road
Bridgeton, MO 63044

Wild Harvest
1010 S. Powell, Box 529
Denver, IA 50622

Minneapolis-Moline
The M-M Corresponder
3693 M Avenue
Vail, IA 51465
712-677-2491

The Minneapolis-Moline
    Collectors Club
409 Sheridan Drive
Eldridge, IA 52748

Prairie Gold Rush
Rt. 1
Walnut, IL 61376

Oliver and Hart-Parr
Hart-Parr Oliver Collectors
    Association
P.O. Box 685, Dept. AP
Charles City, IA 50616
302-945-0549
www.hpoca.org

Oliver Collector's News
Rt. 1
Manvel, ND 58256-0044

Index

Acknowledgments

You might say that there's been a lot of water passed under the bridge since I began work on this book in 2002. Since that time, a number of the people who either had the greatest influence on my life or taught me the most about classic farm tractors have passed on. That includes both of my parents who exposed me to tractors and agriculture on the family farm in north central Kansas. It was there that I got my first experience with tractors that are among the classics today, including a Case Model D, Massey-Harris 44, Farmall C, and Farmall 560—the tractor that I spent more hours on than any other.

Two more people who have recently passed on, who contributed greatly to this and previous books, are Estel Theis and Roy Ritter. Both were John Deere two-cylinder tractor enthusiasts who lived within fifteen minutes of my home in Savannah, Missouri. Consequently, it was easy for me to run out to their farms a couple times a week and take a few more pictures as they completed another step in the restoration process. You'll find plenty of photos of both men in this book, so I want to thank their families for allowing me to reuse the photos and the information that both men provided. They've been greatly missed.

There are a number of other people I'd like to thank for their contributions as well. Among them are Chris and Kim Pratt, who write and edit the *Yesterday's Tractors* online magazine found at www.ytmag.com, which has been a valuable resource; the capable staff at Dennis Carpenter Ford Tractor Restoration Parts in Concord, North Carolina; and Paul Jensen and his staff with Jensales Inc., in Manchester, Minnesota.

The list of collectors and tractor enthusiasts who have helped with information grew longer as the book progressed. And since this revision includes material from some of my previous books that are no longer available, including *How to Restore Classic Farmall Tractors* and *How to Paint Your Tractor*, I'd like to add them to the list as well. So, knowing that I will probably forget someone, here's a thank you to: Stan Stamm, a Minneapolis-Moline enthusiast from Washington, Kansas; Bill Anderson, a full-time vintage tractor restorer from Superior, Nebraska; Jeff Gravert, a Cockshutt tractor enthusiast from Clay Center, Nebraska; Lyle Wacker, a decal vendor from Osborne, Nebraska; Larry Karg, an Allis-Chalmers collector from Hutchinson, Minnesota; Eugene, Gaylen, and Martin Mohr, collectors of Minneapolis-Moline tractors from Vail, Iowa; Dennis Funk, from Hillsboro, Kansas; Paul Cummngs, a Ford and Farmall collector from Amsterdam, Missouri; Francis Gorden, from Agra, Kansas; Larry, Gary, and Mark Manville from Dearborn, Missouri; Gilbert Vust, an Allis-Chalmers collector from Portage la Prairie, Manitoba; Jim Seward, a tractor restorer from Wellman, Iowa; Dave Henderson, a tractor repair and restoration specialist from Colo, Iowa; Arland Lepper from Marshalltown, Iowa; T. W. Cook, a Farmall collector from Georgetown, Texas; Bob Devling, a classic tractor collector from Elwood, Kansas; John Smith, a Ford tractor enthusiast from Peoria, Illinois; Tom Armstrong, owner of N-Complete in Wilkinson, Indiana; and Dallas Mercer, owner of Mercer Restoration in Excelsior Springs, Missouri.

Finally, I want to thank Bill Briner and his staff at Bill's Auto Electric in Savannah, Missouri; Gary Ledford, a paint technician in St. Joseph, Missouri; Jim Deardorff, owner of Superior Coatings in Chillicothe, Missouri; B. J. Rosmolen, owner of BJ's Auto Collision and Restoration, in St. Joseph, Missouri; John Hunter with Maple-Hunter Decals; Travis Jorde, owner of Jorde's Decals; Lyle and Helen Dumont, owners of Oliver Decals; Dan Steiner, president of Steiner Tractor Parts; and Lee Grady, the McCormick-IHC collection archivist for the Wisconsin Historical Society for their help with photos and technical information on paint, decals, electronics, and supplies.

Last, but not least, I want to thank my wife, Barb, who has blessed me with her encouragement and patience during my many years as a writer, and Michael Dregni with Voyageur Press for his expert help in getting this book from written word to printed copy.

About the Author

Tharran E. Gaines was born in north-central Kansas where he grew up on a small grain and livestock farm near the town of Kensington. The only boy in a family of five children, he still feels that he did all of the farm work normally delegated to a full farm family of boys; others say he was spoiled by four younger sisters.

He attended Kansas State University, where he received a degree in wildlife conservation and journalism with the goal of going into outdoor writing. He soon was using his agricultural background as a technical writer for Hesston Corporation, and hasn't left agriculture since.

As a technical writer, he has produced repair manuals, owner's manuals, and assembly instructions for Hesston, Winnebago, Sundstrand hydrostatic transmissions, Kinze planters and grain wagons, and Best Way crop sprayers. As a creative writer, he has crafted and produced everything from newsletter and feature articles to radio and TV commercials to video scripts and advertising copy for such companies as DeKalb Seed Company, DowElanco, Asgrow Seed Company, Rhone-Poulenc, Farmland Industries, and AGCO Corporation.

In 1991, he began his own business as a freelance writer, and today continues to operate Gaines Communications with his wife Barb out of their home office. The majority of their business involves producing all editorial copy for two AGCO Corporation company magazines under contract to *Progressive Farmer*. These magazines include AGCO *Advantage* and Hesston *Prime Line*.

Tharran and his wife live in a 100-plus-year-old Victorian home in Savannah, Missouri.

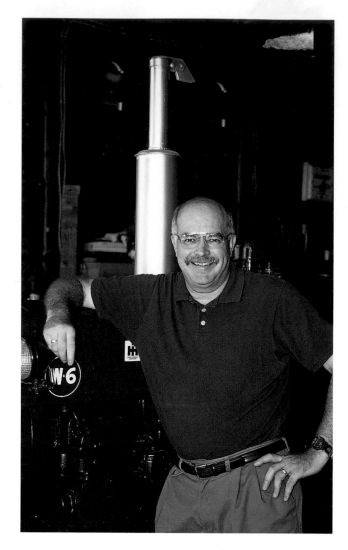